From the Buckeyes to the Bronx

Rick Bay

ISBN: 1-4774-6419-0
ISBN-13: 9781477464199

Dedication

To my beloved Denice

Acknowledgements

This book is nothing more than a summary of the extraordinary events that shaped my life and professional career from 1981 to 1988, none of which would have occurred without the courage of the three men who hired me–the late Dr. Paul Olum, president of the University of Oregon; Dr. Edward Jennings, former president of The Ohio State University and the late George Steinbrenner, principal owner of the New York Yankees. Although my collaboration with these men was sprinkled with debate and disagreement, I respected them all and remain grateful for the opportunities they provided me.

While there was no shortage of memories to draw upon for this volume, the story could not have been so effectively presented without the guidance and masterful editing assistance from my agent, Laurie Hawkins. In fact, without Laurie's tenacious direction, which ranged from designing my first website to counseling me about the importance of using the social media to "get the word out," I doubt the book would have ever been published. I cannot thank her enough—or the person who introduced me to her, fellow writer, Gail Forrest.

Several others poured over various drafts of the manuscript, providing valuable observations and suggestions along the way. For this voluntary service, I thank my mother, Ellen Reinhardt, and her late husband, John; my college roommate, Nick Frontczak; Bill Byrne, athletics director at Texas A. & M. University; my next-door neighbor, David Milner; my long-time friend, Janice Frieder and my wife, Julie. I must also give special thanks to fellow author Eric

Kinkopf, who first put the idea of writing a memoir into my head when I was director of men's athletics at the University of Minnesota in 1991, and who provided sage editing assistance during the writing process. The encouragement I received from these folks and others provided me badly needed momentum, often when my energy flagged, over the four-year life span of the project. Finally, I must credit "Wikipedia" for refreshing my memory and saving me hours of research with such topics as Woody Hayes, Jeb Magruder, Billy Martin and Dave Winfield.

A special thank you goes to Peter Richard, the talented artist and graphic designer who created the book's eye-catching cover.

Finally, I must thank the hundreds of athletes, coaches, administrators, managers, and fans that made the seven years covered here so interesting. Many appear in these pages and, while some are portrayed more favorably than others are, I can only say that the stories are true to the best of my recollection and that I have tried to be fair. Two persons in particular, Don Canham and George Steinbrenner, played important roles in my career, although I was never able to connect with either on a personal level. I had professional differences with both, though my relationship with Canham was more disappointing and perplexing. Because both have passed on in the last few years, I admit to feeling somewhat uncomfortable about discussing our relationships. However, if I am to tell my story truthfully, they are too important to omit. Indeed, while remembrances of things past can differ, I will be disappointed if anyone finds the book mean-spirited.

Introduction

When Forrest Gump's mama said, "Life is like a box of chocolates. You never know what you're gonna get," she could have been talking about me. For nearly 25 years, I walked the unexpected and unpredictable path of a sports executive. And I did it from coast to coast at the highest levels of competitive sports.

A former football player, wrestler, and coach at the University of Michigan, I began my administrative career as the athletics director at the University of Oregon when the program was so short of cash that we played BINGO at halftime of our basketball games just to raise enough money to paint the gym. While there, I tangled with Phil Knight, an Oregon alum, whose company, Nike, sent equipment directly to three All-American track athletes, which required me to declare them temporarily ineligible under NCAA rules.

Despite my Michigan pedigree, I became the athletics director at Ohio State. Soon I had to declare All-American Cris Carter ineligible, and Richard Nixon was delivering the eulogy at Woody Hayes's private funeral. A year later in what *Columbus Monthly Magazine* called "The Week the Town Went Crazy," I resigned in protest when the president fired football coach Earle Bruce, against my recommendation. In a bizarre turn of events, the firing led to a major lawsuit amid insinuations in the media that the president was having an extramarital affair.

New York Yankees owner George Steinbrenner rescued me from unemployment when he named me the Yankees executive vice-president and chief operating officer, a position I held for exactly 100 days. Billy Martin was in his fifth stint as field manager (still the Major League record for most times managing the same club), and Lou Piniella was the general manager. Phil Rizzuto and Bill White were the radio announcers, and Mel Allen was still around. Things happened, as you can imagine. I suffered through countless phone calls with "The Boss," who had an unpleasant habit of hanging up while I was talking. I quit even though, surprisingly, George wanted me to stay.

Clearly, I was better at getting jobs than I was at keeping them. I didn't plan it this way. I would rather have been more stable, but each experience was fascinating in its own way and, now, I wouldn't change a thing. My career has been a bumpy ride, sometimes turbulent and defiant, but I have been left with a rich index of stories and anecdotes that my more sensible colleagues would find impossible to duplicate. And because the media rarely covers sports from the perspective of an executive, the behind-the-scenes, colorful accounts in this book are being shared for the first time.

I am often asked how I came to be an athletics director and all I can say is that there was no clear path.

Sports were in my genes. My father was my high school football and wrestling coach. I was rolling around–in diapers, still–with his early wrestling teams, as were my two younger brothers. We all had rug burns and bruises from grappling on the thinning carpet in our living room and playing tackle football in our balding yard. We lived less than 200 yards from the high school athletic field in Waukegan, Illinois, and when we weren't playing there we were pretending to be one of our Major League heroes in Wiffle Ball games in our driveway.

I went to Michigan on a wrestling scholarship and also played football. I weighed 165 pounds and had no inclination for acting, so I never imagined a career in professional wrestling. Aspiring to play in the NFL also seemed a stretch, so I turned to coaching. I was good at it, but felt overly con-fined dealing with just my own sport.

How to make a career in sports without either playing or coaching left but one avenue for me—administration, where I could mold and lead an entire organization. But the talent pool from which most college athletics directors were chosen did not include former wrestling coaches, and I struggled for many years working and hoping for a break. Finally, when my prospects were bleakest, after failing even to qualify for an interview for the athletics directorship at small Sonoma State University, I was invited to submit my credentials to the University of Oregon. It was the most un-likely turn of events one could imagine, and it is where this story begins.

SECTION I
QUACK ATTACK

1

"B-41; I–16; G–12; O–7..."

The PA announcer's voice boomed through cavernous McArthur Court and reverberated into the concourse and through the double doors to the sidewalk just outside the gym, where I was standing. This was not what I had pictured a Pac-10 athletics director doing at halftime of an important mid-season conference basketball game.

No, I had envisioned myself roaming through the private suites surrounding the court, glad-handing our donors and skillfully laying the groundwork among their guests for future solicitations.

Or perhaps doing a radio interview to talk about the future of Ducks athletics. "Well, thanks, Bill, for that nice introduction," I'd say to the announcer. "You're right—we *are* headed in the right direction, and I think it's only a matter of time before we're competing for the championship."

But this wasn't Pauley Pavilion at UCLA or Hec Edmundson Pavilion at Washington. There were no private boxes, and we were probably lucky to have *any* radio station doing our games. No, this was Mac Court at the University of Oregon in the winter of 1983, and we were playing BINGO at halftime to raise enough money to paint the inside of our decrepit gymnasium. Even though I had approved the humiliating idea because we had to find $7500 somewhere, I hadn't even the courage of my convictions to stay in the building during this bizarre scene.

"BINGO!" shouted someone from the third tier of the building, and the one-minute ordeal was over. It doesn't take long to get BINGO when you have 1800 cards out—and that was the only redeeming aspect of it, because I was standing outside in a cold drizzle freezing my ass off.

My sports information director stuck his head out the door and said, "It's over."

I walked back into the arena, too sheepish to make eye contact with anyone.

It was Bill Byrne's idea. Bill was my director of development, my main fundraiser. He was extremely innovative and terrific at his job. One day we were sitting around the office bemoaning the embarrassing condition of the interior of Mac Court, and wishing that at least we could paint the seating area. We had received an estimate of $7,500 to do the walls and floors of the interior, money that we simply didn't have.

Bill had an idea. "We'll play BINGO!"

"What the hell are you talking about?" I said.

"It will be easy," Bill went on. "At every game we sell three BINGO cards for $5 to any takers. Then, we call out the numbers over the PA system at halftime. The winner gets half, and we keep the other half which goes toward the painting job."

I was speechless for a moment. "Bill, you aren't serious. We can't sit there reading BINGO numbers all during the halftime. People will go nuts; we'll be laughed out of town."

But Bill persisted. "Listen. Let's say 600 people buy BINGO cards, three cards for five bucks. That's $3,000, and 1,800 cards in play. It'll only take about six numbers to find a winner. It will be over in less than a minute, and we will have made $1,500 toward the paint project! We'll have all we need in five or six games."

So we did it, and it worked, although I was never in the gym when the numbers were called out. I couldn't stand it. As soon as the half ended, I headed for the exit, just as the PA announcer was saying, "Ladies and gentlemen, get ready for Oregon Duck Basketball BINGO! Here we go! "B-55, I-43 ..."

About a minute later, from out on the street, I could hear one of our volunteer spotters in the second balcony holler, "We have a winner, up here!"

We had our money in four games and many fans wanted us to keep doing it. But the city attorney had called my office and I was pretty certain I knew why. Fortunately, I was able to stall for time and didn't get back to him until we had covered our budget. Of course, I was positive that the whole thing was illegal, but it was over before anyone in the president's office or city hall really understood what was happening. And although we did paint the gym, it still looked awful. As they say in politics, it was sort of like putting lipstick on a pig.

2

I was in my second year as the Ducks' athletics director, and such was the sorry state of Oregon athletics in the early 1980's. But BINGO aside, I was not complaining. I was lucky to have this job–damn lucky

I was working for the University of Michigan Alumni Association when the position at Oregon opened. I had no business even applying for the job; I was under-qualified to be a Division I athletics director. Because I had no athletics administrative experience to speak of, I knew that I needed a strong endorsement from someone inside the business. Unfortunately, it wasn't going to come from the one person who should have been a slam-dunk reference for me, the athletics director at Michigan, Don Canham.

Don had hired me. I'd been his wrestling coach for four years and had returned the program to an elite status with consecutive unbeaten seasons and a Big Ten championship. But at times I had also been an irritant to him in what I considered matters of principle, but which he apparently felt bordered on insubordination. I was never disrespectful toward him, but he was arbitrary and not open to reasonable give-and-take discussions. He could be ruthlessly vindictive, and, given his evolving stature as one of the most powerful ADs in the nation, he was a bad enemy for me to have.

I had wrestled at Michigan for the legendary Cliff Keen, who coached the Wolverines for 45 years. I'd been team captain and won two individual Big Ten championships before becoming his assistant for four seasons, until he retired. But in the interim, I had failed to form a constructive relationship with my boss. A couple of the other coaches in the department complained to him that I was too rigid in the teaching of a physical education class with respect to my grading policy. He almost didn't hire me to succeed Coach Keen because of it. Later, after I became the head coach, he became agitated over my refusal to award a varsity letter to the son of an important friend, a young man who I had removed from the team.

There was at least a third significant incident that did not endear me to my boss, and this time it was clearly my fault. Upon becoming the head wrestling coach, I had elected to put part of my salary into a university pension fund (TIAA-CREF) before it was mandatory. I did not yet have the seniority necessary to make my participation a condition of employment. The woman in staff benefits who enrolled me assured me that because the contribution was not yet required I could retrieve the money at any time without penalty. Some weeks later I saw a piece of art that I wanted to buy, but my only available cash was in my TIAA-CREF account. When I tried to retrieve it, however, I was told that once deposited the money could not be withdrawn. Of course, this edict was exactly the opposite of what I thought I'd been assured when I enrolled. I was angry and made an impetuous, hotheaded decision to sue TIAA-CREF for the few hundred dollars there. This in itself was ill advised, but what was more stupid was that I did not realize that the university would be listed as a co-defendant.

A few days later I was summoned to Canham's office. The university attorney had just called to inform him that one of his knucklehead coaches was suing the university. Don was livid and I couldn't blame him. I immediately dropped the suit, paid my attorney, and tried to keep a low profile in the office for a while. But Don never forgot, and it later got back to me in my search for a job in athletics administration that he told several prospective employers, "Be careful, he sued the university."

Several years later when I told Canham that I was re-signing as wrestling coach, he was more than a little per-plexed.

"What are you going to do?" he wanted to know.

"I'm not sure," I said. "I just know that I don't want to coach the rest of my life, and if my heart's not in it, I should turn the job over to someone else."

I wasn't going to hang around until I found another job. I was half-afraid that if I made the guarantee of new em-ployment a self-imposed condition for my quitting, I might end up hanging on for the wrong reasons. I thought the fair thing to do was to admit I didn't have the fire, and move on.

But he didn't understand and took my leaving person-ally. Really, it had nothing to do with him, but he was sure that people would think that he had run me off. It was com-mon knowledge that we didn't get along, but a good AD didn't sack a successful coach simply over a personality conflict.

"At least wait until you've got another job," he suggest-ed.

But I told him that I couldn't wait, and besides, I said, he already had a great guy to take over, my assistant, Bill Johannesen. So I left coaching, grateful for the opportunity and experience, but never regretting leaving.

The irony was that the man who hadn't wanted to employ me in the first place, now didn't want me to leave, even though he would never have hired me for an admin-istrative job at Michigan, and would never recommend me to anyone else.

The scenario was bad news for me because by the time I decided to pursue a career in athletics administra-tion seven years later, Canham had become one of the most influential and powerful athletics directors in the na-tion—both a king and kingmaker. Largely on the force of his recommendation, three of his administrative staff had already landed important Division I athletics directors jobs—

Dave Strack at Arizona, Bump Elliott at Iowa and Charles Harris at Pennsylvania.

But for me, as far as Don was concerned, the die had been cast. I had heard from enough of our common acquaintances that he never spoke highly of me. In fact, I was told, it was just the opposite.

3

I was only 31 and had just been voted national coach of the year. Thus, I am sure that my resignation shocked many people, and some probably thought I had been fired. But the job was getting to me. It wasn't fun toward the end of each season and I took losing too hard, going into a shell for days. The thought of having to establish a summer wrestling camp, mostly for recruiting purposes, and the necessity of staying visible as a guest instructor at the camps of other coaches was too much to bear. I didn't want to spend 12 months of the year involved in wrestling. It was as simple as that. Yet, I knew that if I wasn't that committed, it wouldn't be long before the Michigan program suffered. It wasn't fair to hang on, even though the administration didn't really care much about the sport and probably would have let me coach at Michigan forever, even with just an average record. I had enjoyed a great run, but it was time to spread my wings and move on.

But what to do? I didn't know. Athletics administration was not in my thinking initially. Maybe it was just that I feared Canham's inevitable poor recommendation, and believed subconsciously that his testimony would prove insurmountable in any effort to launch a career as a sports executive.

My first inclination was simply to find something that would keep my wife, Sue, and me in Ann Arbor. Sue had become increasingly interested in interior design and was consulting more at the furniture store, where she worked. In fact, it would be only a few years before she established her own interior design business.

I had always loved the public relations aspect of coaching, and I knew that the University of Michigan Alumni Association did a lot of work in that area. Its executive director was Bob Forman, and, after a few meetings, he created a job for me in his operation with the title Director of Field Services.

Michigan had well over 100 alumni clubs around the nation, with a few even outside the United States, and Bob needed someone to keep them organized and energized. Volunteers who lived in the area ran them, but they needed direction and assistance from Ann Arbor.

I stayed with the alumni association for seven years, something I never would have predicted–and something that never would have happened had not Bob Forman so generously accommodated my creative energies. I loved the theater, and he allowed me to pioneer a program in alumni education where I led groups to the Shakespeare Festival in Stratford, Ontario, Canada, and to the Shaw Festival in Niagara-on-the-Lake, New York. He provided me the opportunity to write for the *Michigan Alumnus Magazine*, and he cultivated and nourished my interest in world travel, putting me in charge of alumni tours to China, when the country had just opened, New Zealand, and a cruise on a Russian ship down the Danube, to name a few.

Besides giving me the opportunity to write and travel for the association, Bob allowed me the release time to stay involved in wrestling with the United States Wrestling Federation (USWF), which led to my big break professionally.

I became fascinated with the bureaucratic and political challenges of working with an aspiring national governing body of an Olympic sport, and decided that a career in sports management or athletics administration was my calling. It had taken 15 years to decide on a career path, and, at age 37, though I knew I was starting from ground zero, I felt energized and excited.

4

I had no portfolio for sports management. My strongest attribute in applying for these jobs was my success in coaching, but the sport was wrestling, not football nor basketball, the high profile sports from which most athletic administrators emerged at the time.

Still, my coaching record provided me at least some credibility. In four years as head coach, my teams were 41-5-3 in dual meets, including a 31-2-2 mark inside the Big Ten. In my last two years at the helm, my teams had finished undefeated, winning our last 27 duals over three years, and we had finished 1st and 2nd in the Big Ten, and 3rd and 2nd in the NCAA Championship, respectively. In addition, those two squads had earned team GPAs of 3.0. I felt I embodied some intangible personal qualities that schools should be looking for in an athletics director, and coaches, for that matter. I had an undeniable work ethic; I was honest; I believed strongly in the importance of sportsmanship and fair play; I felt that winning in the absence of academic achievement and good citizenship was relatively meaningless. Just as I had in coaching, I relished the chance to impart this core set of values to a large number of young student-athletes at the highest competitive level. Besides, I loved a challenge and felt I was smart enough to succeed.

Forewarned is forearmed. I knew that I couldn't list Don Canham as a reference, but there was no avoiding my employment history and I knew that prospective employers would call him, regardless. I began to adjust my job search strategy accordingly.

I plowed ahead and began applying for directorships at smaller schools, such as Indiana State and Sonoma State University, a Division III school in California. And I decided to preempt the inevitable by volunteering to the various search committees that the vetting process would reveal a negative review from Canham, and that I would appreciate the opportunity to explain the reasons.

To think that a wrestling coach or any minor sport coach might have the necessary administrative tools for such an assignment—well, it just didn't resonate when schools went looking for athletics directors.

And yet my own school, Michigan, had done just that in 1968 by hiring its track coach, the aforementioned Don Canham, rather than its popular retiring football coach, Bump Elliott, whose 1964 Wolverine team won the Rose Bowl and who was thought to be a shoo-in for the job. Canham's selection over Bump was a big surprise to Michigan fans (many of whom probably had never even heard of Canham), and seen as a huge upset in Big Ten administrative circles. I know I was shocked, and I was on the coaching staff. I don't think Don had even been to a football or basketball game in years, and he was someone you rarely saw around the department. In fact, while his teams won championships regularly, he depended heavily on his outstanding assistant coaches, and didn't even travel with the squad on road trips.

Ironically, the reason for his frequent absences at the athletics department was what got him the AD job. He had been moonlighting as the founder of an extremely successful mail order business that sold sports equipment and coaching aids, such as stopwatches and instructional loop films, the latter for which I was one of the demonstrators in wrestling. When long-time Michigan AD Fritz Crisler retired, the university decided to hire a person with a strong business background, and Canham fit the bill. Whatever reservations existed in the community about the hire evaporated when he immediately recruited little known Bo Schembechler as the new football coach (from equally obscure Miami University of Ohio), who proceeded to upset Woody Hayes's number one ranked Ohio State team in his first year, and whose teams began filling Michigan's 100,000 seat stadium regularly.

But as I evaluated my own situation, I was neither the coach of a major sport nor a successful entrepreneurial businessman. I certainly was not aware of any former wrestling coaches in administration. There was another former track coach, DeLoss Dodds of Texas, whose old profession was comically denigrated when he fired his basketball coach, the irascible Abe Lemons, who said, "A basketball coach being fired by a track coach is like a United States Marine being shot by a Cub Scout."

Nonetheless, the more I thought about becoming an athletics director, the more appealing and glamorous the job seemed. For instance, I knew that an AD got a private booth in the football press box. I'd heard that the Big Ten athletics directors sat around, smoked big cigars, and sipped Bailey's Irish Cream after dinner at conference meetings. I guessed that there would be a fairly generous expense account for entertaining, and that you would have your own private secretary. And certainly, an AD always enjoyed lofty community status.

What I didn't know, but would soon find out, was that along with every private booth in the press box came three or four disgruntled boosters as guests; that for every men's basketball game I would enjoy attending, there would be a snail-paced soccer match at which I was expected; that for every puff piece in the local media extolling my virtues, there would follow two antagonistic press conferences questioning my judgment and intelligence; and that for every generous rights fee check from the television networks, there was a 10:00 p.m. basketball game starting time to be tolerated. And most revelatory and crushing of all, I found that for every thrilling victory, there was at least one heartbreaking defeat.

5

Undeterred by Canham's looming shadow, however, and clueless as to the realities of being an AD, I plunged ahead in search of my destiny.

In 1974, just as I was phasing out of my coaching career at Michigan and starting work for the alumni association at the school, I began serving on the board of directors of the USWF. Two years later, I became the organization's president and ultimately began attending United States Olympic Committee (USOC) Executive Board meetings as an observer. There I had the incredible good fortune of meeting Tom Jernstedt, who was doing the same for the NCAA.

Tom was an Oregon graduate and the leading candidate for the Ducks' athletics directorship when the job came open in the spring of 1981. By then he was the number two man at the NCAA, and the guy the Ducks really wanted to head their moribund athletics department.

Tom and I attended the quarterly meetings of the USOC, and I must have made a good impression, because at one of the gatherings he asked if I would be interested in applying for the athletic directorship at Oregon. He said that he intended to stay with the NCAA and would like to nominate me. I was flattered and excited by the prospect, eagerly gave Tom my consent, and waited anxiously to see what would happen.

When he submitted my name for the Ducks' job, I never thought I had a chance. And even later, when I was excited to be invited to Eugene to meet with the search committee, I considered the exercise a courtesy interview in deference to Jernstedt's recommendation. The fact that I was suddenly a serious candidate at Oregon was fortuitous, to put it mildly.

My trip to Eugene a few weeks later turned out to be an exhausting two-day interview process. It seemed that everyone connected to the school wanted a shot at interviewing the candidates. I appeared before at least six different search subcommittees—the student council, the faculty committee, a coaches' committee, a gathering of school administrators, an alumni committee, and last, but not least, the presidential appointed central search committee, which, after receiving input from each group, would make its recommendation to the president.

The questions I fielded were predictable: how would I raise enough money to cover the athletic department deficit; what was my position on rules compliance; what was my tolerance for poor academic performance by our student-athletes; how could athletics interface more effectively with the rest of the university community; and what was my attitude toward Title IX and women's athletics?

I did my best to answer, but when I had no idea, I simply said that I didn't know, and would have to be on the job for a while to be able to respond. Later, I discovered that my willingness to say, "I don't know," earned me points with a number of folks sitting at the table. They admired my candidness.

When I returned to Ann Arbor, I was very much on edge. I felt that I had interviewed well, but all the other candidates were currently in athletics administrative positions and had far more experience. There was no Internet then, but I tried to keep track of what was happening by calling university vice-president Curt Simic, who had coordinated the search for the president. He simply advised me to be patient while the search committee continued its deliberations. Soon word leaked out that two of the candidates had withdrawn from the search, and another had not fared well with various references. It appeared to me that I might be the last one standing, a fact that Tom Jernstedt confirmed.

"Rick," he said, "they are going to have to pick you or start the search all over again."

A few days later, a couple of friends at Michigan called to say that they had been contacted by Oregon about me. It was clear that they were checking references, which to me was a good sign. But, then one of my co-workers at the alumni association came down to my office to tell me that she had just taken a call from Oregon about my attitude toward women. She had given me high marks on that count, but said that the Oregon person mentioned to her that everyone at Michigan was complimentary except my old boss, Don Canham. Apparently, Oregon head football coach Rich Brooks had been assigned to call Canham, who proceeded to denigrate my candidacy, as I knew he would.

Although I had warned the search committee of what Canham would say, I knew that I needed something stronger to balance the ledger and that the only person who could do that was our own Michigan football coach, Bo Schembechler. Since Canham was Bo's boss, I wasn't sure how Bo might react to my request for his intervention with the Oregon search. In any event, I called Bo, told him what I believed Canham had done in talking with Brooks, and asked if he would be willing to call the Ducks coach and recommend me. Bo agreed to do it, and it must have worked because a day later I had the job. When I called Bo to thank him, he said, in typical Schembechler fashion, "I just told them that you weren't an asshole."

Going home that night I thought I knew how fortunate I was, but the magnitude of my good luck was reinforced when I opened my mailbox and found an envelope from Sonoma State, the Division III School to which I had applied. It was a form letter thanking me for my interest in their job, but notifying me that I had been eliminated from their pool of candidates and would not even be interviewed. Someone was looking out for me, that was for sure.

6

A few days later, I flew back to Eugene for a press conference and a goodwill tour of the Eugene community. I gave interviews to various Oregon newspapers and was featured on a number of radio and television shows.

My most important appearance came at a meeting of the Oregon Club, a large group of alumni and friends of the Ducks' program, which met every Monday at noon during the school year to hear from a coach or administrator from the athletics department. They were the university's main booster organization and they did everything from raising money for athletics to volunteering as manpower in the athletics office. The women volunteers had their own organization called the Daisy Ducks.

The Oregon Club's Monday gatherings were always at the Valley River Inn, a small and beautiful hotel on the Willamette River on the outskirts of town. Crowds of 200 to 300 people would attend, especially on days following big wins in football or basketball, which, unfortunately, were rare occurrences. Folks could ask questions of the coaches, and the lunches usually featured a raffle drawing of some kind for Oregon memorabilia.

My first Oregon Club meeting is the only one that I remember. My guide for the week was the Ducks' perennial associate athletics director, Herb Yamanaka, who had been at the school for more than thirty years and served almost every athletics director in Oregon history. He knew everyone in Eugene and around the state who was important to the program. Herb tutored me well before that first appearance, explaining that the guys who would be at the front table in the banquet hall were our "big hitters" and would expect special attention. Herb suggested that before taking the stage to speak I should approach that table and shake hands with each of the men there, one of whom was former legendary Oregon track coach Bill Bowerman. Bowerman had won several NCAA track and field championships, coached any number of Olympians, and had invented the first ripple-soled running shoe using his wife's waffle iron to craft it in the basement of his home.

Track and field was by far Oregon's most successful sport and Coach Bowerman was revered in the community. The coach was also the co-founder of Nike, along with Phil Knight, who had been one of his athletes. A few years before I arrived at Oregon, Nike became a public company, and about a dozen Eugenians became millionaires overnight. Bowerman was an important guy, and while working at Oregon personified the model of what athletics directors sometimes refer to as a "power coach," a term usually reserved only for highly successful football and basketball coaches. These were guys like Bear Bryant at Alabama and Indiana's Bob Knight, who were often perceived not only as bigger than life but also as bigger than the university they served. Bowerman definitely fit that profile in Eugene, dubbed "Track Town USA," by the sport's aficionados throughout the country, if not the world. Many national and world-class track events had been hosted at the university's Hayward Field, including the 2008 and 2012 United States Olympic Trials, and Oregon track was the town's pride and joy. I took Herb's advice and made it a point to pay special tribute to the VIP table, including Bowerman, before going to the microphone.

It was a surreal moment for me. Remember that, except for having been Michigan's wrestling coach for four years and doing my volunteer work for the USWF, I really had no credentials. I was coming to the job, a Pac-10 athletics directorship, as the former associate executive director of the Michigan Alumni Association. In fact, even the university administration that made the decision to hire me struggled to find the words to justify my selection. University vice-president Ray Hawke was quoted as saying, timidly, "As we looked for leadership, we turned to one of the top universities in the country to find him," inadvertently suggesting, perhaps, that on that basis the chairman of the physical education department at Michigan would have been equally qualified.

Fortunately, I had one credit that trumped all others in this track-crazy community. The year before, I had run the Boston Marathon in two hours, 47 minutes. Bowerman, of course, was very pleased, and for a moment I thought I might become the first athletics administrator in history to get a Nike shoe deal. I joked that I had a couple of creative designs in mind for wing tip dress shoes, but admitting that the "Swoosh" might be a problem.

The meeting went very well, especially when I broke the ice by pronouncing "Oregon" correctly in my first sentence. Oregon is almost always mispronounced by outsiders, so when I said how proud I was to be the new AD at the University of 'Ora-gun,' I could sense a quiet sigh of relief from the audience. I said, "I bet you all thought that I was going to say "Or-ee-gun" didn't you?'" Everybody laughed, and I knew that I had gotten off to a good start. Even Bowerman was complimentary, saying to the *Eugene Register Guard*, that at least I spoke "the King's English."

7

Herb Yamanaka, beyond his self-appointed role as my chief political strategist (a role that I welcomed), was also extremely generous and allowed me to live in his home for several months when I first came to town. Many other new employees in the Ducks athletic department had been guests in Herb's home until settling in permanent housing. I called his place the "Yamanaka Hilton."

When I left Herb's place it was to move into the McMorran House on the Oregon campus, which was normally the official residence of the university president. However, the president at the time, Paul Olum, had resided in Eugene for many years before becoming the school's CEO, and preferred to continue living in his own home, rather than relocating across town. That left the McMorran House vacant and, presumably, more vulnerable to vandalism or some malfunction in the structure that might go undetected for a long time. Someone in the administration knew that I had yet to find housing and asked if I would mind living on the top floor of the place and pay rent of $200 a month. The ground floor of the house featured a huge kitchen and dining room and a large entertainment area. All of the bedrooms were upstairs, but the master was big enough for my purposes to serve as the main living space. Having divorced a year before coming to Eugene, I was single, working long hours and really just needed a place to unwind and sleep. I kept some milk and orange juice in the gigantic downstairs refrigerator and a couple of boxes of cereal for breakfast, which was all I needed. It was perfect; it gave me a place to store my furniture from Michigan and unpack all my clothes, something I really couldn't do while staying with Herb. It was ideal for the university, because it still had the use of the place for official functions and receptions downstairs, as well as me as a caretaker living upstairs.

Everything was fine until someone in the media realized where I was staying, and for only $200 a month. Of course, the reporter only got part of the story, which generated this headline in the student newspaper: *ATHLETIC DIRECTOR LIVING IN MANSION*.

Once the details were known, everything settled down, but a few students quoted in the article were still nettled that I was "making $46,000 a year and only paying $200 a month rent." President Olum responded that I was using only two rooms (plus one shelf in the refrigerator), and that if he were living there, the university wouldn't be getting *any* rent. Still, I thought the headline was hilarious and I mailed it to a bunch of my friends who had wanted to know how I was doing in the new job. "Great," I wrote, "One of my perks is that I live in a mansion!"

The McMorran House dust-up was a light-hearted precursor to the more serious challenges I was about to encounter in my new environment. Being new not only to the position but also to the profession I really had no idea what I was getting into, and the euphoria of all the initial positive press attention wore off very quickly. To begin, I had inherited a job that faced a budget crisis, had no business manager or fundraiser on staff, was facing an NCAA investigation, and had just dropped three sports, including baseball. And the facilities were abysmal. The athletics department offices for both coaches and administrators were located in the bowels of MacArthur Court, the oldest basketball arena in the conference. For those who didn't have to work there, Mac Court was a wonderful vestige of Ducks athletics tradition that was thought to give the men's and women's Oregon basketball teams a huge home court advantage. Triple-tiered with a seating capacity of almost 10,000, the old gym had fans sitting right on top of the action, making it truly a hostile environment for a visiting team.

But the building was a liability in every other way. The locker rooms located in the basement were small and filthy; there was no weight room, as such, although there were barbells available in the dark hallway outside the training room, where players could do a few biceps curls while waiting in line to be taped. The visiting team locker room resembled a janitor's closet that, in fact, it was during the off-season. The ancient wood basketball court had several "dead spots" on the playing surface, which, while well known to our players, were a revelation to our opponents, who in the midst of a fast break were shocked to see that the ball they had just bounced on the floor had stayed there. And the place needed painting, both inside and out, the former of which we accomplished in my second year with our BINGO earnings, but the latter of which was too expensive to even consider.

That first year at Oregon in 1981 was both memorable and life changing. I met Denice Nave, the woman with whom I would share my life for the next 25 years. It happened in the Oregon press box at my first home game. Denice was a gorgeous blonde with a beautiful wide smile and a vivacious personality that could light up a room. At the time, she was working in sales for Kelly Services in Eugene while volunteering her help on football Saturdays by hosting the athletics director's private box and greeting his VIP guests, showing them their seats and serving beverages and snacks during the game. In my first home game as the Ducks new athletics director, we were playing the University of the Pacific, and though we had already lost our first two games, I was agitated that the crowd wasn't larger for our home opener.

"Where the hell is everyone?" I said rather sharply to Denice. I had just met her and regretted the tone of my voice immediately.

But before I could apologize, Denice, undaunted, said, "Well, Mr. Bay, it *is* the first day of deer-hunting season in Oregon—not a very good time to schedule a football game."

I had been put in my place, and deservedly so. I had to laugh—and so did Denice. Three years later, we were married, shortly before I left Eugene to take the job at Ohio State.

8

Another U.S. Olympic Committee delegate who had joined Tom Jernstedt in promoting my candidacy for the Oregon job was long-time University of California/ Berkeley athletics director Dave Maggard. Dave also represented the NCAA at USOC meetings and was the only Pac-10 AD I knew coming into the job. When I called to thank him for his help, I asked what he thought I should do first. He said, "Rick, it's going to take you a year just to find your way around Eugene." He was right. When I looked back on that first year, all I had accomplished was learning whom in the community I could count on for assistance, and trying to sound as positive about the program as possible in an effort to restore public confidence in the athletics department.

During my second year at the school, I hired Bill Byrne away from San Diego State University to be my senior associate in charge of development, better known as fundraising. Bill would later succeed me as Oregon's AD, and eventually go on to the same position at both Nebraska and Texas A&M.

Bill was a great guy: innovative, wonderfully optimistic, terrific with people, and perfect for the challenge we faced in reorganizing and re-energizing our fundraising efforts. Although not much of an athlete, Bill would make periodic token efforts at keeping his chunky body in shape. Usually this took the form of his riding our department's primitive–and lone–stationary bicycle in the basement hallway of Mac Court, very near the barbells, which there was no evidence he ever touched. I didn't have to remind Bill not to overdo it, since he always set the speed so low that I doubt the bike could have remained upright on the open road. He also read paperback novels while peddling, which added to his perfecting what I called the "motionless workout."

We both exercised in the early morning, but my routine included a six-mile run along the banks of the picturesque Willamette River, after which I would return to Mac Court and encounter Bill pedaling at about three mph, while reading the latest Larry McMurtry novel. One day I brought him donuts and coffee to consume during his workout because, I told him, if there was anything I hated to see, it was a malnourished cyclist, forced to quit from hunger pains before finishing his book.

Bill's BINGO brainstorm wasn't our only uncharted entrepreneurial venture. One summer we got into the entertainment business and booked a rock concert in our football stadium, featuring Joan Jett and the Blackhearts. Although the athletics department had done this previously the experience was new to me.

I learned that concert promoters dealt only in cash, and that everyone, including the performers, had to be paid before they left the stadium. I had assumed that we would be writing the appropriate checks a few days after the concert, once we had an audit and a handle on the final numbers. But a few days before the event, my athletics department business manager learned in a conversation with the promoters that they expected cash as soon as the concert ended. That was how they did business, they told us, and they would have to cancel unless we agreed. I strongly suspected that the university administration and its auditors would be apoplectic over such an arrangement and might call everything off, even before the promoters did. But the tickets had already been sold, and the projected income was to be an important part of our next budget.

I decided to say nothing and simply hope for the best. I am not sure what I expected, but when the concert ended, I was mortified to find myself huddled with my business manager and the promoters (not to mention the macabre, leather-clad Joan Jett, herself) in a small tent behind the stage, dividing several hundred thousand dollars. In the midst of it all, I nearly passed out when I heard police sirens outside the stadium. I envisioned a raid from the Eugene Police Department vice squad. Later, I was told that an ambulance had come down the stadium ramp to help a woman who had given birth during the concert.

We made about $75,000 from the Joan Jett gig. In early fall, as we were getting into the football season, we were approached by another promoter who offered us a chance to host a concert featuring The Who, a huge act at the time, which could have netted us well over $100,000. The problem was that they were coming from Seattle on a West Coast swing and could only perform on the Thursday before our home football game against, of all teams, Notre Dame. The Who needed three days to set up the venue, and two days to tear down. It just wouldn't work and the bad luck of the date conflict cost us money that would have been a big bonus for our budget.

9

The game against Notre Dame was the biggest in a long time for our fans. The contest had been scheduled many years before, and, knowing that there would be a huge demand for tickets, I decided to charge a $4 premium for the game. Many supporters were upset, complaining that they had been backing our team when we were losing and now I was gouging them the first time an attractive non-conference opponent came to town.

The $4 premium for Notre Dame made the ticket $15 (actually $15.50 with a 50 cent surcharge, but more on that later), the most ever charged for a Ducks' athletic event. What made the price even more unpalatable was that by the time the nationally ranked Irish came to Eugene, we were 0-6, the first ever-such record in Oregon football history.

The fans and the media were becoming increasingly unhappy with our coach, Rich Brooks, but I pointed to our impressive record a couple of years before and pleaded for patience. Then at the pre-game brunch in the press box, I bravely stood up before a packed room and predicted a 13-10 Ducks victory, joking that although the Irish might have the church on their side, God was merciful and knew a charity case when He saw one. Of course, everyone guffawed, but, astonishingly, I nearly called it!

The Ducks were leading exactly 13-10 near the end of the game when we were forced to punt. The Notre Dame punt returner tried to make an ill-advised over-the-shoulder catch, fumbled, and had to race about fifteen yards back to beat two Oregon cover men to the ball. The Irish then made a couple of first downs and kicked the tying field goal, as time expired.

The Notre Dame tie was a moral victory of sorts, but we still limped into the final week of the season with a 0-9-1 record.

Our rival in Corvallis, Oregon State was no better off with 1 win and 9 losses and our so-called "Civil War" game could better have been called the Frustration Bowl. Unhappy as everyone was, however, more than 35,000 fans showed up on the Oregon State campus for the contest in typical, Oregon rainy weather. What was worse was that the OSU athletics director, the jovial 300-pound former Beavers football coach Dee Andros, and I had to go onto the field at halftime to accept a check benefiting both schools from the Portland area grocers' association, which had run a fundraising in-store promotion during the season. Of course, the money was welcome, but there was a loud chorus of boos from the stands as I was introduced over the PA system, while walking onto the field. However, the introduction was so brief that that the catcalls had not entirely dissipated when Dee's name was announced. I saw it as a perfect opportunity to jab Dee.

I shook my head sadly and said to him, "Geez, Dee, I can't believe these fans would boo you like this in your own stadium!"

He about fell down laughing. "Ricky, boy" he said, "they hate your ass here!"

I couldn't help but laugh with him. Dee was a great guy, known as the "Great Pumpkin" from his coaching days at OSU, when, with his mammoth frame fully draped in Beaver orange, he would lead his team onto the field. He could hardly run (thank goodness the ramp leading from the locker room onto the turf was downhill), but God help any player who dared pass him before he got to the sideline.

In those days, both Oregon and Oregon State (along with Washington State) were the dregs of the Pac-10 Conference, and we had to stick together simply to survive. There were periodic grumblings from the Los Angeles and northern California schools about having to share television revenue with us, given our average game attendance (we shared gate revenue) and the mediocre audience ratings in our small markets, which adversely affected the league's television rights fee. When this issue arose at Pac-10 meetings, Dee and I would facetiously point out that if it wasn't for the cannon fodder generously provided each year by the Oregon schools, USC and UCLA might possibly not have the glittering records they needed to be ranked so high, nationally.

That day we beat the Beavers, 7-6, in a driving rainstorm, weather befitting the futility both schools had suffered throughout the year. We finished 1-9-1 and I wondered how we were going to sell any tickets for the following season. I thought I might have to give up the idea of scaling our ticket prices based on the attractiveness of the opposition and simply make prices for every game as low as possible. I couldn't do anything about the 50-cent surcharge, which had been imposed upon me to pay for repairs to a failing septic tank and drain field at one end of our stadium.

The University of Washington Huskies were our most hated opponent. Somehow, the school managed to escape the "Northwest stereotype," perhaps because Seattle was a lot more fashionable than Eugene, Corvallis, and Pullman, Washington, and it gave them an aura of superiority. While we couldn't stand to lose to Oregon State because we were neighbors, and a loss to the Beavers meant hearing about it incessantly for the next twelve months, the rivalry with the Beavers was not mean-spirited. Washington was winning Pac-10 championships regularly, however, and it felt like they were lording it over us.

Having survived the criticism of the $4 premium for the Notre Dame game the year before, and aware of the emotions the Huskies evoked whenever they came to Eugene, we decided early on to raise the single game ticket price by $2 for that game. The week *before* the Washington game, however, we went down to Tucson and upset Arizona, which gave us a surprising 2-0 record in the conference and tied us for the league lead. Washington was also unbeaten and suddenly we had a "big game" on our hands, a rarity in those days. Tickets were in demand, especially with the many folks who had decided against buying season tickets.

When people realized that the game cost $2 more than usual, they thought I had made it up on the spot. I was accused of wanting to exploit the upset win over Arizona by raising ticket prices while on the plane back from Tucson. It took a couple of days for fans to acknowledge that, yes, the price had been set in advance, but it was still $2, and they weren't happy about it. Whatever they paid, however, was too much. We got clobbered 32-3.

Athletics directors are, of necessity, opportunists. While often accused of exploiting our most loyal fans, most of us have experienced budget dilemmas that require striking when the iron is hot. Sudden ticket demand to a popular bowl game or an NCAA basketball event is an AD's best opportunity to cash in. Requiring boosters to pay a healthy premium for such tickets is highly unpopular, especially if the school in question has been struggling for a long time. "We've been supporting your lousy ass teams for all these years," a typical letter begins, "and you finally have a half-way decent season, and you stick it to us. What happened to rewarding loyalty?" There is no answer except that you are running a business like any other, which means that when demand is high, you had better capitalize on your good fortune.

In 2000 when Arizona State made its first-ever appearance in the Rose Bowl, ASU athletics director Kevin White recognized a golden opportunity to generate revenue badly needed to keep the Sun Devils program viable. Despite the certainty of angry public reaction and media criticism, White announced that each Rose Bowl ticket would require a $100 surcharge, and even $200 for the best seats allotted to the school. Recrimination rained down on the Sun Devils AD, but Arizona State sold every ticket allocated to it, and the athletics department made an additional $3 million in the process, money that was crucial to eliminating its deficit and sustaining the competitiveness of ASU athletics for next two years.

When it came to the Rose Bowl, all twenty Big-10 and Pac-10 schools received and were responsible for selling a minimum number of tickets. Normally, only the two participating schools experienced a demand well beyond their contractual allotment, especially if those participants had not appeared in the game for many years. In fact, it was not unusual for non-participants simply to sell at face value their extra tickets to the conference school playing in the game.

At Oregon, I had inherited a situation whereby a Los Angeles travel agent paid the athletics department a significant premium for our unused tickets in order to sell Rose Bowl packages to tourists. Although this practice amounted to the university scalping its 100 tickets for $75 above face value, the transaction masqueraded as a gift to the department—the agent making a one-time donation to Oregon athletics. Given the Ducks' abysmal financial position at the time and the prospect of a $7,500 windfall, I never took the time to analyze the deal honestly, choosing instead to feel grateful that we had just covered the travel budget for men's and women's tennis.

Except for this annual Rose Bowl bonus, about the only thing Dee Andros and I could count on consistently for revenue was good attendance when we played each other. We were just hanging on otherwise. So one day I said, "Dee, if we were smart, we would play each other *twice* in football—once at the beginning of the season in Portland (where most of the alums of both schools lived), and then our regular "Civil War" game at alternate sites at the end of the year. We'd have two great crowds and make a lot more money." Of course, I might not have made this suggestion except that Oregon State hadn't beaten us in football for nine years.

Dee looked at me. "Good idea for *you*, Ricky boy, but we're not very good right now."

I said, "Really, I'm serious. It's been done before."

"Bullshit. When?" Dee asked.

"1896," I said. "I looked it up, and you were probably there. You guys were Oregon Agricultural College then. We won both games, 2-0 and 8-4. But you guys are better now. I know you'll score more than four points combined."

"I'm not interested, Ricky, unless you guys want to play us four times in basketball," he answered. "We'd draw big there, too."

We already played them twice in the Pac-10 schedule, and sometimes three times if we happened to meet in the Far West Classic holiday tournament in Portland. I couldn't remember the last time we had whipped them on the hard court. Actually, we had lost 13 straight basketball games to the Beavers going back to the early '80s.

"Well, football is different," I countered. "Lots of teams have played twice in a season, especially with the bowl set-up."

"Nice try, Ricky boy, but I don't think so."

We both laughed, as we seemed always to do when we were together.

Our jousting aside, however, the question of whether any of the Northwest schools (except Washington, which was winning championships) should remain a part of the Pac-10 was not only a periodic conference issue, but also fostered debate among the faculty on the three campuses.

In the midst of a discouraging football season, the Oregon faculty senate began to question if, indeed, we weren't out of our league. At one senate meeting, I was asked why we kept beating our heads against the wall against the likes of USC, UCLA, Washington, and, more recently the new and heavily state-subsidized Arizona schools. Why didn't we just move to the Big Sky Conference? Let's play Montana and Idaho, it was suggested. I remember replying that the Pac-10 was more than an athletics conference, that it was to everyone's advantage at Oregon, including the faculty, to be affiliated and frequently identified with the UCLAs, Washingtons and Stanfords, rather than the Montanas, Idahos and Nevadas of the Big Sky. I reminded them that, although often ridiculously out of perspective, competitive athletics was often the most visible yardstick by which a university was measured. Thus, I said, because we couldn't control public perception, it behooved us to field as fine an athletics program as possible, and to be in a prestigious conference

The reality of those remarks probably did not sit well with some faculty, but I walked away feeling as though I had made sense and had given them something to think about.

10

Dee Andros was encountering the same problems at Oregon State. So, bitter rivals that we were on the playing field, we joined forces in other ways to keep our programs afloat. I went to Corvallis to speak at a testimonial for Dee, and he agreed to take part in one of our season-ticket football sales promotions.

It was called "Quack Attack," and came about because we needed something that was catchy but didn't promise too much. "Returning Excitement," our sales slogan from the year before, was based on the fact that we had both the Pac-10's leading punt and kickoff return men on our team. But in the awful season just completed, in which we'd won only one game, the only excitement for me had been sharing a tent with Joan Jett and nervously wading through tens of thousands of dollars in cash with her promoters.

I don't recall who had the idea for the new promotion. The premise behind the catch phrase was that folks in the community who failed to buy a season football ticket for the 1982 schedule could be vulnerable to a "quack attack," meaning that, suddenly and unexpectedly, when they opened their mouths to speak only a quacking noise would emerge from their voice box. It was a little like getting a flu shot as a preventive measure against the flu—buy a season ticket and protect yourself from a "quack attack."

My marketing guys—actually, I think we had only one on our skeletal staff—had some radio spots produced in which an unsuspecting shopper in a supermarket starts to say something at the checkout counter, but when he opens his mouth he can only quack! The person at the cash register says something like, "Aha! You haven't bought your

Ducks season football tickets yet, have you?" After another uncontrollable quack or two from the frustrated customer, an announcer breaks in with, "If you want to avoid a quack attack, you had better get down to the U of O ticket office and get your Ducks season football tickets now!"

It was a cute idea, promised nothing, and was popular in the community, so we decided to do a television spot using the same concept. I called Dee Andros for help. When I told Dee that I wanted him to be in a television spot promoting Ducks football tickets, he thought I was crazy.

"Ricky boy," he said, "are you tryin' to get me fired?"

"Why would I do that?" I asked. "They would just go out and hire a better AD, which isn't going to help me."

"You sumbitch," he laughed, and then agreed to do it.

The ad started with an upper body shot of Dee lying in a hospital bed, his 300-pound torso covered with a white sheet that was large enough to be a circus tent. He is moaning to the nurse and then tries to say something, but the only sound that comes out of his mouth is a loud "quack" along with a tiny, floating white feather. He tries again, but gets the same result. Then, slowly the camera pans the length (and mound) of his body to expose two webbed duck feet sticking out from under the sheet. The message is clear. By refusing to buy Oregon football tickets, even Oregon State University athletics director Dee Andros cannot avoid a quack attack. Dee got a little heat from some of the Beavers fans in Corvallis, but most people loved it, and took it in the right spirit.

The Pac-10 was a great conference for antics like this. Another example involved George Raveling, the head basketball coach at Washington State. As I said, our basketball arena was ancient, and confining, with high school-like pull-out wooden bleachers for the five or six rows closest to the floor. Because the teams had to sit in folding chairs right up against the first row, nearest the floor, the fans could have reached out and touched the players. (The way we were playing I worried more about the safety of our team than I did the visitors.) This allowed for easy dialogue between the opposing team and coach and the Oregon boosters behind their bench. In fact, long time season ticket holders sitting there got to know the visiting coaches well and often talked with them briefly before the game.

George Raveling was a big man, a former outstanding player at Villanova, and very outgoing. He always had a white towel draping over one shoulder when he coached, presumably to wipe the sweat from his face during games. One year, as a joke, the Oregon student section gave him a yellow towel (one of Oregon's school colors) before a game against the Cougars. After that, Raveling never failed to feature the yellow towel whenever WSU came to Eugene to play the Ducks.

One season Raveling's mischievous nature caused a major ruckus in Corvallis. In 1983, Washington State had a great basketball team (as did Oregon State), when it embarked on its annual road trip to Oregon to play the Ducks and the Beavers. In those days, every school had a travel partner and we all played on Friday and Saturday nights. On this Friday, while we were playing Washington, the Cougars were in Corvallis. To get his squad fired up, Raveling came out dressed like his players and warmed up with them. He took a turn in the traditional layup line, and then proceeded to shoot around with the squad for a few minutes. The Beavers' fans went nuts, and the Cougars' players loved it. The stunt eliminated any tension the WSU team might have felt, and they went on to an easy upset victory. The next morning the Pac-10 commissioner dictated that no coach could appear in uniform with his team or take part in any on-court, pre-game warm-up activities.

I could only wish that we had been the team that had come up with a gimmick to beat Oregon State. The Beavers were coached by the legendary Ralph Miller, and we were never good enough to lick them in my three-year run as athletics director.

My second year at the helm, I hired a new coach, Don Monson, who had built a basketball dynasty at the University of Idaho. As good as the Beavers were, Monson's Idaho team came to the Far West Classic in Portland in late December, whipped both Oregon schools, and won the championship—and it did it two years in a row. So when I hired Monson, our fans and I were hopeful that we now had the makings of a program that could compete with our cousins in Corvallis.

Still, everyone knew this would take time, especially Coach Monson. We had one very good player, Blair Rasmussen, a 7-foot center from Seattle whom Monson's predecessor, Jim Haney, had somehow successfully recruited away from the University of Washington. Beyond Rasmussen, however, we were talent thin. Even Blair had his limitations, depending mostly on a little turnaround jump shot from about seven or eight feet from the basket.

The Monday before we were to drive to Corvallis to play the heavily favored Beavers, Don came into my office and said, "Rick, I don't know if you and Denice ought to sit in the stands on Saturday." (The visitors always had about 12 seats behind their team's bench, but they were still surrounded by home fans.)

"What do you mean," I asked, slightly alarmed.

"Well, we can't hope to stay in the game unless we hold the ball, and the fans in that place are going to want to kill me, and anyone else who is wearing green," he began. (This was 1984, before the 45-second shot clock was a part of college basketball.) "They like to run and shoot, you know, play up-tempo, and they're not going to be able to do it, because we're not even going to take a shot, until Blair gets free for his jumper.

"If we can get ahead, we may never shoot again," he continued. "They're going to have to foul to get the ball back, and if we can make our free throws, we might have a chance. Anyway, I just wanted you to know."

Denice and I decided to gut it out, sort of. We didn't wear green and I resisted the temptation to take a couple of Beaver-orange raincoats in case things really got ugly.

We won the opening tip, came right down the court, got Rasmussen free, and he canned an eight-foot jumper. Ducks lead, 2-0. Oregon State quickly inbounded the ball, raced the length of the floor, but missed the shot. We got the rebound and walked the ball up the court, and promptly went into a four-corner offense, passing the ball around the perimeter until Blair gained an inside position, again, and easily made another basket, making it 4-0.

The Beavers charged back, but turned the ball over, and we slowly brought the ball over the 10-second line. Unfortunately, the rule requiring a team to move the ball past mid-court within 10 seconds *was* in effect, or we would have just stayed under the Oregon State basket. Now, with what seemed like a whopping four-point lead, we really began working the four-corner drill, our players simply holding the ball if an Oregon State defender did not come out to pressure them.

Finally, it began to dawn on the sold-out crowd what we were up to. The booing started and then became abusive; profanity and paper cups began raining down on the tiny, reserved-seating area of our official party. I started wishing I had brought those orange coats.

The game went on like this and the half ended with us ahead by the unlikely score of 12-8. More debris showered our bench area, our team was booed off the floor and, finally, someone spotted me, screaming, "Bay, you asshole, why don't you hire a MAN for a coach!"

As strange as this part of the game was, there was another weird occurrence just as the second half began. One of the players noticed a wet spot on the playing floor and that a liquid was dripping from the ceiling of the arena.

When the custodian began to wipe it up, he was startled to find that the fluid was blood. Play was halted while someone investigated the source of the dripping, which seemed to be coming from the catwalk overhead. Someone had hung what must have been a live duck or a newly killed one from the rafters. Dead now, but still bleeding, the bird was finally cut down and play resumed. Because the duck had to be lowered to the floor, at least some of the crowd saw it and roared with delight.

Whether it unnerved our team I can't be sure, but the Beavers began to foul us. We began missing our free throws, Rasmussen grew cold from the field, and once Oregon State got the lead we didn't have enough firepower to catch them. The Beavers became a little cautious themselves. Now that they knew Don's strategy, they didn't want to fall behind again. We ended up losing 29-23, the lowest scoring game in modern Pac-10 history. It was our 10th consecutive defeat at the hands of Oregon State. The odd thing about the game was that we had decided on an ultra-conservative offensive strategy because we didn't think we had much scoring potential, but five days later we let it fly and scored four times as many points as we had in Corvallis, beating Stanford, 91-71.

Don Monson was a disciple of Jud Heathcote at Michigan State and was there during the Magic Johnson years, when the Spartans won the national championship. As did Jed, he would prowl the sidelines during games, growling at the officials on what seemed like every trip down the court, usually stopping short of drawing a technical foul. Still, it became somewhat embarrassing and I finally told him that I thought he was losing credibility with the referees because he contested almost everything. When there was something legitimate to dispute, I told him, the officials had already tuned him out.

For some reason, many college basketball coaches were of the mind that they had to contest everything to improve their chances of getting the "next call." "I've got to let them know I'm here," the thinking went, because, "If the officials think that *I think* I got screwed on one call, they're more likely (subconsciously) to give me a break on the next one."

To his credit, Don acknowledged that I was right, and thanked me for talking with him about it.

Unfortunately, Don never was able to get the program going at Oregon. I left for Ohio State after Don's first year. Eight years later, Bill Byrne, my successor, reassigned him to be the men's golf coach rather than fire him and have to pay him a buyout. It was a move that resulted in Don's bringing a lawsuit against the university.

Having played golf with Don a few times, however, it was the golf team that should have sued. I loved Don, and still value his friendship, but his golf was awful. On his first trip to the Eugene Country Club with me to hit some practice balls, he shanked one through the netting that guarded the nearby practice green. His ball struck another member on the lower leg. Don and I stood there in horror, watching the stunned look on the man's face, and seeing, a second later, blood starting to seep through the pant leg of his lightly colored trousers. After that, Don was encouraged to take his game directly to the course where there were fewer people in a compacted area.

11

In fairness to Don Monson's coaching record at Oregon, we did have the worst basketball facility in the conference. Mac Court was a dump, and I can only imagine what a recruit thought when first exposed to the site where he might play his college career. All we could say was that the close proximity of the fans gave us a big, home-court advantage.

Don raised some money from basketball boosters to spruce up his staff offices, but that was about it. Of course, I knew what he was going through, because my office was in the same dungeon, just around the corner from him. In addition, the football offices were there, too, about 20 feet from my office, in the other direction.

My office was in a new location, in what had been the men's track office. Before my arrival, the AD's office could be found at the back of the building, beyond a maze of cubicles for other staff, and boxes that were filled with office supplies. The workspace itself was a long, rectangular area, divided lengthwise by what appeared to be an eighth-inch thick corkboard. This design created two offices, one of which was the "private" enclave of the director, while the other served as a secretarial space and waiting area for guests. I use the word *private* advisedly, because the thinness of the dividing wall was such that anyone in the secretary's office could probably hear me signing letters.

I knew instantly that this would never do. The athletics director, the leader of the department, needed to be much more visible and accessible. He needed to be at the front of the building, not down a labyrinthine corridor, where he appeared as though hiding in the Paris sewers. The problem was that the only solution was to trade space with the men's track office. Given the great tradition of Oregon track, I knew that the relocation of that office to this area might cause a little heartburn among their faithful. I never imagined the firestorm that broke out. Not only did my track coach, Bill Dellinger, not accept the move gracefully; he put the worst possible face on it and did his best to ensure that Bill Bowerman and his disciples in the community would be outraged by what they saw as the first step by the new director to scale down the track program.

I had explained to Dellinger the reason for the move, saying that it was in the best interest of the department from a public relations standpoint that the new director be viewed as a leader, out front in every way, and easily accessible to the public at large. This meant my occupying a front office, and his was the only space that was satisfactory and could be moved. The location of the football offices were also up front, but formed a kind of suite that could not be re-configured in any other place in the building. The only other front workspace was our ticket office, located under the outside marquee of Mac Court, which had to remain there to be accessible to the public.

Coach Dellinger would not be mollified, and I began to hear about his constant grumblings in the community. I warned him about it, but to no avail. He was undermining the department, and the situation finally got to the point where I actually thought about firing him. How this would have gone down, I don't know. Dellinger, who had been Bowerman's assistant until the old coach retired, had an outstanding coaching record in his own right, but he had a knack of rubbing people the wrong way, and was not nearly as esteemed as his old boss. As it became clear that I might have to terminate Dellinger, I was told confidentially by the personnel office that I would have to give him sufficient notice and an opportunity to clean up his act, which I was more than willing to do. The guy was a great coach. I liked him and I didn't want to get rid of him, but the department's welfare had to come first.

The Human Resources Department required that I implement what was called "progressive discipline," that necessitated my writing a letter of warning to Dellinger, which he promptly made sure that Bowerman saw. Soon the media was asking me about it, and, although I couldn't discuss personnel matters publicly, I was spending way too much time defending myself on an issue that paled in comparison to the many other challenges we faced.

Eventually the controversy quieted down, especially when I would not be goaded into talking about it. But the incident did not help my standing in this track-crazy city, and was a harbinger of other difficulties to come for me connected to the sport.

Nearly 25 years later, in his book, *Bowerman and the Men of Oregon*, author Kenny Moore printed the warning letter to Dellinger in its entirety. Moore, a former two-time Olympic marathoner who ran for Coach Bowerman at Oregon, implied that I was somehow intentionally, maybe even maliciously, trying to disparage the track program. Nothing could have been further from the truth. Moore never bothered to get my side of the story because he typified the bunker mentality of a core group of Bowerman disciples who cared only about the Oregon track program. They demonstrated little or no regard for the athletics department as a whole. The bigger picture was not a consideration for them. If I could have moved the track office to a better space I would have, but the archaic layout of the office space in Mac Court left few alternatives. I had just been installed as the leader of Ducks' athletics and I needed to look like it.

12

In October of 1982, it came to my attention that several of our male track athletes were receiving free equipment—warm-up suits, shoes and other items—through the mail directly from at least two sportswear companies, Nike and Adidas. This was an NCAA rules violation; athletes could only be issued equipment through the athletics department equipment room. Even then, they had to return the equipment at the end of the school year or buy it at fair market value.

We were already on NCAA probation for infractions serious enough to keep Ducks football off television and out of a bowl game for at least a year. Unfortunately, our on-field performances pretty much guaranteed the latter anyway. Although equipment companies had apparently been funneling their products to collegiate track athletes for years, it was something no one talked about or perhaps even considered. Track programs in general were not well funded by their schools; kids needed equipment and if the equipment came directly from the manufacturers, who cared? The athletes wore the stuff openly and I don't think anyone stopped to reflect on whether it was a violation.

However, our probationary status at Oregon made everyone hypersensitive, if not paranoid, about the rules. We could not afford another hiccup, and I was under strict orders to report anything, no matter how seemingly minor, to both the Pac-10 and the NCAA.

Ironically, the matter came to light after comments by Bill Bowerman at a summer luncheon of track boosters, at which the former coach was complaining about the infiltration of Adidas running shoes into the Oregon program. Bill Dellinger had designed a special nylon mesh running shoe that he thought Nike would manufacture, but when Nike rejected the idea, Dellinger went to Adidas. It wasn't long before several Oregon runners were wearing Adidas shoes and Bowerman, giving vent to his anger over the matter, inadvertently brought everyone to the realization that neither company should be sending shoes or anything else to Oregon athletes. Suddenly, the issue of my having "power grabbed" the old track office was dwarfed by the Dellinger-Bowerman shoe controversy.

The unfortunate result of the matter was that we not only had to collect the equipment from the athletes and return it, but, far worse, I had to declare three athletes ineligible for receiving an "extra benefit" and then file for their reinstatement through the NCAA sub-committee for eligibility appeals. The situation was especially controversial, not only because the three athletes involved were All-Americans—Jim Hill, an outstanding 1500 meters runner, and the Crouser brothers, Dean and Brian, who were national champions in the discus and javelin respectively—but also because Nike's chairman, Phil Knight, had become a major benefactor to the university.

Fortunately, for everyone, discovery of the infraction came about during the off-season for track, and the athletes were reinstated without their missing any competition. I knew the violation had been inadvertent. Dellinger was aware that Nike and Adidas were sending equipment directly to the athletes, but reasoned that the direct-mail approach was okay and that it simply eliminated the extra step of having to re-issue the items through the equipment room.

Later, the athletes probably did receive the same equipment, legally checked out to them, through the university. This would have been all right, so long as the clothing and shoes were in keeping with the normal issue for any track athlete. In other words, an equipment manufacturer could not send a fancy $1,000 warm-up suit to the athletics department and stipulate that it be issued to a particular star runner, who would then presumably win all his races wearing their product. Everyone on the team had to receive the same basic equipment.

Although I don't recall what minor penalties the NCAA imposed beyond the temporary ineligibility of the athletes, we avoided a major public scandal. But behind the scenes, Phil Knight was livid. By that time, I probably had only met him once or twice and Lord only knows what he may have heard about me from Bowerman and Dellinger. When I called to let him know what had happened, and told him that Nike couldn't be sending equipment directly to our athletes, he said something to the extent that he was a private citizen, not bound by the NCAA or the university, and he could damn well send free equipment to anyone he pleased.

I could only acknowledge that he was right.

"Mr. Knight," I said, "I agree that you have every right to send our guys free equipment. I can't stop you," I told him. "But every time you do, I'll have to make that athlete ineligible and he'll have to send the stuff right back to Nike."

That was the last we spoke of it, and, as far as I know, Nike did not send any free gear directly to our kids again.

A few months before I left to go to Ohio State I had another skirmish connected with the track program.

It was widely thought around Eugene that Bill Bowerman had lots of money and that he someday would leave it to the university, if we played our cards right. So folks went out of their way to abide his eccentricities, not wanting to upset him or his legion of admirers. Bowerman was a great coach; his track program was Eugene's pride and joy. He was responsible not only for the development of many world-class runners, but also in building the Oregon track program into the most prestigious in the nation. When Oregon built its new football stadium in the late '70s, he was instrumental in transforming the old playing field into a track stadium called Hayward Field, named after the Ducks' first track coach. As many as 17,000 fans would cram into Hayward to watch the NCAA men's and women's championships, the Pac-10 championships, the US Olympic Trials and the famed Oregon Relays. Nearly as many spectators would also show up to watch the great dual meets between Oregon and UCLA, often a battle to see if the Ducks' outstanding distance runners could outpoint UCLA's sprinters.

Eugene became known as "Track Town, USA," and track put the city on the map. The sport had such great tradition that almost all the world's greatest track athletes eventually came to Eugene to compete. Eugene was a small community, 400 miles north of San Francisco and 100 miles south of Portland. The airport was so small (at the time) that when the football team's charter was headed to Arizona, the plane had to make a quick stop in Sacramento to gas up, because the airport's runway was not long enough to accommodate a full load of fuel on takeoff.

I was caught up in track fever like everyone else. I doubt that there was an athletics director anywhere else in the nation that embraced track as I did, not only as an administrator but also as a fan, and, I might add, an actual participant.

Having run a couple of marathons before coming to Eugene, I was now in the perfect setting to continue recreational running. Despite professional differences, I liked Coach Dellinger and we often ran together on the beautiful wood-chip paths that wound along the river.

It was not unusual to be passed by Mary Decker Tabb or Alberto Salazar along the way. In fact, one day Alberto (just out of school and with at least one New York City Marathon title under his belt) slowed alongside me as I was huffing and puffing my way through a six-mile run at about a six-minute pace. He started telling me how glad he was to have a new athletics director who loved track and was a runner to boot. Gulping for air, all I could do was nod, at which point he said, "Well, I've got to get going, Mr. Bay. Nice talking to you," and sprinted off leaving a cloud of Oregon woodchip dust in his wake. He told me later that he had been in the midst of a 15-miler at a leisurely 4:45 pace.

I also worked out with the women's cross country team and its coach, Tom Heinonen, who trained me for my only two 10K races. He knew that I had run a 2:47 marathon, but when I told him that my goal for the 10K was to break 35 minutes (under six minutes a mile), he warned me that I would have to do a lot of speed work to build up my strength.

"This is different from a marathon," he said. "It's not just endurance. You're going to have to get a lot stronger."

So I became introduced to what track coaches call "interval training." At the time, I could easily run six miles in under 40 minutes, or about 6:40 a mile, but getting under a six-minute mile pace would mean having to reach a new level. To do it, Tom and I would meet at the track before six in the morning, and after warming up with some distance running, we would start to run the 400-meter oval in intervals—sprint 200 meters, jog 200, sprint 200, jog 200. My lungs burned and my leg strength dissipated under the pressure of the sprints. After a few weeks of this regimen, however, I felt as though I was in the best shape since my college wrestling days.

Tom also talked to me about diet and about the strategy of running the course, which fell steeply downhill at the start and could easily seduce a runner into a prematurely fast pace that would all but destroy him in the end. I listened to Tom as eagerly as if I was on his team—and I ran the race of my life, finishing in 34 minutes, 36 seconds (5:46 /mile), and 17th out of 228 runners in my age group—and I did it in Track Town, USA!

I think all this was lost on Bowerman, who, when dealing with me, seemed consumed only with who had the power. One day he walked into the president's office and told him that he wanted to contribute $1 million to construct a track building at the end of Hayward Field. It would house the coaches' offices for the men's and women's teams, locker rooms for both, a recruiting lounge and a viewing area on the roof for VIPs to watch the competition on the track below. Ignoring protocol completely, he already had arranged for conceptual drawings for the project, bypassing my office altogether.

According to Moore's book, this was payback for moving Dellinger's office. "Fine (thought Bowerman): If this AD won't give Dellinger a decent place to work, I'll give the university a whole new building," Moore wrote.

The logic was mystifying. If giving the university and athletics a new building was retribution, I welcomed the punishment. But it wasn't that simple. There was one catch. The building was *only* for track, and the athletic director would have no supervisory control of the place. This proviso was both petty and insulting. He further stipulated that no other university or athletics department function could take place on the property without track's consent.

The decision to accept or decline the gift under these conditions was not my call, but I told the president that while I would love to have the facility, I thought that *any* gift to the school should be made irrevocably and not subject to outside control, no matter how subtle. I agreed completely that it was incumbent upon the school to honor the purpose of the gift and that it truly be regarded as the "track building." However, if there were occasions when the building could be put to good, temporary use for the benefit of the department, the athletics director should have the latitude to make that decision.

This policy would have been consistent with the management of all the athletics facilities. The football coach pretty much controlled what happened in Autzen Stadium, as did the basketball coach with respect to Mac Court. However, those facilities were not theirs and we often staged other events at the two venues, sometimes even inconveniencing those sports temporarily for the greater good.

To my dismay, as we began to discuss the issue internally, I could see that the president and a few of his team were leaning toward giving in to Bowerman. The sentiment seemed to be, "Hey, it's a million dollars; there's more where that's coming from, and let's not make the guy mad." I was adamant in my opinion that the university could not allow an outside agency to control any of its facilities, even indirectly, and that to accept any gift under these conditions would be a bad precedent.

Following these initial discussions, things calmed down for a while; no decision was made and it looked as though Bowerman might relent. I finally saw the drawings and noticed that there was great deal of open space in one section of the building for which there was no designated use. If all of the track program's needs were covered, and there was still space left over, the department ought to utilize it for the common good. This was exactly the issue I had raised in the beginning.

The space in question was in a distant corner of the building on the ground floor, adjacent to a kind of utility room. One significant expense for the department was the annual laundry bill. We did not have adequate facilities in the basement of Mac Court to have our own laundry operation, but the proposed track building seemed to have the perfect space, at no expense to its main tenants. When he heard about the concept, however, Bowerman and his people put such a negative, out of perspective spin on the idea that the word around town was that, "Bay wants to turn Bowerman's track building into a laundromat."

Sometime later, when Denice and I were in Ashland, Oregon, for the Shakespeare Festival, there was news from Eugene that Bowerman was so frustrated with me that he would welcome a "wrestling match with Bay in the middle of the football stadium." I laughed, but at the same time could not help fantasizing about where I'd land one of my waffle-soled, Nike-wides, if given the chance. Why all this trouble with former track coaches, I wondered? Canham had coached track, too. It made me want to cancel my subscription to *Runner's World*.

My ongoing insistence that the university adhere to its basic guidelines relative to institutional control gave Bowerman an excuse to withdraw the gift. I honestly don't know how serious he was about the gift in the first place, or if he just wanted to pick a fight with me over the moving of the track office. But if I was the reason that the gift fell through, it apparently took Bowerman a long time to get over it. I left Oregon in 1984, but it wasn't until eight years later, in 1992, that the building finally was completed.

13

While I loved our track program, it was taking up a disproportionate amount of my time. We certainly drew more fans to our track events and generated more revenue from the activity than any other school in the country, but the sport still didn't pay for itself, and I needed to concentrate more heavily on the two sports that could make or break the entire athletics department–football and men's basketball.

The football coach I inherited was Rich Brooks, a former Oregon State player who had been a backup to the Beavers' only Heisman Trophy winner, Terry Baker. Rich had taken over a faltering program a few years before my arrival, and after several losing seasons, led the Ducks to their best record in years. In 1980, Oregon went 6-3-2; including victories over both UCLA and defending Pac-10 champion Washington, while tying powerful USC.

Optimism in Eugene was running high in the summer of 1981. We were to open the season in a kind of warm-up game at Fresno State. We lost, 23-16, in what was a shocking defeat for Oregon fans, not to mention Rich, who unnecessarily apologized to me for the team's performance while walking off the field. What was worse was that we lost eight of our next nine games before ending the season by trouncing hapless Oregon State, 47-17 in the "Civil War" game, in Eugene. The entire year had been a nightmare, and I was worried about what the disaster would do to ticket sales the next season.

I felt sorry for Rich because no coach worked harder to succeed. He had promised the Oregon alumni in Portland (the Ducks' biggest fan base) that if he got the job, he would make the 200-mile round-trip every Monday to speak at their booster's luncheon. And he did it, unfailingly, although I often tried to talk him out of going so that he could concentrate on the team. Rich said that a promise was a promise, and every Monday he would leave the office at 10 a.m., speak at noon, and return just in time for practice at 3:30. It was grueling, especially because so many trips were to explain what had gone wrong the previous Saturday.

Rich was also willing to do anything to help the department, at large. Every year at our biggest fundraiser, the Big Green Auction, Rich let folks bid for a limited number of game-day sideline passes. He once even included game access to a set of earphones, so that the winning bidder could hear the coaches in the press box talking to, or more likely, screaming at colleagues on the sidelines, as the action was unfolding on the field.

Still, we never had a winning season the three years that I was at Oregon and I was getting pressure to fire Rich. But I knew that he was an outstanding coach. We just did not have the facilities or the budget to recruit successfully against the likes of Washington and the southern California schools. It seemed as though I was spending most of my time defending Rich, but I hung in there with him, and it paid big dividends for Oregon when, in 1994, the Ducks went to the Rose Bowl for the first time in 50 years.

After that, money came pouring into the athletic department (most of which was from Nike founder Phil Knight), and today Oregon boasts one of the most spectacular athletics campuses in the country.

A few years later, Rich became the head coach of the Atlanta Falcons, and, today, even though he had an overall losing record at Oregon (because of the lean early years), the Autzen Stadium floor has been named Rich Brooks Field. Rich ended his career as the head coach at Kentucky and had more success at Kentucky than any coach since Bear

Bryant led the Wildcats before becoming a legend at Alabama.

Basketball was a different story. Oregon won the very first NCAA basketball tournament in 1939, defeating Ohio State for the title. The starting five on that team was big for its time (averaging about 6'3") and was known as the Tall Firs. In the years before I arrived in 1981, the Ducks had fashioned a reputation as a "giant killer" at Mac Court, even defeating some of John Wooden's great UCLA teams.

The coach was a fiery guy named Dick Harter, who in 1978 went on to coach in the NBA, leaving the job to his young assistant, Jim Haney. Jim was a great person, but had never had a head job and was overmatched. Somewhat shy, Jim did not have the same charismatic public persona as Rich Brooks and so people weren't as patient with him. After two more losing seasons, while I was there, Jim stepped down and Don Monson took over for the next nine years, though his teams failed to win half their games.

Athletic directors are blamed for lots of things they do and for some things they didn't do. I hired Monson and refused to fire Brooks. Whatever anyone thought of the decisions, they were my responsibility. But I had nothing to do with the poor financial condition of the department when I arrived or the decision to eliminate baseball from the program. In an effort to reduce the deficit, the university administration made the decision to eliminate three men's sports before the new director was in place. It would not have been fair to strap a new AD with the onerous task of cutting sports as his first order of business. Thus, in the months before hiring me, Oregon cut men's gymnastics, swimming and baseball, the last of which caused the most furor.

The Ducks had never had a great baseball tradition; it was a spring sport that played in the shadow of track and field. Still, there were many former players who lived in the Eugene area. In addition, the move threatened to be a precursor for the virtual elimination of the sport in the Northwest, because it was feared that Oregon State, Washington and Washington State might use the Oregon precedent as an excuse to drop their programs. Given the rainy, cold springs in the region, many games were weathered out, and the southern schools in the Pac 10 hated to go north. At the time, I don't believe the folks at USC and the Arizona schools (all national powers) would have been heartbroken if all four northern programs would have been eliminated. But the other three persevered, largely because the Oregon action sounded the alarm that they, too, could be in jeopardy. Unlike Oregon, they each had long-time coaches with strong personalities who now had a window of opportunity to rally advocates in a way that preempted any potential action to eliminate baseball.

Meanwhile, in Eugene, the baseball folks would not give up, and they were lying in wait for me, the new AD, to plead their case further. The central administration had warned me that this would happen and re-emphasized that the decision to cut the sport was final.

As someone who loves baseball, I felt as bad as anyone did that my school no longer had a team and I did not want to come across to the wounded baseball alums as insensitive. So I made myself available when the committee representing the group (which, unfortunately called themselves the SOBs, for Save Oregon Baseball) wanted to meet with me. I believe the budget for baseball when it was cut, was somewhere around $200,000, counting scholarships. The SOBs pledged to raise enough money to extend the sport one more year, which, they said, would give them time to develop a mechanism for supporting the sport indefinitely. I was sympathetic, but the hard fact was that a year-to-year plan would not work. No high school players would come to Oregon knowing that the sport might be cut again at any time, and nobody would schedule the Ducks in Eugene when no return games were guaranteed.

I told the group that the only possible way baseball could be reinstated was for them to endow the sport fully, which meant coming up with at least $4 million cash that could yield about five percent annually to meet the budget and guarantee the sport's existence indefinitely. That proved to be impossible, scuttling the bitter struggle to resurrect Oregon baseball.

Because I was involved in these final discussions, many people believed that *I* was the AD who made the decision to drop baseball. Twenty-five years later, one person who knew the truth maliciously continued to perpetuate the myth. I was the athletics director at San Diego State, then, and changed baseball coaches. The outgoing coach, a disgruntled Jim Dietz, who was originally from Oregon, disingenuously told a local columnist that I had been the one responsible for eliminating the sport–and the *San Diego Union Tribune*, a publication that was often footloose about facts, never checked out the allegation and printed it. Four years later, the hurtful falsehood was still alive. In 2004, when I joined Ironwood Country Club in Palm Desert, California, a member there who had gone to Oregon told me that when he mentioned my name to another Oregon alum in the community, the guy said, "Yeah, I remember him. He is the son of a bitch who dropped baseball."

14

By the spring of 1984, I had been at Oregon for three years. It clearly had not been smooth sailing. We had yet to have a winning football season and the basketball program was struggling to regain respectability under a new coach. Bowerman was still nettling me at every opportunity, and unfortunately, Mac Court had not burned down.

Worst of all by far, however, was that a few months before I left, our wrestling team was in a car accident on its way to Pullman to compete against Washington State. Two of the young athletes died, including Jed Kesey, son of the famous writer Ken Kesey, author of *One Flew Over the Cuckoo's Nest*.

I was in Pullman when I got the news. I had flown over earlier in the day, because our basketball team was also playing Washington State. A reporter from an Oregon paper covering the basketball game had a car and volunteered to drive me about two hours to Spokane to the hospital where the injured athletes had been taken.

One of the young men died before I arrived. We had stopped at a gas station pay phone to get an update and a doctor came on the line to tell me of the death. In what was the most difficult phone call of my life, I phoned his mother in Portland to break the news. I also called Ken Kesey, he a former Oregon wrestler, who was living in Pleasant Hill, Oregon, not far from Eugene, to tell him what happened and that Jed was in critical condition. We continued toward Seattle and, by the time we reached the hospital, Jed, too, had passed away. The team had been traveling in two vans in wintry, but not prohibitive, road conditions. One of the vans, traveling under the speed limit, hit an icy patch and went over a low guardrail and down an incline.

Kesey never blamed the university or the coach driving the van. Instead, he sued the state of Washington, asserting that the guardrail was too low. He also bought the Oregon wrestling team a new fortified van for road trips, one that was equipped with all the medical paraphernalia of an ambulance. Bill Byrne and I attended the funerals of both young men, and we held a memorial service at Mac Court in their honor.

The funeral for Jed Kesey was at the family home in Mt. Pleasant and was one I will never forget. Kesey, a throwback from the hippie culture of the '60s, had a long friendship with the Grateful Dead rock band and several members of the group attended. By the time Bill and I arrived, the coffin was in an open grave that appeared to be almost in the Kesey's back yard. It was night, the yard was barely lit, and it seemed as though everyone was smoking what I took to be marijuana, the thick smoke and pungent odor wafting in the air. Folks continued to arrive, many walking directly to the grave and throwing various items into the hole, including tapes of Grateful Dead recordings. The environment was quiet, eerie, and profoundly sad. Bill and I paid our respects and left.

Later that spring, when I stepped back to evaluate the fruits of my labor at the school, the only achievements I could claim were that we were finally off NCAA probation, our fundraising was better, and the department's budget seemed to be under control. It had not been a great situation when I had signed on and though my staff and I worked hard, I didn't feel that we had made much progress. Still, it was a Pac-10 AD's job and, if nothing else, I now had a bit of a track record removed from Michigan, a new credential of sorts, which could only be positive down the line.

15

When Ohio State announced that it was accepting nominations to replace Hugh Hindman as athletics director, I decided to apply quietly. I figured I had no chance of getting the job, but I thought that if I could get an interview it would be good experience to go through the process. Although I was grateful for the opportunity I had been given in Eugene, I didn't think I would be at Oregon forever.

I called Dan Heinlen, the Executive Director of The Ohio State University Alumni Association, to see whether he would be comfortable in submitting my name for consideration. I knew Dan well from my alumni work at Michigan, and he was a good friend of Bob Forman. He seemed enthusiastic about the prospect of nominating me, and, to my surprise, about a week later I was invited to meet with half of the search committee in Phoenix. The other half was going to Atlanta on the same days to meet with other candidates. Ohio State had divided its search panel to cover more ground as quickly as possible.

I felt honored to get an interview, but given my limited experience and my Michigan background, I was certain that the committee was more curious than serious about my candidacy. While my meeting with the committee went smoothly, I did not expect anything further to come of the matter.

A week later, however, I received a call from Madison Scott, Ohio State Vice-President for Human Resources, who asked me if I could fly to Denver to meet with President Jennings. This was significant and I couldn't help but feel a little excited. But I was also suddenly ambivalent. No one at Oregon knew that I was talking to Ohio State, but now I felt compelled to confide that to my own president, Paul Olum, who had hired me at Oregon and who had given me my breakthrough opportunity in sports management. For the most part, the people and the media in Eugene had been great to me, and I owed Oregon a debt I would never be able to repay. Now, when I was finally getting the hang of it, I might be off to Columbus. I was sheepish, to say the least, but Paul accepted the news philosophically, saying that if Ohio State hired me it would be a compliment to the credibility the Ducks had regained under my brief tenure.

I met with Ed Jennings and Madison Scott in the Denver airport for about two hours. The meeting went well, with Ed and "Scotty" outlining the most pressing challenges for the new AD. The head football and basketball coaches, Earle Bruce and Eldon Miller, respectively, were not popular in Columbus, they said, and the new director would have to evaluate both programs in short order. They emphasized, however, that there would be no mandate to make coaching changes, even though the rumor was that the new AD would be expected to clean house.

Two days later Bob Forman phoned me, and said, "Rick, Ed Jennings just called me, and I think they're going to hire you!" I told Bob that I couldn't believe it and that I hadn't heard anything from Jennings or OSU. No sooner had Bob and I hung up than Madison Scott phoned and asked *if* I could come to Columbus for a news conference two days hence *if* they needed me to. I said that I could and he said, "Good. I'll call you tomorrow." The conversation lasted about a minute.

I was very nervous because there were still a number of "ifs" involved, and I still could not believe that I might get the job. An hour later, Scott called again and said, "We want you here tomorrow. What are your thoughts on a contract?" Ohio State had never awarded a multi-year contract to anyone in athletics, including Woody Hayes, but I said, "I think that I need three years."

He said, "Fine, and we're thinking $75,000 plus full benefits."

"Done," I said. "It's an honor for me to be a Buckeye, and I'll see you tomorrow."

The next afternoon when my plane touched down in Columbus, a driver met me at the airport and took me directly to President Jennings' home where his wife, Eleanor, and Madison Scott were waiting to greet me. Eleanor promptly excused herself. After some small talk, Scotty whipped out a contract, explaining that, instead of the three-year deal mentioned on the phone, a year-to-year agreement would be more palatable for public consumption, because neither Earle Bruce nor Eldon Miller had a multi-year deal. Inasmuch as we hadn't discussed this change and that the document on the table already reflected the alteration, I recall being momentarily miffed that they had been so presumptuous. This was a fleeting reflex, however; I would have probably paid *them* to be the Ohio State AD.

I stayed at the Jennings residence for a quiet dinner with them and Scotty, who tutored me as to the questions I was bound to get the next morning at the press conference. That night I was sequestered in a sparse, dormitory-like guest room in the Fawcett Center on campus, which also housed the OSU Alumni Association offices, where I was to be introduced to the media. The press had been alerted to the imminent announcement and was calling every hotel in town in an effort to break the story. I don't know if anyone checked with the Fawcett Center, but it wouldn't have mattered if they had–not because I had been booked under an assumed name, but because no one in Columbus had the faintest idea of who I was. The next day, when I walked into the alumni association lounge amidst the jungle of cameras and microphones, nearly everyone was surprised. I know that President Jennings, who made the final decision to hire me, was especially pleased at finally being able to conduct a press conference that featured an announcement from the university not known and analyzed beforehand by the media.

In fact, there were only four people who knew of my impending appointment–Paul Olum, Denice, and two men in Ann Arbor. One was my old boss and confidant, Bob Forman, and the other was another old boss, who Forman suggested I call–Don Canham.

The night before, in my room at the Fawcett Center, I called Bob with the great news, and couldn't help but speculate with him how Canham might react. My first thought was that the announcement in Columbus would be a kind of "in your face" vindication for the way in which I felt Canham had treated me during my years at Michigan. But Bob had a much wiser take on the situation and suggested that I call Don in the morning just before the press conference. Tell him what is happening, Bob said, and suggest that because Ohio State and Michigan have always provided the leadership for the Big Ten, that you and he set your differences aside and work together for the betterment of the conference. Bob's advice was priceless.

The next morning, 30 minutes before I appeared at the media gathering, I called Canham. His secretary, Carol, answered the phone, and I asked for Don. There was a slight pause in Carol's response, because she had typed many of the rancorous letters I had received from Don over the years and knew that our relationship did not warrant many personal phone calls. In fact, I had not spoken with Canham since leaving Ann Arbor three years earlier.

When Don picked up the phone I said, "Don, I want you know that I am in Columbus, and that in less than 30 minutes, I am going to be named the athletics director at Ohio State." Dead silence.

Finally Don said, not very sincerely, "Congratulations. That is a very tough job right now."

"Thanks," I replied, and then followed Forman's script precisely. "Don, the reason I am calling is that while I know that we have had our differences over the past few years, Michigan and Ohio State have been the leaders of the Big Ten for a long time and it is going to be important for that to continue. I am hoping that we can work together for the benefit of the league and put those disagreements behind us. In addition, you gave me the opportunity to coach at Michigan and I owe you for that."

Don gave a relatively agreeable replay; we hung up and I went to meet the press.

Two days later, amongst all the congratulatory calls I received, my old friend, former Michigan hockey coach Al Renfrew, phoned me. By this time, Al had given up his coaching position and was now the ticket manager for the athletics department. He told me that as soon as Canham and I had ended our phone conversation Don had come down to the ticket office and said to Renfrew, "Renny, you are never going to believe what those crazy sons-of-bitches in Columbus have done this time!"

I wasn't to start my job Ohio State for a nearly a month. I returned to Eugene to settle my affairs, put my house on the market and, most importantly, talk with Denice. We had been dating for more than two years and I was hopelessly in love with her. Because of my position at the university, we never lived together but we were inseparable whenever I was in town. I remember taking her to New York for one of my bi-annual theater weekends. We saw *Amadeus*, *Grease* and *Evita*. Denice had never been outside Oregon and was dazzled by the bright lights of the city. After my first football season at Oregon, I asked President Olum and the commissioner of the Pac-10, Wiles Hallock, if it would be okay to bring Denice to the Rose Bowl game. All the conference athletics directors and their wives attended, but I wanted to make certain my bringing Denice wouldn't cause a scandal. (The concept of "significant others" was not yet fully developed.) Surprisingly, no one seemed to object, and we had an incredible time.

Although I never took her on team trips, she accompanied me to Pac-10 meetings and hung out with the other directors' wives, who immediately adopted her. She was much younger than they were and really knew nothing about sports, but the women loved her innocent radiance and laughed affectionately at her naïve questions about the business of intercollegiate athletics. They became protective of her, as well, and when it was announced that I was going to Ohio State, the group cornered me instantly, at my last Pac-10 meeting, about my intentions regarding her. I was ambivalent. I knew that I couldn't take her unless we married and I wasn't sure if I should uproot her from her family and friends and thrust her into a position in Columbus, Ohio, in which she, too, would be under a microscope. She would be living in a much bigger city with no idea whatsoever as to the magnitude of Buckeye athletics, and she would be the "first lady" of the Ohio State athletics department to boot.

But the Pac-10 wives would hear nothing of what they called my "stupid and silly" reservations. Lu Andros, the wife of Oregon State AD, Dee Andros, was especially adamant, saying, "And there's no question that you're going to marry Denice and take her to Columbus. Don't even think about it!"

It was at this last Pac-10 gathering that our long-time commissioner, Wiles Hallock, retired, and the search for his replacement began. Tom Jernstedt was one of the candidates we interviewed. During Tom's interview, I said to him, tongue in cheek, "You know, Tom, even though I'm going to Columbus, I don't think I can ever forgive you for the three years I've spent at Oregon."

But Tom's dry wit prevailed, "Neither can Oregon," he retorted.

I proposed to Denice the next week. A few days later, we were married in a civil ceremony at the Eugene courthouse on our lunch hours. Her parents and Herb Yamanaka, who had introduced us, were the witnesses. Then we both went back to work.

A few days later, we drove to the Oregon Shakespeare Festival in Ashland for a weekend honeymoon, a week after which we flew to Columbus for good. Denice's education about Ohio State began on that plane ride across the country, during which she learned the words to the Buckeye Fight Song, "Fight the Team Across the Field." Although we were "rehearsing" in almost a whisper, I'm pretty sure that the people sitting around us could hear, and must have thought we were crazy. I told Denice that all eyes would be on us at the first football game to see if we knew the lyrics. That is exactly what happened. After we had joined 90,000 others and the great OSU Marching Band in belting out "Fight the team ... " in that first pre-game ceremony, Denice turned to me and said, "You were right. Everyone was watching."

But as proud as I was to be at Ohio State, I knew how much I owed to Oregon. Twenty-six years later, after having served as AD for the Buckeyes, the University of Minnesota and San Diego State University, I was inducted into the National Association of College Athletics Directors Hall of Fame. Inductees who have worked for more than one school must choose one for the ceremony, and I picked the Ducks. Easy choice when you think of it.

SECTION TWO
"The High Road Led Out of Town"

16

In May of 1984, in Columbus, Ohio, there was culture shock. I was selected as the new athletics director at The Ohio State University. Not only was I a "Michigan Man," but also I was a Michigan man no one in Columbus had heard of.

My friend, the mischievous Renfrew, used to joke that Canham didn't even know that I was on the coaching staff. One of Renfrew's standard jokes when the two of us spoke at Wolverine golf outings was that he had bumped into Canham that morning in the office and had asked, "Where's Rick Bay?" To which Canham supposedly replied, "How the hell should I know? Look it up in an atlas."

In Columbus that didn't seem so far-fetched. Columnist Kaye Kessler, writing for the *Columbus Citizen Journal*, reported, "Virtually every one of the 88 original candidates to fill departing director Hugh Hindman's shoes had been ferreted out by the media bloodhounds with the exception of the man the persistent (President) Jennings and his board selected."

The occasion was the proudest day of my professional career. Ohio State was at the vanguard of college athletics, and, given my background, I had clearly been selected on the basis of my reputation as an administrator. I was certainly not a favorite son in Columbus, and my track record as an athletics director was limited to three years at Oregon. Even less thrilling for the Buckeye faithful was that I had wrestled and played football at Michigan, had coached there for eight years, and then worked for the U-M alumni association. Two decades at Michigan was not the best pedigree for an Ohio State AD.

To help balance the ledger, I had come to town blessed with one asset that no one had expected and that surprised even me in terms of its sudden impact–Denice. Any concern I had felt about my new wife adapting to life away from Oregon quickly vanished. She was an instant hit in Columbus, and with her at my side I enjoyed a much more congenial and sympathetic presence than I could have ever mustered as a single male.

Denice quickly landed a highly visible job as director of membership of the Capitol Club, a new, upscale, private downtown dining and fitness club. The new Capitol Club was going to be located at the top of the Huntington Bank Building, which was still partially under construction in the center of downtown Columbus. While still in Eugene, Denice had worked for the new Hilton Hotel, and when the already established board of directors heard that the new athletics director's wife had experience in the hospitality industry and was looking for work, she was a shoo-in. With her attractive appearance, vivacious personality, and strong work ethic, she easily captivated both the executives at Club Corporation and Capitol Club board members.

There was a lot of work to do because, although the club had its board in place and had secured a prime location at the top of the building, Club Corporation would not actually start construction on the space until all 600 members had paid their initiation fee of $1,200. Thus, for her first several months on the job, Denice worked as a one-woman gang out of a temporary office on the mezzanine level of the Huntington Building, which, itself, had just opened its doors to a few early tenants. The good news was that Club Corp was the best in the business and had selected both a site and a slate of directors that were irresistible to the social elite of Columbus. The other private clubs downtown, the University Club and the Columbus Club, were well established but old and stodgy, one still requiring women to use the side entrance of their building.

By the time the grand opening of the Capitol Club occurred, Denice and I were as well known to the community as any new couple could hope to be. In some ways, we were the toast of the town. In the 1985 fall issue of *Columbus Monthly Magazine* we were one of the featured couples photographed for a big fashion spread. We were pictured leaning, back-to-back, in new leather jackets. "Decked out in outfits that would be perfect for a brisk day in Ohio Stadium," the caption read. Denice was wearing a bright red $450 Maglia jacket and $112 Anne Klein wool gabardine pants. I was sporting a $230 black Beau Geste jacket with a fur collar and looked about as good as a thoroughly airbrushed picture could make me.

We loved the place and began to do all we could to support the community. I did some television spots on behalf of Ronald McDonald House and the children's cancer hospital in Columbus, and we helped with the fundraising efforts of the Columbus Opera. We were season ticket holders for the local ballet and several theater companies, and one weekend I performed with the Ohio Sate Symphonic Band as the narrator for Aaron Copeland's *Lincoln Portrait*. I felt like Charlton Heston, as my voice boomed out over the music. One day the public radio station in town asked me to do a two-hour show about my favorite classical music. The host and I talked about how I became interested in the genre, and I was able to play favorite excerpts from operas and symphonies.

I attended Columbus Clippers games when I could and invariably would be invited into the broadcast booth with announcers Tom Hamilton and Terry Smith, both of whom went on to call games for Major League Baseball with the Cleveland Indians and Anaheim Angels, respectively. I was a frustrated play-by-play guy and occasionally they would let me do an inning or two. I vividly remember botching the description of my very first play. Jay Buhner, who went on to star for both the Yankees and the Mariners, was batting for the Clippers.

"Here's Buhner," I intoned mellifluously. "Here's the first pitch. Buhner swings and lofts an easy fly ball to center, and that will be one away ... oh, no, the centerfielder dropped the ball, I think! Wait ... the umpire who ran out see if the ball was caught ... and now Buhner is standing on second base. Let's see if we can recap exactly what happened ... "

I'd blown my professional debut, big-time, and Tom and Terry about fell off their chairs laughing.

The various press briefings and many public appearances the first few months on the job went well. Self-deprecating humor and jokes about my Michigan background helped Denice and I quickly gain acceptance to and by the Buckeye nation. I reminded everyone that I had not come directly from Michigan to Ohio State, but had spent three years in Oregon being "cleansed" of my Wolverine heritage.

I told of my first meeting with Woody Hayes who, although no longer coaching, maintained a campus office at the ROTC Building, and was not too keen on the fact that the Buckeyes had hired a guy from "that school up north." Woody still could not bring himself to say "Michigan."

I had not been on campus for very long when I went to introduce myself and pay my respects. I remember his office vividly. Behind his desk were giant shelves filled with dozens of books on military strategy and war history. There were football pictures and memorabilia, of course, but any visitor knew instantly that this man had many interests beyond his beloved sport.

The coach welcomed me but said almost immediately that, while he wished me luck (now that he was stuck with me, I think he meant), he thought it only fair and honest to tell me that he had wanted an Ohio State man to get the job. (Former Buckeye All-America quarterback Rex Kern was rumored to have been in the running.) Further, he admitted that he never envisioned a guy from "that school up north" becoming the OSU AD, and especially someone who had played on the school's football team.

I had somewhat anticipated this topic of conversation, and I replied to Coach Hayes, "Coach, you can get out all the old game film, all the statistics, and all the press clippings and you'll see that I never did anything to hurt Ohio State in football."

He loved that answer. We laughed together and were friends the rest of his life.

Meanwhile, back in Ann Arbor, all my old friends were happy for me. Wolverine football coach Bo Schembechler was reported to have said dryly, "We'll at least we know they won't cheat." And Will Perry, Michigan's sports information director observed, "He'll have to change his jokes. He used Ohio State material a lot when he was with the alumni association." Will was right and I was glad that he didn't repeat any of them to the media.

17

The Ohio State-Michigan rivalry is legendary and has produced good-natured ribbing from both sides during the
week of the game.

Every year, on the Thursday before the Ohio State-
Michigan football game, the two rival local alumni chap-
ters held a joint cocktail party in Toledo, Ohio; just across
the Michigan-Ohio state line. Tradition required that each
school send three representatives to speak at the function,
which normally attracted more than 500 boosters.

The format was a "roast" of sorts, in which speakers from
the schools would alternate, each attempting to insult the
other, but with the promise to do so cleverly and to "keep it
clean," as some of the boosters brought children with them.
However, this pact was made in the early evening prior to
the opening of the bar, and the pledge was a distant memory by the time the program was underway two hours later.
Often the comments from both sides became a bit tacky, if
not downright obscene. There were derogatory comments
about the Olentangy River, which runs just outside of Ohio
Stadium, raising facetious questions about its relationship to
the Columbus sewer system.

For several years running, I was the cleanup hitter for
the Michigan contingent. One year I suggested that Ohio
State officials had been considering closing the open end
of their horseshoe shaped stadium in order to accommodate more spectators. The only problem, I said, was that it
would be too confusing for Buckeye fans trying to find their
way out when the game was over.

Another time, Dick Finn, the Ohio State baseball coach,
represented the Buckeyes in Toledo. At about five-foot-sev-
en, Dick was only slightly shorter than me, but it didn't stop

me from saying that I had mistaken him for the lifeguard at the whirlpool. Later, when I wound up in Columbus, Dick kidded me that if I didn't give baseball more scholarships he would release audiotapes of my disparaging remarks he had supposedly recorded at the Toledo gatherings.

For several years, one Michigan booster published a "newspaper" that week, called *The Obliteration Bowl News*, which suggested the series had been so one-sided in favor of Michigan, "due to Buckeye ineptitude," that Canham and I had agreed that the rivalry should be cancelled for lack of interest. The paper went on to allege that, "The Michigan Athletic Department, magnanimous to a fault, has offered to discontinue their bi-annual trip to Columbus, substituting Slippery Rock, Shippensburg, or some other high-caliber team for the bungling Buckeye squad."

There were many stories about Woody and the rivalry. It was said that, on one occasion, when Coach Hayes and an assistant were recruiting in Michigan, their car ran out of gas on the way back to Columbus, very near the Michigan–Ohio border on Highway 23 just north of Sylvania, Ohio, but still *in Michigan*. Refusing to buy gas in Michigan, Woody made his assistant walk across the state line to purchase a can of fuel in Ohio.

When I was on Michigan's freshman football team in 1961, I watched my first Michigan-Ohio State game from seats just behind the Wolverine bench in Michigan Stadium. Freshmen were not eligible for varsity competition in those days.

The Buckeyes scored late in the fourth quarter to take a 42-20 lead, and Woody appeared to take all his regulars out of the game. But with just a minute or so remaining and the Wolverines simply trying to run out the clock and get off the field, Ohio State recovered a Michigan fumble and Coach Hayes put all his starters back in. Then, in what was essentially, the last play of the game, quarterback Joe Sparma (who later pitched for the Detroit Tigers) threw a short touchdown pass to Sam Tidmore to make it 48-20. To add to Michigan's misery, the Buckeyes converted a two-point conversion to make it a perfect 50, as time expired.

As an Illinois native, yet unschooled in the bitterness of the rivalry, I was stunned at the way in which the game had ended. I turned to my freshman teammate beside me and said, "Boy, this is a serious rivalry!" Later, when Woody was asked why he had gone for two points at the end of the game, he replied, "Because I couldn't go for three!"

The next year, in 1962, my first year as a reserve quarterback on the Wolverine varsity, we played at Ohio State and were so depleted with injuries that even I made the traveling team. With less than a minute to go in the game, and trailing 28-0, our coach, Bump Elliott, tried to get me in. As my name was called, I was thinking that I would always be able to claim that I had played in Ohio Stadium against the Bucks. But with no timeouts remaining and with the clock running, by the time I found my helmet and started toward the huddle, time expired. Inasmuch as I was already running in the direction of our locker room, I just kept going, later joking that the head start allowed me to elude the autograph seekers pouring onto the field and be first in the shower.

Because I did not play football when I was a senior, when the Wolverines next visited Columbus in 1964 (and, incidentally, beat the Buckeyes 10-0 for the Big Ten championship), I never expected to see the inside of the famed Ohio Stadium horseshoe again, much less set foot on the field. Now, 22 years later, in 1984, amazingly, I found myself the new athletics director at Ohio State.

18

The irony of ending up at Ohio State (and a secret that I closely guarded at Michigan) was that I had fantasized about the Buckeye program when I was growing up.

Howard "Hopalong" Cassady, the great Buckeyes' halfback, was the first college football player to capture my imagination, and, in basketball, my favorite players were the terrific little Ohio State guard Robin Freeman and the team's mammoth center, Frank Howard. My dad took me to an Ohio State-Northwestern basketball game in Evanston, about 30 miles from our house, and I remember Freeman scoring well over 30 points with jump shots and free throws so pure the net barely moved as the ball whispered through. Howard, who, at 6'7," 260 pounds, was a giant even by today's standards, went on to play Major League Baseball, hitting 382 home runs, several more than 500 feet.

Because there were not many televised college football games in the 1950s, it may have been Howard Cassady's nickname, "Hopalong," which first inspired my interest in Ohio State. Like me, Cassady was not very big, but he could dart through the smallest of openings and speed past any defender.

A Chicago radio station carried a Big Ten "Game of the Week" on Saturdays, and, on Sundays, ABC's Bill Fleming hosted a college football highlight show that featured film from five games from the day earlier. I was particularly excited whenever Ohio State was spotlighted. I recall listening anxiously whenever Hop got the ball, or when Tad Weed, Ohio State's place kicker, attempted a field goal or extra point, or when Dean Dugger, their split end, caught a pass. The quarterback was Dave Leggett and big Jim Parker (later an NFL Hall of Famer with the Baltimore Colts) was the massive offensive tackle that opened the holes through which Cassady scooted for big gains.

A couple of years later, in the late '50s, when Woody Hayes was becoming more famous for his bone crushing "three yards and a cloud of dust" offense, fullback Bob White was the workhorse. Going into his senior year, White had become legendary for never having been tackled for a loss. I was caught up in the action vicariously, as though I was carrying the ball every time it was handed off to White. Because Ohio State fullbacks usually carried the ball 30 times a game, I didn't see any way that White could sustain his unblemished record. I gulped each time the announcer said, "The handoff is to White, and he ... !" I panicked if the play-by-play guy started with, "White gets the ball and is *hit in the backfield* ... "–and then I would feel a rush of relief, as he continued, "But he sheds one tackler, moves across the line of scrimmage for a gain of four." I became so personally involved that I became upset with Woody that he would call on White on every obvious, short-yardage situation. If *I* knew White was getting the ball, so did the defense, and the chances of his being thrown for a loss was substantially increased. I don't remember whether Bob White made it through his senior season with his record still intact, but he wouldn't be the last Buckeyes fullback to drive the opposition crazy. There was big Jim Otis.

A former classmate of mine at Michigan hated Ohio State and Jim Otis in particular simply because his name was called so often on the Ohio Stadium public address system.

In those days, Ohio State beat Michigan regularly with Woody Hayes' grind it out offense using the fullback as the primary weapon. It seemed as though every time the Bucks got the ball they would embark on a 20-play drive that would eat up eight or nine minutes of the clock with the fullback carrying most of the load.

The PA announcer would drone, "OTIS CARRIED THE BALL. A PICK-UP OF THREE; SECOND AND SEVEN." On the next play it was the same thing. "OTIS CARRIED THE BALL. A PICK-UP OF FOUR; THIRD AND THREE." Then yet again. "OTIS CARRIED THE BALL. A PICK-UP OF FOUR; FIRST DOWN OHIO STATE."

The constant voice, monotonous, like Edgar Allen Poe's "Tell-Tale Heart," never shutting up. The fact that it was *always* Otis, that Michigan was losing and couldn't get the ball, and that the clock was running—all of this, in the heat of the game, was too much and drove my buddy nuts. While he couldn't have been happier for me when I became the new Buckeyes AD, he had one request when he called to congratulate me.

"Do me one favor," he said, "Get rid of the goddamn PA announcer—you know, the 'Otis guy.' He drives me crazy every time we come to Columbus!"

Whether it was Bob White's line plunges or Hop Cassady's improbable scampers, I was always enthralled with Ohio State as a youngster, and, in my imagination, I could actually see myself someday playing football at Ohio State.

That never happened. Woody Hayes knew football talent when he saw it and he never recruited me. I was an all-state high school quarterback in Illinois (on the same all-state team as Dick Butkus), but at five-foot-10 and 170 pounds, with average speed and an iffy arm, I was not Buckeyes material.

At Waukegan High School, where I played for my dad, we ran the West Coast offense before it became known as that. I operated out of the shotgun formation, executing about as many variations of the pass/run option play as any football mind could conjure up. And I'd played against some very good players in our league, some who distinguished themselves at higher levels—Jim Hart of Niles High School, later a star with the NFL St. Louis Cardinals and

Chuck Mercein of New Trier, who played with the Green Bay Packers for Vince Lombardi.

More surprising than Woody's indifference was that Ohio State wrestling coach Casey Fredericks did not recruit me either.

I had just become only the third high school wrestler in Illinois history to win three state championships, winning my last 71 matches, to boot. I could have gone almost anywhere in the nation on a wrestling scholarship, but I never heard from Ohio State.

My parents had divorced when I was 17. By the time I was a high school senior my dad had married Ellen Hershberger, another teacher at the school. She taught honors English. Ironically, her parents lived in Gahanna, Ohio, just outside Columbus. Ellen had received her undergraduate degree from Baldwin Wallace University, near Cleveland, and had earned her Master's Degree in Elizabethan theatre from Ohio State. Thus, I had a new set of grandparents and I would call them whenever my Michigan team would wrestle the Buckeyes in Columbus.

Invariably, my grandmother would come to the meet to watch me or my teams wrestle, and, without fail, would take great pleasure in calling Coach Fredericks the following Monday to give him holy hell for not recruiting me. Coach Fredericks supplicated her for forgiveness, saying that he knew I was already committed to Michigan. The fact that neither our team nor I ever lost to Ohio State gave her even greater satisfaction.

By the time I became the athletics director at Ohio State, Coach Fredericks had retired, but would still come around the department occasionally to kibitz. The first time I ran into him after taking the job, he asked about my grandmother, who had passed away by then.

Casey said, "Man, she used to jump me big time after every Michigan match about not recruiting you. I told her that everyone knew that you were going to Michigan, and that I had to put my energies where I had a realistic chance of signing someone. I tried to explain that I simply couldn't waste time recruiting someone who had already made up his mind to go elsewhere. But she kept saying that if I'd tried harder, you would have come. I was really glad that she never actually came to see me. I would have had to hide out in Woody's office, and blamed the whole thing on him! Boy, that would have been interesting, your grandmother against Woody!"

19

I hadn't been in Columbus long when I began to realize that there was a troubling perception in the community that the Buckeyes athletics program was languishing, at least in terms of image. The notion gave me pause. I had just come from a program–at Oregon–that sponsored only 16 sports on a paltry $6 million budget. Further, neither the Oregon football nor basketball programs were winning, we were just coming off NCAA probation and, as painfully noted earlier, we had to play bingo at the halftime of our basketball games to generate enough money to paint the inside of our gym.

Conversely, the Ohio State program included 30 sports supported by a $13 million budget with a good cash flow, had wait lists for season tickets in football and basketball, and was coming off five consecutive nine-win seasons on the gridiron. How bad could things be?

When I looked only at the raw figures, the impressive revenue streams, the near-capacity attendance for football and men's basketball, the huge numbers of sports and student-athletes being served, and the countless championships the Buckeye teams had accumulated, I became a bit apprehensive. How could I possibly make it better? One thing I had already discovered about college athletics, though, was that most things are never quite as good or as bad as they might seem.

After a few months on the job and countless speaking engagements throughout Ohio, I found that most of the uneasiness about the program was not about winning or beating Michigan, but, rather, how the Buckeye nation felt about itself and its public image.

Prior to my arrival, for example, Buckeye starting quarterback Mike Tomczak had been declared temporarily ineligible by the NCAA for modeling clothing for a retail outlet in Columbus. Tomczak thought would be fun. It was an inadvertent violation and Tomczak had not been paid.

Previously, however, it was revealed that former Ohio State quarterback Art Schlichter was battling a serious gambling problem that some blamed on football coach Earle Bruce. This perception was misguided but developed, in part, because Bruce, himself, loved horseracing and was known to bet on the ponies. In addition, Bruce had a television show that included an innocent "pick the winners" segment that was eventually declared illegal by the NCAA because it seemed to promote betting.

Finally, two men's basketball players had recently been declared academically ineligible, and one other male athlete had been investigated for rape, though he was later exonerated.

It turned out that, except for Schlichter's gambling addiction, which wasn't connected to OSU but which sadly led to his imprisonment, the issues were not serious. But it was clear to me that while the community certainly wanted the Buckeyes to win, it was even more important to its psyche that it never feel embarrassed by anything that happened in the program. I knew this instinctively, of course, but now I felt a need to be able to articulate my expectations to the coaches and athletes.

I met with every team and presented what I called the WAC Concept. (This had nothing to do with the old Western Athletic Conference.) With this concept, we had three goals: Winning; reasonable Academic success; and exemplary Citizenship. All three must be achieved in order to be genuinely successful. Accomplishing only two of the three would not cut it. My logic was that a team could win a championship, but if the athletes were plagued with eligibility problems, poor graduation rates or by trouble off the field, then, deep down, the university and many of its boosters would feel sheepish, if not embarrassed by the achievement, that somehow it had been tainted. However, the converse was also true, I said. Give me a team made up honor students who are also wonderful citizens, but rarely wins and, again, deep down, no one would feel truly proud of it, either.

To me, the ultimate achievement in college sports was to win a championship with a roster of responsible and successful students who were also good citizens. I had coached such a group my last two years at Michigan.

As previously mentioned, my 1973 and 1974 Wolverine wrestling teams finished undefeated, won a Big Ten championship, finished third and second in the NCAA Tournament, respectively, and had cumulative team grade point averages of about 3.2 on a four-point scale. Of the fourteen letterman on the 1973 squad, all graduated, three became lawyers, two were engineers, two were successful businessmen, one was a dentist and five became high school coaches and/or educators. Everyone at Michigan truly felt proud of these teams.

Still, I wasn't going to kid myself: winning was important any way you cut it. This was particularly true in Columbus where, although I had inherited very successful football and basketball coaches by most standards, there was a contingent of fans that felt the teams hadn't won enough.

Although this reasoning did not necessarily permeate the community, the dissatisfaction was sufficient to have generated a rumor that I had been hired to fire Earle Bruce and Eldon Miller. One magazine ran a headline, "Rick Bay: The Axeman Cometh?" SMU athletics director, Bob Hitch, who had been another candidate for my job, had been quoted as saying he had turned down the position because he was expected to come into Columbus "to fire everybody and reorganize the entire department."

This speculation had resulted in some angst within the department. I felt that it was time to reassure everyone.

20

I met Ohio State head football coach Earle Bruce for the first time at the 1984 Fiesta Frolic Golf Tournament in Scottsdale, Arizona. This annual event was sponsored by the Fiesta Bowl and was designed to build mutually beneficial relationships between the bowl and college football's power brokers. Still many years before the formation of the so-called Bowl Championship Series (BCS), the Fiesta Bowl was striving to establish itself as an upper echelon game that could attract the nation's best teams. Backed by many prominent executives in the greater Phoenix area, the bowl spared no expense in attracting the upper crust of college athletics.

The initial Fiesta Frolic had begun as small, semi-private stag affairs, limited almost exclusively to Big Ten and Pac-10 football coaches and athletic directors. I attended my first Fiesta Frolic while at Oregon and was dazzled by the incredible hospitality the bowl offered.

Headquarters for the event was the five-star Arizona Biltmore Hotel, where the complimentary menu of food and drink was endless, and where we often received free golf apparel and equipment. Each day we were invited to play an exclusive Phoenix area golf course, such as Troon and the Boulders. On at least one occasion that I recall, a fleet of helicopters airlifted us from the Biltmore to our golfing destination, inasmuch as driving that distance would have reduced our afternoon sun time at the hotel pool. Another time, the Fiesta Bowl committee arranged for a squadron of corporate jets to fly the group to Lake Powell, in northern Arizona, for an evening cookout.

The committee members were good guys and master hosts, when it came to entertaining. Their persistence paid huge dividends. The Fiesta Bowl has hosted many national championship games and is, perhaps, second only to the Rose Bowl in college football prestige and status.

One evening at the '84 Frolic, on the veranda of the Wrigley Mansion, just above the Biltmore, the cocktail hour was well underway when Earle Bruce came over and introduced himself to me.

"I hear you're being interviewed for the Ohio State job," he said.

Although surprised that he knew this, I admitted that I was and asked him point blank, "Is it a good job?"

Earle never hesitated. "It is always great to be a Buckeye," he said, "but I never thought they'd talk to a Michigan guy."

"They haven't." I said. "I'm an Oregon guy."

We both laughed and at that moment formed a lasting friendship.

Earle Bruce was a great football coach. Standing less than six feet but burley, weighing about 240 pounds, Earle looked nothing like a former Maryland high school state sprint champion. In fact, this achievement seemed so improbable that, even when documented in print, few believed it.

Once during a Buckeye football practice, one of the players mentioned the story to a small group of teammates. Earle heard the chuckling, was irritated by the distraction in the first place, and then was just plain pissed off that anyone, especially a player, would intimate that he was not a sprint champion. Finally, Earle could no longer contain himself and said that he goddamn well had won the Maryland state high school 100-yard dash and that, furthermore, he could still beat anyone the team put forward to race 30 yards! This reckless challenge caused so much whooping and hollering that custodians working in the bowels of the stadium thought that 50,000 fans had showed up for practice.

Because this little fracas transpired near the close of practice, which usually ended with wind sprints that the players hated, it was decided that if the player won the race there would be no wind sprints.

At 55 and badly overweight, Bruce had not sprinted 30 yards in the last 30 years, but in his mind's eye he was back on that cinder track in Maryland, where he had outrun everyone in the field. As the two unlikely combatants took their starting positions at the goal line, the team, assistant coaches, managers, and trainers formed a funnel to witness what might be the most famous four seconds in Ohio Stadium history.

"On your marks, get set, GO!" yelled the starter.

To everyone's astonishment, Coach Bruce appeared to lead for the first 12 yards, but by 20 yards he had blown out a hamstring and the race was over. There would be no wind sprints for the Buckeyes that day, but the event captured perfectly the fiery competitive nature of the coach, and turned out to be one of those spontaneous occasions that bring a team closer together.

Earle was beginning his sixth season as the Ohio State coach when I arrived in Columbus. He had compiled an outstanding record. In five seasons, his team had never been worse than 9-3, winning two Big Ten championships, three of five against ultra-rival Michigan, and three bowl games. But football expectations are high at Ohio State and 9-3 was wearing thin. True, the Buckeyes had gone 11-1 in Earle's first year—with only a 17-16 Rose Bowl loss to USC keeping them from the national title—but they had gone 9-3 since, inciting some to begin grumbling about "old 9-3 Earle."

I said publicly that I held Earle in high regard, and that I certainly did not intend to change football coaches. Still, the questions persisted: should we settle for 9-3 at Ohio

State; and why hadn't we won a national championship in 15 years? I had been making public appearances all over the state, talking about the merits of our program. Yes, I said, our goal every year is to end the season as unde-feated national champions. But, I asked rhetorically, is it fair to consider anything just short of that a failure?

I didn't feel that I should have to apologize for Earle, and kept trying to put his record in perspective. Except for Tom Osborne at Nebraska, Earle, in his five years in Colum-bus, had the highest winning percentage in college foot-ball. However, one night in Columbus, after speaking to a group of businessmen and their wives at a private club, one of our most generous boosters came up to me, saying, "Rick, you're right. Earle's done a great job. But you're new in town, and let me give you some friendly advice. No one in Columbus wants to be told that 9-3 is acceptable. Intel-lectually, of course, we know that you cannot win all the time, and that 9-3 is better than most teams can achieve. But we don't want to hear it."

When I finally found time to visit with Earle in an ex-tended conversation, it was clear to me that he was feel-ing unappreciated, and justifiably so. Among other things, he was working on a one-year contract, better described as a year-to-year agreement, at the pleasure of the presi-dent and athletics director. Although coaches' contracts and salaries then were nothing like they are today, (I be-lieve Earle was making about $80,000), many of his peers had multi-year deals. The problem at Ohio State was that the school had never awarded a multi-year contract to anyone. This was precisely why President Jennings had ul-timately decided not to give me the three-year deal that Madison Scott had implied would be forthcoming in our phone conversation, before I came to Columbus. Besides, never mind that times were changing, Woody Hayes had never had a contract, but had worked under 29 consecu-tive, one-year agreements.

The real reason for this impasse, however, was that Ed Jennings was not enamored of Earle Bruce. Earle was not his kind of guy and Jennings did not want to be contractually obligated to him, especially when he probably hoped that I would come to the same conclusion. I told Ed that if ever we did have to hire a new coach (although I certainly was not thinking along those lines), the marketplace was such at the time that we would have to offer a multi-year deal to attract the person we wanted. In what was hardly a vote of confidence for Earle, Jennings responded by saying that if that time came, he and the board of trustees would do what was necessary.

21

The president's bias toward Earle notwithstanding, I liked the coach immediately. He was my kind of guy—honest, no nonsense, competitive as hell, and possessing a great sense of humor.

I felt as though he sensed immediately that I was not the hatchet man he had been expecting, and that I would defend him whenever necessary. Earle's record was better than that of both Woody Hayes and Bo Schembechler in their first half-decades. I wanted to do something quickly that would reduce the tension of the football staff, but with no additional job security to offer them, I thought demonstrating a decent sense of humor myself might help achieve that goal.

During my football playing days in both high school and at Michigan, I was not only a quarterback, but a place-kicker, as well. My first fall practice at Columbus, a week before our first game, I put on a pair of shorts and laced up an old square-toed kicking shoe that I had kept from college and trotted onto the field in Ohio Stadium. That's about all I had ever done for the Wolverines—trot onto the practice field.

The team was nearing the end of practice at the closed end of the horseshoe. Traditionally, the team concluded their workout by practicing the kicking game and I joined a surprised group of Buckeye place-kickers, warming up at the other end of the stadium. Having never seen their athletics director participating in football practice, the kids were initially dumbfounded. And being all soccer-style kickers, they had never seen a straight-ahead kicker with a square-toed shoe. A second later, they embraced the moment and insisted I try a couple of short field goals.

A few minutes later, Coach Bruce called for the kickers, and each player tried a few extra points before Earle called loudly for the "fifth-string kicker." He had seen me working with the kickers a few minutes earlier and decided to carry matters one step further. In the spirit of bonding, I wanted the coaches to see me practicing with the players. That was the whole point. But I had not expected Earle to test my good will so directly. At first, no one present knew who the "fifth string kicker" was; when I realized that it was I, I had no choice but to run onto the turf and into the huddle. The play was for me to attempt an extra point, and everyone lined up as if we were playing for real. Thankfully there was to be no live rush by the defense, which was a relief considering I had no pads and was at least 50 pounds lighter than anyone else on the field. Now, I had to attempt the kick and the tension around me suddenly became surprisingly palpable, as I am sure that everyone was concerned that I might embarrass myself—which is just what I did, shanking the ball off the side of my foot, and nearly decapitating the right tackle in the process. The reaction on the field was stunned silence. No one knew whether to laugh or cry.

Thankfully, Earle came to the rescue, blamed the miscue on a bad snap and questionable hold, and added that the defense had been offside. Thus, I was granted a reprieve. The offside penalty moved the ball one and one-half yards closer to the goalposts, the ball was snapped and placed again, and I floated one through, albeit barely.

Everyone cheered, and I reacted in such a way that the coaches knew they could kid me about the botched kick anytime they wished. Earle never forgot it, and even today still accuses me of ruining the Ohio Stadium Astroturf, my first attempt having supposedly taken a divot bigger than a Frisbee from the artificial surface.

Our first game in 1984, and my first game as Buckeyes AD, was in Columbus against my old nemesis from the great Northwest, the Oregon State Beavers, which had already been unintentionally maligned by the Ohio State student newspaper the day I got the job.

Confusing the Oregon and Oregon State mascots–we were the Ducks–*The Ohio State Lantern* ran a headline that read, "OREGON SORRY TO SEE BAY LEAVE; HE CLEANED UP BEAVER PROGRAM." I couldn't stop laughing and immediately sent the column off to Oregon State AD Dee Andros, saying that he owed me a big debt of gratitude for straightening out his program even while I was working at Oregon.

As mentioned previously, the Ducks and the Beavers played each other on the last Saturday of every season in what was billed as the "Civil War" game. Often the two teams were so bad it wasn't a question of who was favored, but rather could either team win? But this was Ohio State, not Oregon, and the Beavers were three-touchdown underdogs coming into Columbus—and Dee made the most of it. He loved telling the media that with his old buddy, Ricky, getting the job at Ohio State, he now had a realistic chance of convincing the Buckeyes to cancel the game. With self-deprecating humor, he claimed that Oregon State was so obviously out-manned that he wouldn't be able to coax his coach and team out of the locker room for the kickoff. For my part, I moaned that because we were such heavy favorites, if we lost, Earle and I would need two seats on the Beaver charter back to Corvallis.

Not surprisingly, however, a game often is close when one team believes itself to be a shoo-in, and my new school barely survived 22-14. This outcome was considered a shaky omen in the community, and by Saturday evening, everyone in Columbus wanted to know what was wrong with the Buckeyes.

Not to worry. Earle's boys hit their stride the next week by trouncing Washington State, 44-0, and then beating

Iowa in the Big Ten opener the following Saturday, 45-26. We won our first road game at Minnesota a week later to go 4-0, but then were upset at Purdue, 28-23, in a loss that left the Buckeyes faithful more than a little disgruntled. A defeat so early in the season, especially against a conference foe, not only all but ruled out a run at the national championship but also put the Big Ten title, and a shot at the Rose Bowl, at risk.

The future looked especially bleak the following Saturday when visiting Illinois took a commanding 24-0 lead early in the second quarter. I stood terrified in my "escape booth" in the press box, as I thought I heard scattered booing in the far reaches of the stadium. I had two private boxes in the press area, one with 15 seats to entertain VIPs important to the support of our program. My "escape booth" had only two chairs and was located in a much more remote area of press row.

Whenever the Buckeyes were doing well on the field, my guests and I enjoyed a love fest in our large VIP booth. There were cocktails, jokes and pithy comments all around, and Denice and I were blithely happy to be the center of attention, pleased to be hosting an event so important to the Columbus scene. However, when the Buckeyes began to falter, the offense suddenly gone impotent and the defense more porous than cheesecloth, the happy chatter abated rather abruptly. All eyes became trained on the field, and Coach Bruce became the target of derogatory second-guessing.

Down 24-0, my competitive juices took over. I wasn't happy with the comments in the booth, but I was more upset that we were losing. I headed for my second booth, where I could cuss in private and even kick a chair against the wall. Simply put, there are times in competitive sports where you need either to be alone or be with someone who truly understands how you feel. I was very intense whenever my school was competing. I hated losing and there was no consoling me. I was almost always embarrassed by defeat, but despised anyone's sympathy when it occurred.

Fortunately, we staged a remarkable comeback against the Illini and won the game, 45-38, so the win meant that I didn't have to accept the well-meaning, but infuriating condolences of my guests as they left the stadium. Further, Earle loosened me up with one of his periodic malapropisms during the post-game press conference. Asked how he felt being down 24-0, the coach said, "It's never over 'til the fat lady dances." Eat your heart out, Yogi.

22

The tension in the press box during the Illinois game exposed more than people's raw nerves. Not only was the game important, I discovered, but also so was the perceived pecking order of who enjoyed the privilege of being in the press box in the first place. At Oregon, press box access was informal. There were invited guests each week to my booth, but both important and semi-important boosters sitting in the stands were welcome to come by and say hello. There were no private suites, as such, beyond my box and that of the president. At Ohio State, however, seating in the press box was a jealously guarded status symbol.

My box could accommodate about 20 people, but the president and the board of trustees occupied the largest suite. There were nine Ohio State trustees, all appointed by the governor to serve nine-year terms, one coming on and going off the board each year. Each trustee received two free seats in the president's box, and, at times, I would have guessed that certain trustees had campaigned for their appointment to the board simply to enjoy nearly a decade of front row seats to Buckeye football. Beyond my box and the president's, however, were four other smaller booths, whose occupants were important symbolically and sometimes, proved to be an irritant to the current leadership at the university.

In the years just prior to the 1984 season, five other persons of note had their own small private boxes in Ohio Stadium. These were the governor of the state, Dick Celeste; the former long-time governor, Jim Rhodes; immediate past president of the university Novice Fawcett; former OSU athletics director Ed Weaver and Woody Hayes. I had inherited this line-up and though I could have put several of these suites to much better use, I wasn't about to blow myself up by kicking someone out. Fawcett and Weaver had been retired for years, Rhodes had been out of office since 1978, and I had several donors who would have given big bucks to take their places.

To make matters more complicated, I now felt compelled to make room for my predecessor, former athletics director Hugh Hindman. This was more than a little awkward because Jennings had just fired Hindman, so I knew he wouldn't be pleased to pass him in the hallway every football Saturday. Still, Hugh had been on Woody's coaching staff, had worked in some capacity for the university for more than 30 years, and had many friends in Columbus. Even those folks who felt that it was time for a change at the top for OSU athletics respected Hugh and did not want to see him treated shabbily. With Hugh's mentor and predecessor Ed Weaver comfortably accommodated in the press box, I didn't see how I could do anything less for Hugh.

Predictably, President Jennings was miffed by my decision but apparently empathized with my dilemma because he said nothing about it for the first several weeks of the season. But in the week following the Illinois game, he finally said, "Why don't you get Hindman out of the press box. Weaver, too. Give them some great seats in the stands and be done with it."

I responded that such a move would be very difficult, would cause people to feel embarrassed for them, and would generate unnecessary ill will toward him, as the president, and me. However, when Ed pressed his point, I finally said, "Ed, I'll make you a deal. When you get rid of Fawcett and Rhodes, I'll get rid of Hindman and Weaver." That was the last we spoke of the matter.

Having called Jennings' bluff in what I privately called "press box politics," I worked hard to establish respectful and friendly relationships with both Hindman and Weaver. I believe that we bonded on the sad occasion of the death of University of Michigan faculty athletics representative Marcus Plant.

Plant had been a friend since my student days in Ann Arbor. A mild mannered law professor, he was one of the elder statesmen in the Big Ten and greatly respected around the country, once serving as president of the NCAA. Marc's longevity meant that he had worked with both Weaver and Hindman on various Big Ten committees and was well liked by both men.

When news of his passing hit Columbus, I prepared to travel to Ann Arbor to represent Ohio State at the funeral. I reserved a small university plane for the trip and asked both Hugh and Ed to accompany me as part of the official Buckeye delegation. While I will never know if the invitation surprised them, they were clearly pleased. That trip in the close quarters of the airplane gave me a perfect opportunity to get to know both men better and to ask their counsel on the many pressing issues facing Ohio State athletics. Later, I wrote to Mrs. Plant about our trip to Marc's memorial and observed, to her delight, that even in his passing, her husband had continued to help me.

After the Illinois scare, we won a big game at Michigan State, but then were upset again, this time by Wisconsin, in Madison. The student section in Camp Randall Stadium is notorious for its hijinks and it pulled off a beauty during our game.

It had been a wild week for Badger athletics director Elroy "Crazy Legs" Hirsch. Elroy was, himself, a free spirit and a jokester, but during the week that we played them he was badly upstaged by two student groups.

For years, the women's crew team had been pleading for a locker room near the lake where they competed. They had no dressing area and were changing clothes in their cars before and after practice. Finally, a few days before our game, they appeared en masse in Elroy's office, shut the door, promptly undressed before Elroy's bulging eyes and refused to leave until he promised to build them a facility.

At this same time, Elroy was trying to convince the student section in the stadium to curtail its tradition of selecting a sometimes terrified, underclass coed from the one of the lower rows in the stadium and passing her up to the rim of the bowl, nearly 80 rows and situated about about forty feet above ground on the other side. Hirsch was scared to death that it was only a matter of time before someone was hurt or the university was sued.

Midway through our game, I was standing in the press box near a glass window overlooking the student section, when I noticed some commotion in the lower section of the stands. Suddenly, what appeared to be a lifeless body was being passed up, row by row, toward the top of the stadium, exactly what Elroy feared. It took me a few seconds to realize that it was a mannequin dressed as a female student, but most people in the press box were not close enough to make the distinction, and many of them thought the form was a real person. Only a few seconds elapsed before the mannequin reached the top row and was then promptly thrown over the rim and out of the stadium.

I'm not sure how much of this Elroy saw, but some of the people around me nearly fainted before comprehending the prank. For me, it was the only amusing moment of the day, because the loss to the Badgers meant that we would have to win our last three games, including the battle against Michigan, to get to the Rose Bowl.

The situation being urgent, the team played with greater intensity the next two weeks, easily defeating both Indiana and Northwestern. "That school up north" was next.

On the Sunday after the Indiana game, however, I received a call that one of our players, reserve running back, Roman Bates, had been arrested and charged with sexual imposition on a 19-year-old female student Saturday night. The press was on it immediately, and, by Monday night, an activist women's group on campus had organized a picketing demonstration outside our offices, demanding that Bates be removed from the team.

I called Bates into my office the first thing Monday morning. Earle had already spoken with him and told me that Roman was a good kid, and that he, Earle, believed that he was innocent. Awaiting his arraignment in a day or so, Bates arrived scared to death. He told me that the woman had come on to him and became belligerent when he showed no interest. He said that the only contact between them occurred when he tried to restrain her from attacking him. Like Earle, I felt he was telling the truth. I told him that I wasn't going to decide on his team status until the case played itself out in the courts.

No sooner had I made this decision then President Jennings called me asking why Bates was still on the team. I explained my philosophy on due process, but I could tell that the president wasn't comfortable with my reasoning. He was getting outside pressure, especially from women's groups, to at least suspend the player, but he didn't overrule me. A few days later Bates was arraigned, and his court date was set for early December. It would be a jury trial.

Unbelievably, the day after Bates' arraignment there was a story out of Morgantown, West Virginia, that two West Virginia players had been arrested for sexual assault and had been immediately dismissed from the team. My phone rang. It was an agitated Jennings and he wanted to know how it was that West Virginia could take such decisive action in such a similar case, while we were doing nothing. I said that I knew nothing more than what was in the paper and that I would get more details. Fortunately, I knew Don Nehlan, the Mountaineers coach, very well. He had been one of Bo's assistants at Michigan while I was coaching wrestling. When I described to Don the situation with Bates, and the apparent similarity with what had happened in Morgantown, Don said that there was no comparison.

"Rick," he said, "the guys I kicked off were constant troublemakers. I warned them in front of the entire team that they would be history if they were anywhere near trouble this season, even if they were innocent bystanders. These guys were bad news, but I gave them one more chance, and here they are implicated again. I'd had enough!"

In the meantime, Roman Bates had been going through hell, and had become a distraction for the team, as well. Reporters were showing up at practice every day to take his picture or try to get a comment on his case.

Before calling the president back about Coach Nehlan's action regarding his players, I summoned Bates to my office again. I reiterated to Roman that I was not going to suspend him, but suggested that he consider voluntarily withdrawing from the team temporarily to prepare for his defense. This action, I said, would not prejudice his case (as I thought my suspending him would have), and would allow his teammates to prepare for the last two regular season games without having to worry about protecting him.

To Roman's credit, he agreed. The president calmed down, and the team went over to Evanston and throttled Northwestern, 52-3, setting the stage for the showdown with Michigan, another of the many games in the famous series that the Buckeyes and Wolverines would play with the Big Ten championship and the Rose Bowl at stake.

One of the many great Ohio State football traditions is "senior tackle," held at the end of the Thursday practice before the Michigan game. The seniors who will be playing in their last regular season game for the Buckeyes line up one by one, and, on the coach's whistle, charge the blocking sled for the last time. When Coach Hayes was alive, Earle would have him address the team just before the ceremony, talking quietly about the importance of beating Michigan and how the memory of that game would be with them forever. It was a poignant moment, and often several thousand people would attend that practice. I felt proud to be there in 1984 and even prouder when we whipped the Wolverines, 21-6. We were off to Pasadena, and Denice's picture was on the front page of the Columbus Dispatch, smelling a beautiful, bright, red rose.

Two weeks after the Michigan game, a jury in Columbus acquitted Roman Bates of all the charges against him. Earle and I felt vindicated, and were certainly happy for our player. But Roman, apparently in too much of a hurry to spread the word, was arrested several hours after the verdict for going 70 miles an hour in a 35-mile zone. This time, he pleaded guilty.

23

Planning for the airlift to California for the Rose Bowl was logistically challenging, and I created a stir at the university by offering to take anyone in the athletics department, plus a spouse, at our expense. This idea was not as fiscally irresponsible as it first appeared. We had to charter a large plane, anyway, just to move the team and its supporting cast to the West Coast. Why not offer the otherwise empty seats on the charter and game tickets to my staff? With the trip covering two weeks, including Christmas and New Years, many people with family obligations could probably not go, but I hoped the gesture would earn me some good will early in my tenure. The only objection came from the other side of campus; some folks resented the notion as preferential treatment for athletic department employees. But I pointed out that the president's official party would require a charter of its own, including all of the university vice-presidents, the board of trustees and their families, important politicians and donors to the university, among others. Surely, I argued, the people on the athletics staff who had helped Ohio State to get to the Rose Bowl in the first place, the people in the trenches, deserved an equal opportunity to make the trip. Happily, my reasoning prevailed and I was a hero with all the folks working for me.

One day before we left for Pasadena, Earle came to my office.

"I wanted to talk to you about our bonus," he said.

I had been waiting for him to approach me about it. Although he didn't have a contract, it was becoming customary in college football for the coaching staff of a bowl team to receive a bonus for a job well done, usually amounting to an extra month's salary. I was never quite sure of the rationale for this accommodation, so I decided to inquire further.

"What bonus," I asked, feigning innocence.

"You know, for winning the championship and going to the Rose Bowl," the coach replied, a little agitated.

"That's what you're supposed to do," I said. "That's what we pay you for, to win championships. Are we saying that your salary is for an ordinary season, but that if you over-perform, you deserve a bonus? By that logic, if you have less than an ordinary season, you would owe me money."

Earle thought for a moment, and then exclaimed, "Well, the Michigan coaches are getting a bonus, and they're sure as hell not going to the Rose Bowl!"

"That's good enough for me," I said, laughing. "I'll take care of it."

In fairness to Earle, he and his coaching staff probably were among the lowest paid in the league, especially considering the prestige of our program and his success in running it. The reason for the disparity was Woody Hayes' inattention to such matters. During Hayes' tenure, the coach was so engrossed in his job that salaries and job security were afterthoughts. To his staff's dismay, he almost never approached the administration on its behalf regarding compensation issues. As a result, by the time Earle took over, Ohio State football staff salaries had fallen way behind the rest of the league. Earle was a lot like Woody. He loved Ohio State. I don't think he would have ever left the Buckeyes over money. However, he wasn't ignorant about what was happening in college football in terms of salaries, contracts and bonuses, and he had far too much pride to allow himself to be taken for granted. Just as a matter of principle, he wanted to be appreciated and treated like his peers, most of whom he was beating regularly.

His salary and bonus aside, Earle did receive outside income for television and radio coach's shows, the latter of which eventually caused him trouble.

Until the 1984 season, two major radio stations in Columbus originated the play-by-play of Ohio State football—WTVN, a Taft company out of Cincinnati, and WBNS-AM in Columbus, owned by the Wolfe family, which also owned the town's only newspaper, *The Columbus Dispatch*. Earle had been doing his television show with WBNS-TV, but one of his good friends, Perry Frey, was the general manager at WTVN and offered Earle more money to move his show there. While this switch may have benefited Earle's pocketbook for the moment, he had apparently not given much thought to the long-range impact of his decision. Had I been there, I would not have allowed him to switch. I would have made up the financial difference to him, somehow, because you simply do not want to alienate the owner of the lone newspaper in a city.

In fact, it was only a year or so later that Neale Stoner, the athletics director at the University of Illinois, lost his job in a similar scenario. The publisher of the *Champaign News Gazette* owned the local radio station that carried Fighting Illini football and basketball. But when Stoner got a better offer from another station in town, it made financial sense to switch. Shortly thereafter, his administration was negligent on a relatively minor bookkeeping issue and the newspaper came after him and his senior associate as though it were a major scandal. The paper blew the matter out of perspective and it was finally perceived in the community to be a colossal impropriety. Stoner and his colleague were forced to resign.

Almost twenty years later, I suffered a similar fate at San Diego State. *The San Diego Union Tribune* misreported a story about the hiring of our new football coach, which damaged the search process. The paper became hostile when I publicly called them into account for the error and it took the next opportunity that came along to discredit the athletics department beyond all reason. This irresponsible and vindictive action was clearly retribution and was a distasteful reminder of the arrogance of power that is sometimes exercised by the media.

WBNS and WTVN, the dominant AM radio stations in the Columbus market, were bitter rivals, not much different in their feelings for one another than Michigan and Ohio State, and both wanted to be the Buckeyes' flagship station in Columbus. In previous years, we sold our broadcast rights to a single entity for a substantial fee. The station, in turn, peddled all available network and local advertising for the games to cover the rights fee paid us, and then some. It was a clean deal for the university because we just took the check and the station did everything else. Upon further analysis, I thought that we could make more money by taking a lesser rights fee from the flagship station, retaining the more lucrative network advertising and selling it ourselves. This left WBNS and WTVN to fight it out to carry Buckeyes' football, knowing that the winner would have only local advertising spots to sell, the estimate of which would dictate how much they would bid to be the flagship.

The university issued a call for proposals from any station that aspired to be the voice of Buckeye football and men's basketball. Only WBNS and WTVN bid for the flagship rights, and, while cash was important to the university, there were other factors to be considered, such as air time for related coaches' shows, promotional spots during the broadcast day, and the station's willingness to put together and monitor a statewide network of stations to carry Ohio State games. When the dust had cleared, and all the elements of the two bids were factored, WBNS prevailed by an eyelash in the opinion of the university's bid evaluation team. WTVN didn't believe it and appealed to the president's office for a review. Thus, an independent auditor familiar with the bid process in the broadcasting industry conducted the reevaluation. Although I do not recall the specific tiebreaking criteria, WBNS again carried the day.

Because the process had been so rancorous, however, we were going to be tested in protecting the WBNS now-exclusive broadcast rights, when the season began. WTVN still qualified for media credentials and it decided to push the envelope. Although only WBNS had a broadcast booth from which to do the play-by-play, WTVN had a reporter in the press box (along with other radio stations covering the games), doing periodic updates from the stadium as "news." Far from being a good loser, WTVN advertised the week before our opener that they would be bringing their listeners ongoing updates from the "Shoe" and urged them to stay tuned during the game. What this meant, it turned out, was that the WTVN reporter in the press box began doing "updates" after almost every play. WBNS, suspecting this kind of chicanery and already monitoring the situation by listening to WTVN, reported the activity immediately to our sports information director. He, in turn, warned the WTVN reporter to knock it off, which he did for the time being. On Monday, however, when we confronted WTVN and cautioned them that a repeat performance at the next game could put their press credentials at risk, they said only that they were exercising their right of free speech and would continue to do so.

At the same time, WBNS had brought Earle's show back under its umbrella, paying more money for the privilege. However, Earle still had friends at WTVN, and he did not fully grasp the meaning of "exclusivity," which is what WBNS had already purchased. Early in the season he was easily lured into extensive interviews with crafty WTVN sports reporters, the length of which was almost greater than his exclusive coach's show on WBNS. All of this eventually worked itself out, but the radio wars dispute left me more exhausted than some games.

On the more positive side, the task of selling all of the network advertising in-house, while new for both the university and me, proved to be interesting and profitable.

Many big businesses in town wanted to be a part of Buckeye football. In years past, the radio stations carrying our games never had a problem enlisting major sponsors for the broadcasts, so I decided to test the marketplace further.

All of the companies we considered as prospects for sponsorship had hired advertising agencies that fielded all proposals for their clients. The seller would have to meet with the agency, which would then take the proposal to company executives, along with some sort of recommendation based upon the projected audience the advertising would reach. For its trouble, the agency would receive a commission, a percentage of the sale price. In a captive market such as Columbus, which had no major sports sponsorship opportunities except the Buckeyes, I thought we could bypass the agencies, saving the commission, and go right to the CEO or his designate and make the pitch ourselves.

I had just hired Ohio State's great, two-time Heisman Trophy winner, Archie Griffin, as a special assistant to the director's office. Archie had been working in human resources on the other side of campus when a position on our football staff opened. Earle needed a new running backs coach and I wanted Archie in the athletics department, one way or another. Earle needed no convincing, and so I offered Archie the job, and just happened to mention the open position in my office as an afterthought. Archie surprised all of us by saying that if he had a choice; he would like to take a crack at the front-office stuff. That was great, and now the two of us were off to sell our broadcast advertising.

Given the billboard nature of network advertising, as in "Ohio State football is brought to you by ... " most broadcasts can only comfortably accommodate four to five network sponsors. Thus, we picked our categories (insurance, banks, auto dealers, and fast food) and set out to make our pitches. We went to the most recent sponsors, initially, explaining that we were giving them right of first refusal in their category, but that we had a price in mind. This was a polite way of saying, take it or leave it. We tried not to appear arrogant, but we were the only show in town and I felt confident that we would be successful in signing our sponsors, even if the price we set did not pencil out for the companies we approached. This was going to be an emotional buy for them and it drove their advertising agencies to distraction. In fact, their reaction was reminiscent of the famed Edvard Munch painting, "The Silent Scream." "Don't do it!" was the silent scream from their agency people when we met with company executives. It was not worth it, they warned their clients. All you had to do was look at the demographics— the broadcasts would have to damn near reach New York City to justify the fee we demanded. However, the allure of Ohio State football was too much to resist. Everybody signed up immediately and we more than doubled our radio revenue from the previous year.

As for establishing the network across the state, from Akron to Youngstown and Findlay to Chillicothe, we simply made games available to any station outside the Columbus area that wanted them. They had to carry the network advertising, but beyond that, could sell their own local spots. However, there was one important caveat that some of the smaller stations didn't like. The catch was that if a station wanted the football games, it also had to carry Ohio State men's basketball. Many stations hated the basketball schedule because there were so many games, many at mid-week, which interfered with their regular broadcast schedule. The only programming that we allowed to pre-empt Buckeye basketball was local high school basketball. It sounds harsh, but Ohio was a football state and we would not have had wide coverage of Ohio State men's basketball without holding football hostage. Even in a major Ohio market such as Cincinnati, there was little interest in the radio broadcasts of Buckeye hoops. With the Queen City just across the river from basketball crazy Kentucky, there was actually more attention paid to Wildcat basketball than that of Ohio State.

One day Archie Griffin and I were talking about this reality, when I said that I sometimes wished *I* had played basketball instead of wrestling. I think I could have been a good player, I confided. Archie, who was also a high school wrestler, said he often felt the same way. Soon we were telling each other of our intramural exploits in basketball, a discussion that somehow led to our agreeing that we should play a little one-on-one the next day at lunchtime. I don't think either of us had really played the game or even shot baskets for a long time, but we decided that the contest would be a two out of three series, with each game to 11 baskets. Despite the grace and athleticism that I had envisioned for myself in this duel, my performance was pathetic. Thankfully, so was Archie's. In the first game, playing like the wrestlers we were, we went 10 or 11 minutes before either of us made a shot. And we were already winded.

Unfortunately, word of our epic battle had spread through the office and a few of our colleagues ventured into the arena to watch. Archie and I couldn't hear the snickers that we knew were there and we finally started to make some buckets. In the end, the Heisman winner prevailed, two games to one. By that evening, when there was a real basketball game in the arena, my hamstrings were so tight that after I had wished the team luck in the bench area, I had to use the handrail to get myself up a small incline from the floor to the concourse. It was embarrassing.

24

My pre-bowl trip to Pasadena was a dream come true. Traveling with Big Ten Commissioner Wayne Duke, we met with the Rose Bowl game committee, Pacific-10 Conference Commissioner Tom Hansen and University of Southern California AD Mike McGee. While at Oregon, I had attended three Rose Bowls, but only as a spectator representing the conference. Rose Bowl officials always wanted as many Big Ten and Pac-10 ADs and presidents as possible to attend the festivities, if only to maintain the lofty status of the event in the media.

If your school wasn't in the game, this trip was about as relaxing and carefree as an athletics director could want. We received two VIP tickets to the Rose Parade, the game and every elaborate party before and after. There was little anxiety connected with the outcome of the contest. Of course, you wanted the team from your conference to win, because the outcome invariably led to unbridled generalizations in the media as to which conference played the superior brand of football. Even money wasn't an issue, as the leagues each received an equal share, no matter who won, and each share (minus expenses for the participating schools) was divided evenly 10 ways.

While all 20 schools received a minimum number of tickets, only participating schools experienced a demand well beyond their contractual allotment, especially if those participants had not appeared in the game for many years. It was a common practice for non-participants to sell, at face value, their extra tickets to the conference school playing in the game.

The 1985 Rose Bowl game would be Ohio State's first in five years, a long time by Buckeye standards, and its first since Earle's initial season in Columbus in 1979. The Bucks went 11-0 that year only to lose a gut-wrenching 17-16 Rose Bowl to Southern Cal and the national championship in the process. Since then Coach Bruce had led his team to four consecutive 9-3 seasons. As I said, they had included three bowl wins, two victories over Michigan and a Big Ten co-championship—but they were still all 9-3.

Now, as I made the requisite appearances in Los Angeles and Pasadena a good six weeks before the game, I was being asked about a 9-2 Buckeye team that could fall to 9-3 yet again.

Choosing to, temporarily, ignore the advice of the Columbus booster about "trying to put 9-3 in a favorable light," I talked a great deal about the advancing parity in college football. "The days of the dynasties are over," I said, "and they are gone for a variety of reasons."

It was true. Up until the early '80s there were seemingly two schools in every major conference battling for the league title, with a chance at the national championship. In the Big Ten, it was a foregone conclusion that Michigan and Ohio State would play for the Big Ten title, and would face the winner of the USC-UCLA game in the Rose Bowl. In the Big Eight (now the Big Twelve), it was Oklahoma against Nebraska for the annual Orange Bowl berth. Alabama from the Southeastern Conference pretty much determined who would play in the Sugar Bowl, as did Texas in the old Southwest Conference in the Cotton Bowl, or so it seemed. Throw Notre Dame into the mix, and there was your power structure. What's more, it was not unusual for many of these teams to be undefeated when they met their rival at the end of the regular season. But those were the days of only a few bowl games, and when only a handful of teams had a realistic chance of upsetting a dynastic program. By the early '80s however, the landscape had begun to change.

By 1984, there were 18 bowl games and of the 36 teams competing, 20 had at least three losses. Until 1972, there had been no NCAA limit on the number of football scholarships a school could offer. Southern schools and Big Eight schools were said have had as many as 150 players on scholarship, of which only 90 or so players ever really saw action. The benefit of the other 60, some of whom must have been talented, was that they weren't playing against you. But in '84, with the scholarship limitation set at 95, and then 85 in 1992, the super powers could no longer stockpile players, and the talent became more reasonably distributed.

Freshman eligibility also had taken hold. High school kids who wanted to play immediately usually had better opportunities in struggling programs and that worked against the previously dominant schools.

The gradual demise of racial segregation in the South played a key role in establishing parity in college football, too. For many years, African-American players who were not welcome at Southern schools were forced to go north to participate, which hurt southern football. By the early '80s, southern schools had many African-American players on their rosters and the football conferences in that region were equal to any in the North. Alabama's legendary coach Bear Bryant was said to have almost single-handedly broken the color line in the Southeastern Conference after his team was upset in Tuscaloosa in 1970 by a USC team with many African-American players, including its great fullback, Sam Cunningham. Apparently, having seen enough of racial discrimination (at least on the football field), the Crimson Tide began to recruit African-American players, many of whom later played key roles on Bryant's national championship teams.

All of these developments evolved slowly over time and fostered parity in college football to the extent that, by the '80s, on any given Saturday, anyone could beat anyone—and that 9-3 was nothing to sneeze at. Or, so I said.

But the 1984 Buckeyes were not 9-3, yet. In fact, on January 1, 1985, we got off to a good start toward 10-2. Early in the game against the Trojans, Keith Byers ripped off a long run from scrimmage that had us first and goal to go at the USC two-yard line. A touchdown seemed inevitable, but on the next play, our right guard jumped offside and we were penalized back to the seven. I was sitting in the Rose Bowl press box with Woody Hayes when our lineman flinched, drawing the crucial penalty. Coach Hayes and I were sitting side by side at a long, wooden plank serving as a makeshift table. It was not very sturdy, and if someone at the opposite end of the table leaned forward, you felt it at your end. When the penalty was called, Woody, knowing how much more difficult it was going to be to score from the seven than from the two, instinctively slammed his fist so hard that every coffee cup, soda can, typewriter and binoculars resting there jumped six inches. At the same time, he hissed, "Goddamn it! Where's the discipline! That will cost us!" Coach Hayes was distressingly prophetic. We had to settle for a field goal and lost the game, 20-17. It was a long trip home for the team, old 9-3 Earle and me.

The Rose Bowl loss made a grey January in Columbus seem even darker. Buckeye fortunes on the football field always had a way of casting the short-term, general mood of the city. A Buckeye defeat on a Saturday afternoon in Columbus created a palpable sullenness among the citizenry until at least the next Tuesday, when the tenor would finally yield to the creeping anticipation of the next game. But a bowl defeat, especially the Rose, meant a longer period of gloom. The victory over Michigan had been forgotten, reminding everyone in the athletics department that the outcome of the last game was what really counted, no matter the opponent.

I would happily recall this axiom two years later when we lost to Michigan at home to give the Wolverines a share of the Big Ten title. Ann Arbor partied until Christmas, until being upset by Arizona State in the Rose Bowl, while we went on to defeat Texas A. & M. in the Cotton Bowl. Later, our coaches ran into a number of Michigan coaches on the recruiting trail, and their guys were dragging. They confided to our staff that they felt as though they'd had a losing season, a co-Big Ten championship notwithstanding, and could hardly recall the ebullience of their victory in Columbus. This drama was played out in both Big Ten cities every season, giving the coaching axiom "you're only as good as your last game" even more substance.

25

For me, there was no time to sulk. Basketball was well underway, and Coach Eldon Miller was no more popular than Earle. Eldon was in his ninth year and had led the Buckeyes to several consecutive successful seasons. In the time he had been in the league, his winning percentage was second only to the legendary Bobby Knight at Indiana. However, he had been unable to bring a Big Ten championship to Columbus, finishing second for two years in a row. Being a runner-up in any sport in a tough league is laudable, until you become a perennial runner-up. Then, suddenly, it's a case of you "can't win the big one."

It was particularly painful for Eldon's teams in that they had gone into the final week of each season needing only a single victory in their last two games to clinch the championship. But in each case they failed, and in the year before I arrived in Columbus did not even advance to the NCAA Tournament. To add insult to injury, they had ended that season with a humiliating first round loss in the National Invitational Tournament (NIT). Still, I had not seen Coach Miller in action and, as with Earle Bruce, was under no mandate to replace him.

But just as Earle was laboring in the shadow of Woody Hayes, Miller had his own ghost with which to contend. Eldon had succeeded Fred Taylor, the coach who had guided the great Jerry Lucas, John Havlicek teams of the mid-60s to three straight NCAA championship games, winning the title in 1960. Even though Taylor was eventually fired as the program faltered in the late '70s, Buckeye basketball fans remembered the glory days and were tired of what many considered encroaching mediocrity.

Even more galling to some was that the dominant team in the Big Ten–Indiana–was coached by Bob Knight, a reserve guard on those same Lucas/Havlicek squads. Many boosters thought that Knight should have succeeded Taylor, that he was an obvious and natural choice. But the scenario to replace Taylor that finally evolved put Eldon, or any other possible successor, in an impossible situation.

When Fred Taylor was fired at the end of the 1976 season after a rancorous, and sometimes public, feud with athletics director Ed Weaver, many of the Ohio State faithful felt the time was perfect to bring Bob Knight back to Columbus. Knight had firmly established himself as one of the most successful coaches in America, having won several Big Ten championships at Indiana, as well as the NCAA title in 1976. Before that he had even won at Army, which, in basketball, was about as likely as Radcliffe winning the Rose Bowl. Although Taylor had coached four Final Four teams at Ohio State, the program had deteriorated badly in the '70s. Most observers felt that the game had passed him by, especially in recruiting where even the best Ohio high school players were leaving the state.

But Knight also had his detractors, mostly because of his reputation for boorish behavior on the sidelines and with the media. There were a number of folks both within the Buckeyes athletics department and the central administration that were not anxious to have him back in the family. He could be extremely disruptive internally and an embarrassment to a university publicly.

Whether this consternation affected Ed Weaver's thinking at the time is unclear, but OSU's approach to Knight was insulting to him from the outset and precluded any serious discussion of the Indiana coach returning to his alma mater. For starters, Weaver, reportedly feeling ill at the time, did not travel to conduct the first interview with Knight personally, but instead sent associate AD Hugh Hindman to the meeting. This in itself probably ruined any chance of a deal, but its fate was sealed when Hindman reportedly started the meeting by asking Knight what qualifications he possessed to warrant the head coaching job at Ohio State. There are no minutes from that meeting, but one can assume that it was promptly adjourned.

Ultimately, Weaver decided to hire little known Eldon Miller, who was then the coach at Western Michigan University. Since coaching searches in college athletics remain about as confidential as a politician's most recent sexual indiscretion, it quickly became known that Miller had been selected over Don DeVoe, a former Buckeyes' player from the great teams of the early '60s, who soon got the head job at Tennessee, where he was an instant winner. Although DeVoe was not ultimately any more successful than Miller as a Division I head coach, his early triumphs in Knoxville provided ammunition for the harpies, who were still vexed over the bungled recruitment of Knight and not inclined to embrace Eldon under any circumstances.

Surprisingly, however, especially to those who thought Miller bland and uninspiring, the new coach turned out to be an excellent recruiter. Within two years he had attracted the likes of Herb Williams and Clark Kellogg to Ohio State and the Buckeyes began to win. Ironically, it was Eldon's recruiting success that contributed most to the criticism that dogged him during his decade in Columbus. "He has the best talent in the league," fans would complain. "Why can't he win a championship?" Most observers had predicted just the opposite for the new coach. "I'm sure he'll be a good teacher, but he has no charisma and won't get the players," they would say.

A major contributing factor in Eldon's inability to capture a conference title was that his team seemed always to have to play its last Big Ten games on the road. This situation was not a quirk in the schedule, but rather brought on by the school itself. The Ohio State High School boys' and girls' basketball finals, and the state wrestling championships, almost always conflicted with the final weekend of the Big Ten's regular season. In fairness to the Buckeyes basketball team, the high school championships should have been moved out of Columbus every other year. But both the university and the city wanted perpetual "ownership" of the events, and feared what might happen if the Ohio State High School Athletic Association (OHSAA) were to sample the hospitality of a rival city such as Cincinnati or Dayton or Cleveland, all itching to host more OHSAA events. Ironically, even the men's basketball program had mixed feelings on the matter because Ohio State's St. John Arena was the traditional site of the boys' championship, and because the tournament brought the state's best players to the Buckeyes' home court, the event served as an extra unofficial recruiting visit to the campus that didn't count against the NCAA limit. In addition, the city loved the tourist traffic that streamed into the community and the resulting positive economic impact that it produced.

So, almost every first or second weekend in March, Eldon took his act on the road for the final conference games of the season and the results were not pretty.

In 1979 the Buckeyes were leading the league, but lost their last three games (the final two at Wisconsin and at Purdue) to finish 12-6 in the Big Ten, which tied for fourth place. In 1980, on the final day of the season, Ohio State lost at Indiana to finish second, again with a 12-6 conference mark. The same scenario occurred in 1982, the Buckeyes losing their swan song at Minnesota for another second-place tie and 12-6 record. 1983 produced another season-ending defeat (again to Bob Knight's Indiana Hoosiers) and another second-place finish, this time 11-7.

In 1984, the year before I arrived as AD, Eldon's team struggled to an 8-10 mark in the league, losing its final five games, including an embarrassing defeat at the hands of Xavier in the first round of the NIT. Embarrassing, perhaps, but not totally unexpected, as the NIT selection committee took fiendish pleasure in sending traditional powerhouse programs to play in hostile environs they never would dream of otherwise visiting.

It is extremely important for every basketball program to win its way into post-season play simply as a validation of its superior status. Since only 64 schools earned their way into the NCAA bracket, the leftover near misses had only one other chance to continue play and that was in the NIT.

The NIT, the first ever tournament to determine the national collegiate champion, chose 32 schools to compete for its championship in a playoff that ended in Madison Square Garden the Monday night before the weekend of the NCAA's Final Four. Many of these teams despised being there, especially a heretofore-major power that, in that year anyway, didn't quite make it to "the big dance," the NCAA Tournament. Still, they sometimes had to beg for the lesser invitation, or face a worse alternative, which was no post-season play at all, an acknowledgement that of the 310 Division I men's basketball programs you were not in the top 96.

The problem was that once your wish was granted, you had no way of controlling what the sometimes-sadistic NIT selection committee was going to do to you when they set the team match-ups. As one example, under normal circumstances The Ohio State University would almost never consent to play fellow Ohio school Xavier University at Xavier. The state's mother school might be willing to play Xavier—or Dayton or Bowling Green—in Columbus, but even this might be a risky proposition if the opponent happened to have a good team, because the Buckeyes would have nothing to gain in winning, but plenty to lose in losing. "WHAT? We lost to Xavier! What the hell is going on over there!" an otherwise disinterested alum would be liable to shout into his morning coffee while perusing the sports page, having no idea whatsoever that Xavier just had a 20-win season and beaten one or two other Big Ten teams in the process. It's the perception that comes with losing to smaller schools that haunts the powerhouse programs.

The NIT (which is now owned and operated by the NCAA) knew this, and it was fully cognizant of the fact that the Xavier student section at basketball games had been waiting all of its existence to mock the Buckeyes, to taunt their every move, to jeer their coach, to ridicule their cheerleaders, to heckle those few courageous Ohio State fans who might venture warily to this alien Cincinnati campus—all players' parents, if truth be told—to deride the 20-piece Buckeye pep band and to lampoon the school's proud fight song, *Fight the Team Across the Field*, in the process.

And since the NIT met its budget primarily through gate receipts, the committee knew that more, many more bloodthirsty Xavier fanatics would pay for tickets in Cincinnati than downhearted Ohio State fans would in Columbus. The NIT loved these in-state match-ups, laughing up its sleeve while sentencing the likes of Texas (in an off year) to Texas, El Paso; Oklahoma to Tulsa; UCLA to Fresno; Michigan to Western Michigan, or Illinois to Bradley. The underdogs packed their gyms with boosters and students all licking their chops at the prospect of slaying Goliath. Such was the case in 1984 when the Musketeers of Xavier pummeled Eldon Miller's Buckeyes, a team so deflated by its failure to make the NCAA bracket that it looked as though it was playing simply to get the season over with.

The 1983-84 season notwithstanding, however, I was unaffected by public opinion, determined instead to come to my own conclusion about the state of our men's basketball program.

As was the case with Earle Bruce, I liked Eldon personally and knew that he possessed all the personal values that I sought in my coaches. He was loyal, honest and a disciplinarian with his players. And, like Earle, he was feeling underappreciated and somewhat insulted that, unlike many of his peers, he did not have a multi-year contract, never mind that Fred Taylor (even after appearing in three straight NCAA championship games) never had an extended deal. Eldon took it personally that he was a year-to-year coach. I reminded him that I was in the same boat contractually, and, that in any case, coming off a season ending in a five-game losing streak (including the Xavier debacle) did not make him a very sympathetic figure for a contract extension.

26

Eldon's 1984-85 team, my first basketball season at Ohio State, made a big turnaround. The Buckeyes tied for third place in the Big Ten standings, posting a conference record of 11-7 (three games better than the year before) and winning their final game of the season against Michigan State (at home, for once) to earn a berth in the NCAA Tournament. The team won its first-round game against Iowa State before being eliminated by Louisiana Tech and "The Mailman," Karl Malone. Overall, the season appeared to be a good omen for both my relationship with Eldon and his long-term prospects at the university.

But the 1985-86 season turned out to be anything but positive, and it brought a bizarre ending to Eldon's coaching tenure at Ohio State.

The Buckeye five got off to a decent start, winning its first five games against so-so opposition and owning a 10-3 record going into the Big Ten schedule. The team split its first six league games, including a big win over Purdue, which was ranked 15th in the nation.

But on that same day in Madison, Wisconsin, following the Wisconsin-Minnesota game, several Minnesota players were yanked from the team bus and arrested just as they were about to start for the airport for their flight to Chicago for their next game against Northwestern. The players were charged with having gang-raped a local woman the night before the game. The central administration at Minnesota was apoplectic and ordered the team back to Minneapolis, thus forfeiting its next game at Northwestern. Gophers head coach Jim Dutcher was so incensed at the decision that he resigned on the spot. The incident not only was catastrophic for the Gopher basketball program, but, strangely, was also the catalyst for Eldon's "resignation" at Ohio State, a few days later.

The Buckeyes had the misfortune of playing the first game at Minnesota after the Madison incident. I was scheduled to travel with the team for the two-game road trip, which also included a game at Iowa. While it was customary, if not expected, for Division I athletics directors to travel to every road football game, basketball travel for an AD was rare, at least until the NCAA Tournament. However, since I wanted to demonstrate my support for Eldon whenever possible, I had cleared my schedule to make the Minnesota-Iowa trip with the team. Cynics in the media suspected that I was simply using the trip to evaluate Eldon more closely in anticipation of a possible coaching change at the end of the year. In any event, any early expectations anyone held about the game at Minnesota were now completely overshadowed by the debacle at Madison the week before.

The Gophers' roster had been decimated by the arrests, and by other university-initiated discipline. It soon became known that Minnesota had only seven scholarship players for its weekend games against Ohio State and Indiana. In order to even practice for our game on Thursday night, the Gophers had to recruit three or four players from the football team who had played high school basketball. By Wednesday it was clear that the football players would also have to suit up for the games, just in case the remaining basketball players got into foul trouble or were injured. Suddenly, it seemed as though the players still in a Madison jail were forgotten, and the media attention shifted, at least temporarily, to the ragtag roster of what was left of the Gopher squad and its quest to salvage Minnesotan pride in the face of incredible adversity.

The setting could not have been more deadly for Ohio State, or even the Boston Celtics, had they encountered such a bizarre situation. The media around the country had by now zeroed in on the unlikely scenario and were quizzing the Buckeye coaches and players as to their feelings about playing a "pick-up team" in a Big Ten basketball game. The local fans, embarrassed by the events in Madison but buoyed by the perseverance of the "magnificent seven," were also won over. And on a Thursday night, bitterly cold even by Twin City standards, 7,000 fans braved the weather to watch their Cinderella team take on Ohio State.

Having flown in the day of the game, I took a cab to Minnesota's cavernous Williams Arena (seating capacity 17,000), arriving well behind the team. Because of the drifting snow the taxi could not make it to the building, so I trudged the last 100 yards to the entrance, the icy walkways crackling beneath my steps. Once inside, I made my way to the Buckeyes locker room to wish Eldon and the players luck. I could tell instantly that no one was looking forward to playing. It was truly a no-win situation. A victory over these Gopher scrubs would be viewed as meaningless by most everyone, while a loss would probably get us laughed out of the conference.

Having coached and competed at the Division I level, I knew instinctively how difficult the game would be for our guys. I had a flashback to the time in high school when we wrestled the Illinois School for the Blind. The only rule alteration that day was that you had to stay in physical contact with your sightless opponent throughout the match. My opponent was quick, strong, and, most of all, fiercely competitive. I won, but it was not easy, as I knew would be the case when we first locked up.

There is always something psychologically inhibiting for a competitor battling an opponent whom he and just about everyone else knows is at an obvious disadvantage. Unless you are Woody Hayes playing Michigan, it is simply difficult to set yourself mentally to mercilessly dominate an antagonist that clearly has no chance of winning. Understanding this, I was still well aware that few others could ever appreciate the magnitude of the challenge facing me against the blind boy, but that it would be considered disgraceful to lose.

Such was the Buckeyes' dilemma that night in Minneapolis. Leaving the locker room Eldon was pale, I was petrified, and the 7,000 nuts in the stands were already drooling over the remote possibility that their makeshift Gophers bunch could jump-start the long rehabilitation process from the catastrophe in Madison.

Ohio State never had a chance. A few of the Gophers football players—in basketball shorts so small I imagined trying to stuff three pounds of potatoes in a two-pound bag—quickly made outlandish three point baskets to shock the arena to life. Another player—weighing in at 270 pounds—ripped down his first rebound since 12th grade and nearly demolished the backboard in the process. The Buckeyes pretty much kept their poise but could never overcome the extraordinary emotional energy of Minnesota, losing the game, 70-65.

I was proud of the team's effort and told Eldon so in our grim locker room afterwards. Neither of us had to guess what the media would report about the game. As far as they were concerned, we had lost to what was now a JV program.

I knew that we could not recover in time for the game against Iowa in Iowa City on Saturday, and we lost again, 86-75. To say that Eldon and the team limped home is an understatement. Unfairly, the program had been cast as incapable and there were more cries for a coaching change. But on Monday morning I reiterated to the press that I was fully behind Coach Miller, that the Minnesota game was a blip on the screen, and that we still had half the season to play.

Almost no sooner had I issued this heartfelt vote of confidence than Eldon appeared in my office, saying, "You better find yourself a new basketball coach. I'm not quitting, but you need to find a new coach."

I was almost speechless, but finally said, "Coach, what are you saying? I am certainly not firing you, and we've still got lots of games left."

We continued in this vein for a couple of minutes, until I finally asked Jim Jones, my senior associate AD to join us as a witness. Eldon elaborated slightly by saying that the university didn't support him, and that we needed to find a new coach. I pleaded with him to think matters over and to wait until the end of the year before deciding anything. But he left the office and twenty minutes later a couple of the reporters who covered the Buckeye basketball beat were at my doorstep, saying that Eldon had just held a press conference, alleging that he had been fired–not by Rick Bay, mind you, but by the university. I felt foolish trying to convince them that Eldon had not been fired by anyone.

"But Eldon says he's not resigning, and you need a new coach," they insisted. Eldon and I looked like Abbott and Costello doing "Who's On First," but what was there to say?

It turned out that Eldon stayed until the end of the season, continued to say that he was fired (by whom, no one knows, to this day) and finally left Columbus to become the new basketball coach at Northern Iowa. But that is not the end of the story.

After the horrific trip to Minnesota and Iowa, we lost five of our next seven games, including the usual last two on the road, and finished 8-10 in the conference. Incredibly, however, we were selected to play in the NIT. Given Eldon's pitiful situation, I felt sure that this time the tournament would compassionately allow us to host a first round game or, at least, not farm us out to a place like Xavier again. I gave the committee too much credit and was shocked to learn that we would be playing Ohio University in Athens. The scenario was Xavier revisited, but this time our guys rose up as if there was something to play for, and we prevailed by two points in what was a great college basketball game.

We were assigned to host Texas in the second round, and won convincingly. We then beat BYU in Columbus, earning the right to travel to Madison Square Garden in New York for the NIT's version of the Final Four. In the semi-finals we exacted some revenge on Louisiana Tech from our NCAA loss the year before (although "The Mailman" had by then graduated to the NBA), which put us in the championship game against Wyoming. We won the title game, 73-63, Ohio State's first national championship of any kind in basketball since the Jerry Lucas team of 1960.

It was the only time that I ever felt awkward about winning a championship. The victory was a great sendoff for Eldon, and he never once reconsidered revisiting his earlier decision. We had continued to work together, were still respectful of one another, and I had attended every game the team played in the tournament. And yet, except for his frustration of not having a multi-year contract or his occasional rough treatment in the press, I could never fully grasp why he had resigned but continued to allege that he was fired. By season's end he had convinced himself (and many others) that he had, indeed, been dismissed, although who exactly had dismissed him was still a question he would or could not answer.

As for me, I felt absolutely silly trying to explain what had happened in my office that Monday after the Minnesota/Iowa trip. Trying to recreate my conversation with Eldon back then for some curious listener sounded more absurd each time I tried. When finally I decided to quit trying, Eldon made sure that I had one more chance. At halftime of the NIT championship game against Wyoming, which found us with a comfortable lead, long time basketball announcer, Bill Raftery, interviewed me on ESPN.

"Rick," he started, "how does it feel to have fired the coach who is probably going to win the NIT?"

27

Most people in Columbus were as puzzled by Eldon Miller's strange departure as I was. Stoic to the end, Eldon said little publicly about the matter and neither did I, except to reiterate that he was leaving of his own volition and that I wished him well in his new job at Northern Iowa.

All the attention switched immediately to the question of who would succeed Eldon. As far as the public is concerned, this is where an athletics director earns his stripes: in a crisis. The hiring of a new football or men's basketball coach is the most scrutinized project an AD undertakes. Closest to this would be the handling of a highly publicized disciplinary matter involving a coach or a high-profile athlete whose possible suspension or expulsion from a team can make or break the season.

The one advantage to Eldon's announcement in February that he was leaving was that it gave me a head start in finding a new coach. Most coaching searches follow a familiar script. The scenario almost always begins when a coach finds himself in the midst of his third consecutive losing or even mediocre year, with rumors about that he will either quit or be fired at season's end. Stopping far short of a vote of confidence for the embattled coach, the athletics director will say only that he will evaluate the program after the last game. The local newspaper, having asked the question in the first place, uses the AD's predictably noncommittal response as a license to immediately publish a list of possible candidates. The AD, not wanting to seem disingenuous, contacts no one, while at the same time frantically searching the Internet to have his short list ready when the deed is done. Finally, usually in mid-March, the coach either resigns gracefully or forces the university to fire him. In either case, a financial settlement is reached ("settlement" being an outgoing coach's favorite word,) and the coach states that he worked hard and at least left the program in better shape than he found it. The university thanks the coach for his service, speaks briefly to the difficulty of making such a tough decision, wishes the coach well in his future endeavors and says, finally, that it's now time to turn the page and move forward.

Except for my wishing Eldon well, none of this scenario unfolded in Columbus that winter. Once I was certain that Eldon meant business, and made sure that he knew there would be no turning back, I embarked upon my search. Buckeye fans wanted a big-name coach or something very close to it. But it was a more complex issue than most people understood because the outcome would also have an impact on football. As I had warned President Jennings the year before, we would never attract a well-known basketball coach to Columbus without the offer of a multi-year contract. This time there was little choice in the matter. We were not going to hire the coach from Otterbein or Wooster simply to avoid a five-year contract for Earle Bruce. The situation gave some people in the community pause because, while there was no reason to think about firing Earle, there also existed a perceptible reluctance to commit to him for the long term. This dilemma aside, however, I locked a telephone to my ear and started down my list.

Inasmuch as I had been an AD only four years, and a high profile guy only one, I surprised a few of my colleagues at other schools by asking permission to talk with their coaches. Existing contracts notwithstanding, it was not unusual for head hunting athletics directors to contact coaches directly (on the sly, of course) to discern their interest in the job. While no formal interviews could be conducted until everyone's season was over, a pre-emptive contact could save a solicitous AD like me a lot of time once the year ended. The coaches themselves were extremely cautious about these informal contacts since any rumor that they were talking with another school would badly disrupt their current team, not to mention the recruiting they had been doing since the season started. At the same time, the Ohio State job was big and I knew very few coaches would dismiss it out of hand. But several athletics directors did.

Homer Rice, the well-respected AD at Georgia Tech was adamant that I could not speak to his coach, Bobby Cremins. "I appreciate your going through me, but he's under contract," he said.

Surely, I said to Homer, I could at least talk to Cremins on the phone.

"No, he's under contract."

Next, I dialed up Tom Butters at Duke wanting to visit with Mike Krzyzewski, a young coach who was finally starting to show some promise. This was 1985, well before Coach K's string of NCAA appearances, not to mention his championships.

"Sorry, Rick, but Mike doesn't want to talk to anyone about another job," Tom said.

"Well, would it be alright if we chatted on the phone?" I asked.

"No," Tom patiently added. "He asked me specifically to shield him from any inquiries in person or over the phone."

I gave it one more shot. "Tom, you're an experienced AD. How's it going to look for me if I have to tell the folks here that I didn't even talk to Mike, that I accepted from his current employer, who doesn't want to lose him, that he has no interest in Ohio State, that even though he doesn't know I called, he's not interested," I was rambling now. "It would help my credibility in Columbus to hear from Mike that he's not interested."

Tom Butters knew a frustrated AD when he heard one. "OK," he said, "I will tell him you called, but I will leave it to him whether to call you back."

Coach did call back a couple of nights later. He thanked me for my interest, said he was flattered and that Ohio State was a great job. But he also said that Duke had hung in there with him when the Blue Devils weren't winning many games in his first few years, and now that the program was turning around (was it ever!), he felt obligated to repay that loyalty with some of his own. Thanks, but no, thanks, he said. Good luck to you and the Buckeyes.

I was zero for two. This wasn't going to be as easy as I thought.

Next in line was fiery Boston College coach Gary Williams. I phoned Bill Flynn, the venerable athletics director at BC, to ask permission to call Gary. Bill wasn't happy to hear from me, but said that he appreciated my going through him, and to feel free to give Gary a call.

Gary's team was on a roll and promised to be a factor in the upcoming Big East tournament. Although preoccupied with his season, he was excited to hear from me and we made plans to talk seriously as soon as the year ended. In the meantime, I decided to travel to Boston to catch a BC game without Gary's knowledge. We had never met, so I knew he wouldn't recognize me. But I wanted to see a Gary Williams team in action and catch a glimpse of his sideline demeanor in the process.

He had already established a reputation as a very animated personality during games, and that night in the Boston Garden he more than lived up to his image. Sweating profusely, even through the armpits of his suit coat, and cussing just as vigorously, Gary was up and down the coaches box and beyond, venturing so far onto the court that he might as well have been in uniform, instructing his team and exhorting the officials to pay closer attention to the atrocities being inflicted upon his "pitiable" Golden Eagles team.

I was amazed that he didn't draw any technical fouls, and several times felt embarrassed for the referees for giving him far too much latitude in his frequent tirades. Easy for me to say, but I would never have taken the abuse those officials were subjected to that night. Still, I was captivated by how his team responded to him and reminded myself that the Buckeyes program really needed a coach with a personality that could excite our fans, especially the student section, which, if motivated, can unnerve even the most poised opponent.

Eldon's decorum during games was somewhat staid, even when he was angry with either the team or the officials. The students didn't connect with him, and this, along with the team's recent mediocrity, had resulted in a significant decrease in student season tickets. Because my own personality was much more like Eldon's than Gary's, I had to overcome my own bias regarding Coach Williams' sideline antics. But my gut told me that Williams might be just the kind of coach we needed to stir up St. John Arena.

My next stop was also in the Big East and it involved the highly successful Jim Boeheim at Syracuse. Boeheim had already won more than 150 games in fewer than seven seasons with the Orange. I had heard through the grapevine that Jim, who had been at SU in several different capacities for many years, might finally be ready to make a move. I was energized by the possibility that I could get him because he would bring instant credibility and name recognition to our program and it would be a feather in my cap for attracting such a high profile coach. Thus motivated, I called long time Syracuse AD, Jake Crouthamel, to ask about Boeheim. His response was shocking and far different from anything I had encountered earlier.

"Jake, this is Rick Bay from Ohio State," I started. "I know that you were probably hoping not to hear from me (by this time everyone was aware of my pursuit for a new coach), especially before your season ends, but I need your consent to talk with Jim. I'm sorry, but ... "

I was interrupted by uproarious laughter from the other end of the line.

"Jake, I'm serious ... "

More laughter. "Sorry, Rick, but I go through this about twice a year. Of course, you can talk with Jim, but he's not going anywhere," Jake chortled. "Jim has been at Syracuse his whole life, and he will never leave here no matter what he says or what anyone else thinks. He's kind of a baby, and whenever he begins to feel unappreciated around here, he lets people know that he might leave. But he won't, no matter what. Sure, Rick, call him anytime, and good luck in your search."

"Thanks, Jake," I said, somewhat disheartened.

"You're welcome," Jake chuckled, and hung up.

I was undeterred, however, and Boeheim sounded very excited when I reached him. He invited me to meet with him at his home in Syracuse within the week, well before the Big East tournament. A few days later I was at his door-step in Syracuse, met his family and had a great discussion surrounding the wonderful opportunity at Ohio State. The coach said he was serious about the possibility and was anxious to visit Columbus as soon as the season was over. Despite Jake Crouthamel's assertion to the contrary, I left Syracuse happy to know that Jim Boeheim was one of my finalists for the job.

I no sooner arrived back in Columbus than I received a return call from University of Louisville AD Bill Olsen. I had phoned him about approaching his legendary coach, Denny Crum, the former UCLA assistant to John Wooden, who was now enjoying phenomenal success at Louisville. Bill said fine, but warned me that his coach would be expensive. I talked with Crum that night, who said that he would be very interested but that I would have to absorb his "annuity plan," if he came.

"What annuity plan?" I asked cautiously.

"Well, I get $1 million if I stay at Louisville 10 years," said the coach. "I've got seven years in, so I'd need $700,000 when we sign a contract."

"I see," I offered weakly. "Coach, I don't know if I could do that but I'll check and get back to you."

No checking was necessary. Scratch Denny Crum.

The time was drawing close, of course, when I would no longer be able to put off talking with Bob Knight. His great coaching record aside, Knight's sometimes crude behavior was well documented, and I knew from our conference meetings how little control the university was able to exercise over him. But Bob had many admirers at Ohio State, his alma mater, and I had pledged to everyone in Columbus that I would hire the best coach attainable. Now I had to make the call that Ed Weaver should have made years ago, while, at the same time, half hoping that the Indiana legend was not available.

Before dialing the Bloomington area code, however, I had a brainstorm to call upon famous Ohio State alum, John Havlicek, newly retired from the Boston Celtics and a future NBA Hall of Famer. Havlicek had never coached but he obviously knew the game and would be a tremendous recruiting attraction. John declined immediately but was extremely helpful in reinforcing my growing attraction to Gary Williams. As a Beantown resident, John had seen many of Gary's games and thought he would be a great fit at Ohio State. I bounced a few other names off him, but Williams was at the top of his list.

The next evening, after talking with Indiana AD Ralph Floyd, who wished me every success with his coach and really meant it, I reached Bob Knight. My strategy was to make Bob feel as though I was offering him the job, as I was sure he would expect me to do, but not really wanting to go that far, for fear he might accept. I admired many of the values Bob embraced, including his penchant for team discipline and his players' graduation rates, but I felt certain that he and I would clash, and sooner rather than later. In short, I could foresee a relationship steeped in one crisis after another that would become public and reflect poorly on the university. Perhaps I sold both of us short in my thinking, but that was how I felt. When I shared my plan with Jim Jones, my senior associate AD, who had worked at OSU for many years and knew Knight well, he sent a shiver up my spine when he said, "Be careful, he might accept."

When Bob came to the phone we made some small talk, and then I said, "Bob, there is no question that I am talking to the finest basketball coach in America." Then, remembering Hugh Hindman's meeting with Bob years before, I continued. "Credentials aren't even a question. The only issues are whether you're interested in Ohio State and whether Rick Bay and Bob Knight can get along."

Then I held my breath.

"Well, I made a commitment here," Knight said. "I know that Bob Knight and Rick Bay can get along, but I don't think I'm interested. But you know if Ohio State had handled this thing this way a few years ago, I might be at Ohio State right now."

I exhaled. I don't mean to be flip about this. I wanted Bob Knight to feel wanted by Ohio State. He deserved to feel wanted by the Buckeyes. I just wasn't sure I wanted to be his athletics director. You never knew when he might explode, and I didn't want to be the guy in charge when he did.

The season ended a few weeks later, and by then my two finalists were Gary Williams and Jim Boeheim. The final plan was for President Jennings, Chairman of the Board of Trustees, Dan Galbraith, and me to charter a plane and interview both candidates in their home cities before making an offer to one of them.

A few hours before leaving Columbus, however, Jake Crouthamel's prophecy materialized and Boeheim withdrew. "Sorry, Rick," he said, "but I've been at Syracuse all my life and..." Where had I heard that I would hear that? I could almost hear Jake chuckling.

We signed Gary Williams to a five-year contract, the first multi-year deal in Buckeye history, after which the university grudgingly agreed to award Earle a measly three-year deal. I was embarrassed for Earle and knew that it was a slap in the face to a coach who had done great things at Ohio State. But to Earle's credit, he accepted the situation gracefully and began preparing for the 1986 season.

28

At the January 1986 NCAA National Convention, the NCAA approved new academic standards for incoming athletes to become immediately eligible, which included a minimum score on the Standard Aptitude Test (SAT) of 700 in high school. Those failing to meet the initial standard would have to wait until their second year to compete.

Many African-American leaders in college athletics had fought against the measure, claiming that standardized tests were culturally biased and negatively affected minority athletes in a disproportionate way. The high school grade-point average was a fairer indicator of a student's aptitude for college work than a test, they argued. Advocates for the new standard countered that high school students who couldn't achieve this very modest score would probably not succeed in most college academic settings, and, at the very least, should not be playing freshman sports.

The debate brought some powerful coaches, rarely seen at these gatherings, to the NCAA convention floor microphones. Georgetown basketball coach John Thompson, an African-American, thought the new rule discriminatory against African-Americans, while Penn State football coach Joe Paterno, a white man, urged the voting delegates not to water down standards and, therefore, sell the athletes short. Black or white, they will rise to the challenge, he promised.

The new standards were approved and have undergone many progressive changes since with respect to everything from the minimum allowable grade point average (GPA) in high school core courses (English, math and the natural/physical sciences, for example) to the minimum allowable standardized test score. The NCAA now uses a sliding scale to match test scores with core grade point average to determine initial eligibility, that is, the lower the GPA, the higher the test score must be, and vice versa. Also, the number of core courses required of high school graduates has increased and, once enrolled in college, student-athletes must demonstrate progress toward a degree-granting academic program beginning their third year to be eligible to compete the following year.

Until the early 1980s, college athletics eligibility standards on a national level were almost non-existent. Once a school granted admission to an athlete, there was no requirement for him or her to make academic progress toward a degree. Some athletes were allowed to major in "eligibility," taking just enough hours to be able to compete, but not advancing toward earning a diploma.

In 1968 *Sports Illustrated* ran a three-part series by Jack Olsen entitled "The Black Athlete—A Shameful Story." The article chronicled the exploitation of the African-American athlete by many schools, how colleges recruited them, kept them barely eligible to play, used their talents to win games and make money, and then, with their eligibility and scholarship exhausted, discarded them far short of having earned a college degree.

Fulfilling degree requirements in a specific academic major was often not a consideration. In addition, it was not uncommon for various schools and athletic conferences to establish minimal academic grade point averages for athletics eligibility that were lower than the 2.0 ("C" average) that was required to graduate. As Olsen pointed out in his *SI* series, many African-American athletes would burn their four years of eligibility, and their scholarship financial assistance, only to find that they were nowhere near completing either the coursework for an academic major or the required "C" grade average required for graduation.

African-American athletes were particularly vulnerable to this sort of exploitation because many had come from economically and educationally deprived backgrounds. The schools recruited these athletes, many academically marginal coming from high school, but then took no responsibility for their academic welfare. There were virtually no academic counselors in athletics departments and no financial aid beyond the four years of eligibility. Once eligibility was exhausted, the athletes were often left to fend for themselves, which meant many returned to their former, sometimes hopeless, environments no better off than when they left, if not worse off for the disillusioning experience.

In 2003, the NCAA adopted the "satisfactory progress rule," mandating that athletes demonstrate incremental progress toward earning a degree to retain their eligibility to compete. For example, an athlete's university must now certify that he or she is 40 per cent toward earning a degree in a specific academic program at the end of the second year to be eligible for the third year; 60 per cent at the end of the third year to be eligible the fourth, and 80 per cent finished to be able to play a fifth year, if, for some reason (having been red-shirted perhaps), a fifth year is forthcoming. Also, fifth year financial aid is often available for those who have exhausted their eligibility, but need more time to complete their degree.

Most schools today have entire academic counseling operations within the athletics department to help keep student-athletes on the right track, and with good reason, I might add, because there is more at stake regarding a school's graduation rates of their athletes than ever before. Individual teams that fail to graduate roughly 60 per cent of their athletes within six years of enrollment can be penalized up to 10 per cent of their scholarship allotment in subsequent years and disqualified from post-season competition.

These proactive measures have all but eliminated the exploitive practices of college athletes that once existed, and they have resulted in higher graduation rates for student athletes in general. According to NCAA calculations, 79 per cent of Division I student-athletes who entered school in 2003 left school with their degrees by 2009, a few percentage points higher than the general student population.

Still there is ongoing debate within the NCAA as to what and how demanding the eligibility benchmarks should be, especially for freshman eligibility. Set the standards too low, and some argue that student athletes are vulnerable to exploitation; set them too high, and some will claim that they are discriminatory.

I think the Ivy League has it right in principle. The Ivy schools have argued that national eligibility standards should not exist at all, that such rules improperly infringe on institutional autonomy. They advocate leaving the entire issue to each school's own integrity. Admit whom you please, they argue, and set your own eligibility standards. If a university can rationalize having a starting senior quarterback, for example, with a 1.4 GPA and 40 hours short of graduation representing your institution, so be it. Sadly, the concept is more than a bit too idealistic for an enterprise that counts on quarterbacks being eligible to help generate millions of dollars for many programs. But it is an idea that I love and respect.

29

Shortly after the 1985 Rose Bowl, I added Notre Dame to the football schedule. This was big news in Columbus, because Woody Hayes had always resisted playing the Irish. It had nothing to do with being afraid of Notre Dame, but rather his concern that the game would distract everyone from his top priority each year, which was to win the Big Ten championship and play in the Rose Bowl.

Bo Schembechler at Michigan felt the same way. When Bo arrived at Michigan in 1969, I was already there as assistant wrestling coach. I vividly remember his printing and erecting a giant copy of the season schedule inside the football locker room. Three of the games were in bright red capital letters—his "red letter games,"—and invariably included the Wolverines' Big Ten opener (whoever it happened to be), Michigan State and, of course, Ohio State. In Bo's mind, a team could reach fever pitch no more than two or three times a year, with the other games taken in stride. Like Woody's, Bo's focus was on the Big Ten title, which required getting off to a good start in the conference opener, beating your intrastate rival and, finally, getting by Ohio State. This was his formula for getting to Pasadena, and he would entertain no distractions. But Notre Dame was already on the Michigan schedule when Bo arrived, and so he was forced to deal with it, which he did, grudgingly.

The first time Bo had to play Notre Dame was in his ninth year in Ann Arbor, in 1978. By then I had left coaching to work for the University of Michigan Alumni Association. I went down to the football locker room one day just before fall practice started. I had a locker, there, that I used for my noontime runs. Sure enough, the schedule was up on the wall, the three red-letter games being Illinois (the Big

Ten opener), Michigan State and Ohio State. Notre Dame was there, but in black and white, thus assigned the same significance as another non-conference opponent, Duke.

Bo happened to be there, so I said, "Bo, how come Notre Dame is not in red?"

"Because they're not a red-letter game," he said rather abruptly.

I knew I had him. "But I thought you put the most important games in red. Notre Dame is big. We haven't played them since the war. Everyone in town is pumped."

"Goddamn it, Rick, Notre Dame doesn't have anything to do with the Big Ten," he barked.

"Yeah, but the team doesn't care if the game's in red or not, you're not going to be able to downplay it with them. Everybody wants to beat Notre Dame," I reiterated, pressing my luck.

"I'll worry about the football schedule; you worry about the wrestling team," he said evenly, ending the conversation.

A few weeks later a fired up Michigan football team, oblivious to the fact that the Irish were not a red-letter opponent, whipped Notre Dame, 28-14. The next season, and from then on, whenever Notre Dame appeared on Bo's schedule there were four red-letter games.

My predecessor, Hugh Hindman, deserves credit for starting the negotiations with Notre Dame, but I followed up with Irish AD Gene Corrigan as soon as I saw a draft contract in Hugh's old files.

When the news broke that we'd be playing them, many people thought I was nuts. The two football powers had not met since 1936, and several folks wrote me that the series was broken off because the Irish enjoyed an unfair advantage. One elderly lady, who claimed to have attended the last OSU-ND game in Columbus, in 1935, wrote me in frail strokes on a postcard that I still have:

April 6, 1985: Mr. Bay–I am 80 years --I object to Ohio State playing Notre Dame. Every Catholic man (on the OSU team) will throw the game to a Notre Dame player. I saw the game in 1935. The last two minutes we had the game won–with Ohio having the ball and time running out–Pincura (the OSU quarterback)–a Catholic had the ball & instead of freezing it–passed it to a Notre Dame player–who just had time to score. The same thing will happen again! No game with Notre Dame–ever! Bernadine Irwin.

There were others who questioned the wisdom of risking an early-season, non-conference loss that would surely affect the national rankings. But I felt that, as one of the premier football programs in the country, we ought to be playing the most respected opponents we could, not only to raise our profile nationally, but also to give our alumni around the nation a chance to see us in their own backyards. I began filling in our future non-conference schedules with Washington, LSU and Colorado.

30

With Gary Williams now in the fold and Earle preparing for his 1986 spring football practice, I started campaigning for new athletics facilities on campus. Ohio Stadium was ancient, having been built in the 1920s, and St. John Arena, our basketball venue, was almost as decrepit. Furthermore, and perhaps most important, we did not have a legitimate indoor practice field for football, which would not have been such an important issue if Michigan hadn't already built one.

Keeping up with the Wolverines was a priority and I began making my case. In inclement weather, the football team used the Quonset hut-like building that our indoor track team utilized, but the roof was barely high enough to accommodate a shot putter, much less a forward pass. Kicking was out of the question—unless I made an encore appearance—and the playing surface was only 40 yards wide. When I began explaining that Bo and his players spent their November practices getting ready for us inside a building that included a full field with goal posts, while our team was running around in the snow if it wanted to practice its passing game, people paid attention.

Nonetheless, few were inspired to rush to my office with cashier's checks, so I initiated a solicitation drive for a project that we estimated would cost nearly $10 million. Seemingly paltry by today's standards, our total operating budget in 1984 was $16 million, while in 2009 Ohio State's athletics budget was well over $110 million. With no state money in the offing, I knew that we would need several very significant gifts of $1 to $2 million each to have any chance of launching the project in a timely manner. Popular opinion to the contrary, no general fund drive of our season-ticket holders was going to be successful. I knew from experience that ordinary boosters, no matter how gung ho, either cannot or do not make willing contributions above the cost of their tickets, which most feel are already overpriced.

Many people thought that I had underestimated the generosity of our fans, and that an all out appeal for funds would generate millions of dollars in gifts. That theory was put to a stern reality check when Woody Hayes died in the spring of 1987. My private capital campaign was already in full swing. I had been aggressively soliciting, one by one, our most capable boosters, ruffling a few feathers along the way, and making the president nervous because of the priority-seating plan attached to it. Coach Hayes' death prompted some wishful thinking among university fundraising folks to insist that we now had a memorial project that would motivate thousands of friends, boosters and former players to donate all the money necessary to proceed. In fact, many people did participate, but with small gifts totaling less than $100,000.

Because Ohio Stadium was ancient, even in 1984, we had no skybox suites to sell. Already we had increased from $750 to $2,000 the donation necessary to procure two tickets between the 40-yard lines, but this money was to fund our scholarship bill, which covered nearly 300 of our 700 athletes receiving financial aid. In addition, I was worried that we might run out of available donor seats because the president was also using those locations to raise money for other departments at the university. His declaration that "a gift is a gift," and that anyone willing to contribute $2,000 for *any* campus cause was worthy of preferred seating in the stadium made sense, but the policy was encroaching on one of the few resources available to me to raise money for athletics. For example, a $2,000 donor to the law or dental schools could claim two premium seats in the stadium, just as a donor to athletics.

This approach to the distribution of donor seats was unprecedented in the Big Ten, which I claimed put our program at a disadvantage. Not everyone in the university should be able to feed off athletics, I said, especially if we were expected to be self-sufficient. Ohio State athletics received no money from the general fund, which certainly was not the case in law or dentistry, which, if forced to provide *their* donors with perquisites would have to consider free legal advice or a complimentary root canal. Finally the president agreed that if and when the stadium exhausted its supply of $2,000 donor seats because of demands from other university departments, he would make up the difference, somehow.

Although football tickets of any kind in Ohio Stadium seemed always difficult to come by, I was shocked to discover that thousands of ducats were available for the first two games of my tenure, simply because fall classes had not yet started and the games were not included in the student season-ticket package. Since no one had bothered to begin marketing these tickets, the general assumption around town that every Buckeye game was sold out was allowed to exist until we made a concerted effort to advertise that, indeed, opening-game tickets were available. The response was overwhelming, as many Buckeye fans that could not buy season tickets finally had a chance to buy a seat from someone other than a scalper.

One of the most intriguing aspects of Ohio State football was that nearly half of the seats occupied on those sellout Saturdays were filled by students, faculty and staff. At every other Big Ten school, season ticket holders from the general public filled the vast majority of the seats in the football stadium for the regular season.

In the early '80s, when the horseshoe's capacity was about 90,000, we sold nearly 25,000 student season tickets and over 17,000 faculty/staff season tickets. This drove other Big Ten athletics directors to distraction, because our revenue-sharing formula with respect to gate receipts did not apply to the sale of these university-family tickets.

Because the university never turned down a season-ticket order from students, faculty or staff, we were left with only 48,000 tickets for public sale. But 12,000 of these were reserved for alumni who were on the waiting list for full season tickets, which meant they had not been out of school for at least 15 years. If not a donor, Ohio State alumni would have to apply for season tickets through the lottery for each of those 15 years to qualify to buy a full season ticket.

When season-ticket holders died, their ticket privileges perished with them and could not be passed to relatives, other than surviving spouses. These tickets were put back into the system, so that newly qualified alumni would have a chance. Our ticket manager kept a close eye on the newspaper obituary page, and we also closely reviewed every ticket application to make certain that the customer was who he or she claimed to be. Still, each year hopeful relatives of a deceased ticket holder would try to beat the system by posing as the departed loved one. It rarely worked, but we used to kid that there was never a shortage of cadavers in the ticket line.

Because donations tied to the seats near midfield went to support our huge scholarship bill, I needed to identify some tickets even more special than those to raise money for capital projects. There were a number of "box seats" close to the field on the home side. These were very much like the boxes in a Major League baseball park and, because they were different from the rest of the seating in the stadium, I was able to justify using their uniqueness to attract major dollars for capital improvements. The problem was that many of the people already sitting there were important, but now would have to pony up a major gift or be moved to the more ordinary $2,000 seats for which most of them were already qualified. Some did make generous gifts, but a few others lobbied the president for special exemptions, and I had to make sure that he did not agree to an exception that would undercut the entire plan. Holding firm was challenging to both of us, because many of those impacted by the new financial requirements were either long time supporters of the university or former or would-be trustees.

In the end we raised or financed about $10 million for the new Woody Hayes Center, a beautiful, indoor-practice facility with handsome coaches' offices, team meeting rooms, a spectacular weight room, and elaborate display cases chronicling Ohio State's storied football history. The building was so spectacular that it far surpassed what Michigan had built, and, in fact, caused the Wolverines to start construction on its second such facility

The building was completed in the early fall of 1987 and was dedicated on the Friday before the Iowa game in November. Woody Hayes had passed on, so both Earle and I spoke at the ceremony.

Seventy-two hours later, Coach Bruce had been fired, and I had resigned. But more on that debacle later.

31

In the fall of 1985, my second year at the helm, I made unwelcome history at Ohio State by agreeing to play our opening game against the University of Pittsburgh at night. Never had a Buckeye football team kicked off a game under the lights in venerable Ohio Stadium. We had ended games at night the year before, in what was already an unpopular precedent, by playing late afternoon games beginning at 3:40 p.m. that were not over until about 7 p.m. But never in 95 years of OSU gridiron lore had we started a game after dark, or at 7 p.m., to be precise. It was simply a tradition that almost all Buckeyes football games kicked off at precisely 1:30 p.m. All that was about to change, and, while I took much of the blame, the real culprit was television.

Until the summer of 1984, the NCAA controlled the television rights for all of Division I football. The NCAA periodically put the rights out for bid, and one or two of the major networks (usually ABC and CBS) would pay a significant fee for the exclusive privilege of selecting and telecasting the games. Normally, on a college football Saturday, the networks would televise several regional games that only fans in those specific geographic areas would see, as well as a single national game that would be carried across the entire country. For example, a typical Saturday menu of games might include Michigan-Iowa in the Midwest, Boston College-Syracuse in the East, and LSU-Florida in the South, all of which might be followed a Notre Dame-USC telecast, nationwide. The rights fees for those games would then be doled out to the conferences based upon the number of times their schools had appeared over the course of the season. The conferences, in turn, would distribute the money among their own schools, using their own revenue sharing formulas.

Because the NCAA tightly controlled and limited the inventory of games offered to the networks, the rights fee was high. And because only a few games were televised each Saturday, only a handful of schools appeared regularly. Having paid dearly for these games, the television networks were aggressively trying to recoup their investment with the sale of advertising, the price of which was largely determined by the size of the audience. Because the size of the viewership was dictated by the marquee value of the teams playing, the networks naturally wanted the "power" schools every chance they could get them. The networks wanted Ohio State, Michigan, USC, UCLA, Notre Dame, and any other school likely to draw big audiences and they wanted them often. This meant that games considered unattractive—the Indiana-Northwestern scrum or the Baylor-Rice "showdown" for example—would always be played in relative obscurity, with respect to any television exposure.

In agreeing which games would be available to the networks, however, the football schools were ambivalent. On the one hand, the Ohio States and Michigans worried about overexposure negatively affecting attendance, that fans would stay home and watch the games on television rather than buy tickets. These schools argued against appearing more than three to four times a season, no matter how much networks wanted them. On the other hand, the Northwesterns and Indianas, the Big Ten's lower division, chafed at rarely being selected, asserting that no television appearances diminished their programs and killed their recruiting, making it virtually impossible for them to be more competitive.

Among the power programs, the fear of over-exposure hurting the live gate was such that that some conferences allowed for an attendance "hurt factor" for any school forced to televise a home game, granting them additional monies for estimated lost attendance. At the same time, however, these schools were often not above lording their television allure over the have-nots in the recruiting wars, reminding prospective athletes that enrolling at a place like Northwestern was tantamount to playing a college football career in virtual anonymity.

Television was becoming a bigger conundrum for everyone. Schools and conferences loved that fact that they were guaranteed money from the networks for the length of the contract. That was a positive. But no one was quite sure to what extent it adversely affected attendance, and everyone hated giving up control of exactly when the games would start.

In August of 1984, the United States Supreme Court stunned college football by ruling, 7-2, that the NCAA contracts with CBS, ABC and ESPN were illegal, a violation of anti-trust law. The lawsuit had been originally brought by the universities of Georgia and Oklahoma, that by then had become part of the newly formed College Football Association (CFA). This group comprised virtually all the major college football conferences except the Big Ten and Pac-10 and had broken from the NCAA with respect to football television. The CFA schools believed that if given free rein to manage their own TV packages they could generate a lot more revenue than they were currently receiving from the NCAA.

The Court ruling dashed all of the television plans previously established for the 1984 season, and the Big Ten/Pac-10 and CFA went their separate ways to design new ones.

The Big Ten and Pac-10 went with CBS, and the CFA with ABC and ESPN, while NBC continued to do the Rose Bowl in a stand-alone deal. And because there was now no restriction to the number of games that could be televised, local stations began to examine the possibility of putting together local packages for games not picked up by the networks. The conferences, now free of any NCAA oversight, began to negotiate their own deals and expected big money for their trouble. But landing such a deal required making major concessions to the television companies, which would pay increased rights fees so long as the games were played at times that would draw the largest audiences. And the best starting times for television were not necessarily the traditional kick-off times that home football crowds were used to and expected.

It was in this dramatic new television environment that I consented to a 3:40 p.m. kickoff against Washington State, our second game of the 1984 season, and my first at Ohio State. This was the first of many starting time compromises with CBS to ensure that the Big Ten could maximize its TV revenues. The 3:40 kickoff meant that darkness would have enveloped Ohio Stadium by the time the contest ended, and, so, three temporary, gigantic light towers had to be leased and positioned around the ancient edifice to make television, not to mention live, viewing possible.

The Washington State game was not an exception. Our home games against Iowa, Illinois and Indiana were also to kick off at 3:40 p.m., while the only other two home games, Oregon State and Michigan, would begin at 12:10. The noon start against Michigan was not new, the network having moved that time up years before to accommodate what had become a traditional doubleheader package that included the USC-UCLA game, and served as precursor to the Rose Bowl game.

When these time changes were made public, *The Columbus Dispatch* ran a banner headline in the sports section that blared: "OHIO STATE YIELDS TO THE DARK AGES."

The story by veteran *Dispatch* writer, Tim May, began:

"Wrigley Field (home of the Chicago Cubs who refused to play home games at night until 1988) won't give in, but Ohio State has.
"For the first time in Ohio State football history, there will be lights on the upper rim of the giant horseshoe

for a few games this season. Portable lights, mind you, in case you're worried about the architectural integrity of the hallowed gridiron mausoleum, but lights nonetheless."

But even these times were not set in stone, because the network still had limited flexibility to make last-minute changes in unusual circumstances. For example, in the unlikely scenario in which the season-ending Indiana-Purdue game would be played for the conference championship, it might replace Michigan-Ohio State as the national TV game. Everything was so up in the air that, from that season forward, our game tickets carried no starting time, but rather the letters "TBA," to be announced.

The public reaction to the new schedule was one of resigned frustration. Fans were not going to give up tickets, but they were not happy campers, either.

Some of our fans, especially those who traveled to Columbus from long distances, were truly affected. The city is located in the absolute middle of the state, and Ohio State football drew boosters from every corner of its borders, many of them driving over 200 miles, one way, to the games. With a 1:30 p.m. starting time they had been used to the game ending by 5:00 p.m. and getting home by 10:00 p.m. A 3:30 p.m. kickoff would change that, as would the night games. Columbus hotels and restaurants loved it, but fans with kids weren't pleased.

I tried to put the dilemma in perspective, and was quoted extensively in Tim May's article.

"Yes, you can take the position that you're not going to be flexible, that the starting time of 1:30 is sacred, and come hell or high water, we're not going to move. But if we take that position, and let's say Michigan takes that position, and then the Big Ten doesn't have a television package.

*"What it comes down to is, you can't have it both
ways. You can't sit back on your high horse and say,
'By God, we're going to start at 1:30, and that's it, and
the television money be damned!' without it sooner or
later affecting your programs...We're talking about a
lot of money, over $700,000."*

$700,000 was the amount we predicted we were go-
ing to receive under the old NCAA package and was a
lot of money at the time. And we did make $700,000, as
I recall, but we had to appear on TV a lot more than usual to earn it. We certainly didn't make what Georgia and
Oklahoma thought each of us would generate when they
filed their lawsuit, mistakenly assuming that in a free market, without NCAA restrictions, they could sell their games in
their own markets for much more than they were receiving
from their shares of the national package. Actually, just the
opposite occurred, at least temporarily. With almost every
game available for television, it was a buyer's market, and
rights fees were drastically reduced.

Tim May closed his tome with this lament:

*"...as Ohio State fans would probably agree, a game
at night beats no game at all. And, don't forget, the
last one out has to turn out the lights, OK?"*

Besides calming the waters among our fans, it seemed
as though not a day went by when I didn't have a new television issue with which to deal.

There were unexpected property rights questions. If
Nebraska (a CFA Big Eight school) played at USC (Pac-10/
Big Ten), it was conceded the home school and its network
partner owned the rights to the contest. But how was the
rights fee to be divided? Fifty-fifty? It sounded logical, but a
bitter debate ensued about the possible disparity in value
of the respective television packages. For example, if the

Nebraska-USC game was played in Los Angeles, it was considered a part of the Pac10/Big Ten television package and was broadcast by its television partner CBS. If, a year later, the return match was played in Lincoln, it was considered part of the CFA package and was telecast by its TV network ABC.

If, hypothetically, CBS was paying a $100,000 rights fee to the Big Ten/Pac10 for the game, but the next year ABC was paying only $80,000 for the same game, why should USC have to split its $100,000 with Nebraska and give them $50,000 when they would receive only $40,000 (in a 50-50 split of $80,000) for the same game when they played in Lincoln? This was a so-called "crossover game" issue, which affected many contests between CBS and ABC/ESPN schools, some of which were contested in court before being settled.

Of all these challenging issues, however, the most vexing took place behind the scenes (at least, for awhile) within our own conference. Immediately following the Supreme Court decision, the Big Ten athletics directors and commissioner, Wayne Duke, met at O'Hare Field in Chicago to discuss our options. The consensus was that we would all make whatever reasonable sacrifices were necessary with respect to starting times, night games and the like to wrangle the most lucrative possible television contracts from the networks. Among other things, this meant that the strongest programs in the league at the time would have to change traditional starting times and televise many more home games than usual over several years, possibly impacting attendance. We all agreed, all ten schools, including Michigan and Michigan AD Don Canham. No minutes were ever taken at these meetings. It was a handshake deal. So I went back to Columbus and announced the good news.

A few days later Michigan coach, Bo Schembechler, was quoted as saying that the Wolverines had made no starting time compromises to accommodate television coverage. His athletics director, my blood oath colleague from our conference meeting at O'Hare, Don Canham, said nothing. Since the Ohio State faithful loathed any situation where they compared unfavorably to Michigan, I became a lightning rod for some rude questioning. Why were we changing starting times when Michigan was making no sacrifice whatsoever?

Eventually, Michigan fell in line with the rest of us, but Bo's pronouncement that Michigan was not making any kickoff time concessions for TV foreshadowed a confrontation at the next meeting of our AD group, several weeks later.

As we were discussing future scheduling issues with respect to television the subject turned to each school's previous commitment to allow the telecast of one night game at home, so long as it was done before the end of October, when the weather was still not too cold. I reported that I had agreed to let CBS have our opening game against Pittsburgh in the coming season. Bump Elliott, the AD at Iowa and my own former football coach at Michigan, confirmed that he had scheduled a home game at night, as well. Suddenly, it was Don Canham's turn, and he said that Michigan would not play a night game at home.

"What do you mean," I said. "We all agreed to do one."

Silence in the room. Two things were certain. Bo had gotten to Canham. And: no one there was about to support a rookie Big Ten AD over the most powerful guy in the conference.

"You said that you would do one," I reiterated.

"No, I never said that," Canham said, a bit sheepishly.

"Don, you know the situation in Columbus. I, on behalf of Ohio State, never would have agreed to do a night game if you and Michigan hadn't made the same commitment," I said.

"Well, I never said I would do one," he repeated.

Then, I appealed to Bump. "Bump, you're doing a night game. Didn't we all agree to do one?" I asked, hopefully.

Bump was an associate AD at Michigan following his coaching career in Ann Arbor, working for Canham before taking the job at Iowa. But he was about as confrontational as a Baptist minister, and here I was dragging him into the middle of a discussion no one in the room was comfortable with.

"Rick, I don't remember exactly what was said. I think we all said we'd consider it," Bump said quietly.

I'd lost, and I knew it, but I turned to Canham and said hotly, "You said that you would do it, and we all know it!'

Later, Purdue AD, George King, another veteran, told me that I should never have confronted Don the way I did. He felt that it was wrong, no matter what Don had promised about night football in Ann Arbor. I told George that I understood how he felt, especially as a long-time colleague of Don's. I said that I was sorry he felt that way, but that I had to stick up for Ohio State.

Although not totally honest about his night game commitment, Don was always forthright in terms of how we got along. Before the Ohio State-Michigan game my first year in 1984, he was asked about me for a *Detroit Free Press* article about my days in Ann Arbor, where Don had hired me as the Wolverines' head wrestling coach. "He and I were never close. I don't have any feeling one way or another about him," he said. "He's all right."

32

Ohio State's first game of the 1985 season was truly one for the ages, or the "dark ages," as *The Columbus Dispatch* had said in reference to our several 3:30 p.m. starting times a year earlier. But some fans thought this was far worse. The Buckeyes were playing the University of Pittsburgh in the first night game in the history of Ohio Stadium, a 7:30 p.m. kickoff. Many letters to my office and the newspaper established that more than a few people were concerned. Would this strange new environment be safe? They knew that the field would be well lit, but what about in the bowels of the horseshoe and the surrounding parking lots? Would there be more police security on duty to protect people going to and from their cars?

While folks initially thought of these as safety issues, what they were really uncomfortable about was the disruption in their traditional routine. Until 1984 virtually every home game in the annals of Ohio State football had begun at 1:30 p.m. This night contest against Pitt was playing mind games with our fans, and I tried to calm them down. First, I pointed out that while the starting time was a result of our new television contract, college football was already played at night all across the country. The Southeastern, Atlantic Coast and the Pac 10 conferences had been playing night football for years, safely, and without incident. Nearly all of the high school games in Ohio were played on Friday nights, I reminded everyone. And almost all of us, I said, attended movies, concerts and the theater at night, for crying out loud! I reiterated that the university had taken every reasonable precaution to make the Pittsburgh game experience safe for all, and I urged everyone to take a deep breath. I was certain, I said a little mockingly, that Columbus was strong enough to make it through the night.

The fans, it turned out, were equal to the challenge, but the team barely got by. Our offense sputtered the entire game, and we edged Pitt, 10-7, duplicating our nail-biting opening victory against Oregon State the year before.

The following week, however, the Buckeye offense did get on track, scoring early and often in a 36-13 victory against Colorado in Boulder. While I don't remember much about the game itself, the Colorado mascot left a lasting impression.

CU's mascot was a full grown, 2,000-pound buffalo named Ralphie, a mammoth creature that led the team onto the field just before kickoff. Folsom Field, where the Buffaloes played, was a smaller version of the Ohio Stadium horseshoe, seating about 60,000.

On that sunny Saturday afternoon in Boulder, the Colorado team entered the playing area from one corner of the open end of the stadium and sprinted about 60 yards, pulling up in front of the home bench on the far side of the field opposite the press box. Ralphie, however, who was leading the charge, kept going. The animal's six handlers seemed to be flying in every direction. Clearly, the buffalo had done this before, and knew that on the other side of the field was a large enclosed van containing his lunch. Appearing almost prehistoric from my vantage point in the press box, the great animal thundered the full 100 yards down the far sideline, shedding a couple of his handlers in the process. It turned the corner at the closed end of the stadium, bolted back up the near side of the field where the visiting bench–our bench–was located and charged another 100 yards to the waiting, reinforced trailer, which nearly disintegrated upon Ralphie's crashing arrival.

I viewed this extraordinary event from about 70 yards away, and immediately began scanning the field for casualties. It had been a mini-stampede. While apparently no one was hurt, I was incredulous that Ralphie was allowed this nearly unescorted freedom every football Saturday at Folsom Field.

Colorado was scheduled to visit Ohio State the next year, 1986. The Buffalo AD, Bill Marolt, approached me near the end of the game, offered his congratulations and asked nonchalantly if they could bring Ralphie to Ohio Stadium. I gaped at him.

"You mean let him run on the field?"

"Yeah," Bill said, "just once around the field, nothing more than he did today. Your fans would love it."

"Bill," I said, "are you crazy? Our band sits on the field, in chairs. If Ralphie got spooked, he could wipe out our tuba section. No way."

"Rick, I'm not asking that he dot the 'I.' But it would be neat for our team and fans if we could bring him."

"Bill," I repeated, "no way."

Years later I ran into Bill McCartney, the former Colorado football coach, who in 1990 had coached the Buffaloes to the national championship. Bill had been an assistant at Michigan for Bo when I coached wrestling in Ann Arbor. He laughed when I told him of my conversation with Marolt that day in Boulder, but he had even a better story.

He said that, traditionally, just before Ralphie led the Colorado team onto the field, it, the team, would huddle just outside its locker room, which was barely out of view of the spectators. Ralphie was always positioned just in front of the players, the animal's handlers waiting for their cue to rush onto the field. By this time the dressing room doors had been closed behind the team, and the players and coaches were standing *behind* Ralphie, ready to go. For a moment it was very crowded in this tunnel area as the team, Ralphie and his handlers were bunched together waiting for the signal to charge forward.

"One game I had given my best pre-game talk to the team," Bill said. "Our collective testosterone level was at an all-time high, and we were primed to run over anyone or anything between us and victory. We were fired up, lots of head butting and butt slapping, absolutely ready to kill. But all of a sudden Ralphie gets fidgety, begins to paw the ground, and somehow gets turned around, so that instead of facing out toward the field, he is staring straight at us. Panic sets in, and suddenly the only thing anyone is fired up about is how to get their asses back into the locker room. Nothing happened, of course. They got Ralphie turned back around, but it showed what a short life span my pre-game speeches have, especially under dire circumstances."

We played back in Columbus the next week and, firing on all cylinders, thumped Washington State, 48-32. But the Big Ten opener at Illinois the following Saturday was a huge disappointment, as we lost on a field goal on the final play of the game, 31-28. It always feels devastating to start 0-1 in conference play, but we won our next five Big Ten games, including the scariest of nail biters at Minnesota, 23-19. Lou Holtz had revitalized the Gopher program, moving all its home games to Saturday nights inside the Metrodome in downtown Minneapolis. The place was packed, as this was a "hump game" for Minnesota, a serious test against a quality opponent to see how much progress they had really made.

The Gopher quarterback was a kid named Ricky Fogge, who could run like a gazelle and was a magician at running the option play. We had failed to stop him all night, and when the home team got the ball with less than two minutes to go, I was worried. With Fogge running the offense to perfection, Minnesota quickly moved down the field and seemed certain to score the winning touchdown. With one time out left, the Gophers had the ball on our two-yard line with about 20 seconds to go, plenty of time to run at least two plays. But on the next snap our defense, though totally exhausted, swarmed Fogge, tackling him at the one.

In what was the worst possible break for Minnesota, Fogge was shaken up on the play, meaning not only did they have to use their final time out, but that Fogge had to come out of the game for at least one play, which was all that the Gophers had left. On the final play of the game the back-up quarterback for Fogge tried the option, himself, only to get stuffed at the line of scrimmage as the game ended. We had survived; that was all anyone could say.

Although unnoticed by the media, one of the most interesting aspects of the week was that I had allowed Earle to talk me into waiting until Saturday morning to fly the team to the Twin Cities. It was a night game, so there was plenty of time to fly over in the morning—if nothing went wrong.

In retrospect, it was a crazy, if not irresponsible, decision. There was absolutely no room for error. If we had had bad weather–and we're talking late October in Minnesota—or a mechanical problem with the charter aircraft, the game probably would have been cancelled (I think the Vikings were to play in the Dome the next day), and we might have been forced to forfeit. But Earle did not want to play at night to begin with, and he hated the idea of arriving Friday and sitting around a Twin Cities hotel room all day Saturday. So, reluctantly, I agreed to delay our departure until Saturday morning, thus arriving at our downtown hotel at noon, eating lunch, resting and then, finally, at about 4 p.m., driving the short distance to the stadium. Everything turned out all right, but it could have been a disaster.

33

The win in Minneapolis set the stage for a crucial game against Iowa the following Saturday in Columbus.

The Hawkeyes were undefeated in Big Ten play and leading the league. A win would put us in the driver's seat and in a position to control our destiny. But the game was also vitally important for another reason, totally unrelated to the Big Ten standings.

With the guidance of our long time team physician, Dr. Bob Murphy, I had crafted the first ever drug-testing program for Ohio State athletics. I had vowed that we would run a clean program, and that our student-athletes would be expected to be decent students and good citizens. In my mind, this included doing all we could to discourage our kids from using illegal drugs, at least those we had the resources to test for, which were marijuana and cocaine.

Dr. Bob and I made an instructional video (to be viewed by every team) describing the health hazards connected with these drugs and spelling out the penalty system connected with the program.

The protocol dictated that any Ohio State athlete could be tested, using a urine sample, at any time and without cause. A first positive test result would result in a warning and required the athlete to meet with Dr. Murphy and me to discuss the problem. An athlete with a first positive underwent mandatory counseling and was tested frequently thereafter. A second positive meant the coach and parents would be notified, and a third positive resulted in an automatic suspension from the team.

We needed to convince both our athletes and the public that our policy was not simply cosmetic, that we were serious and that we really wanted to know if we had problems in our program. At the time, there was a mentality among some college administrators that the less you knew about what your teams and coaches were doing, the more insulated you were from allegations of mismanagement. Some ADs didn't want to know what their head coaches were doing, and some head coaches were not anxious to audit closely the activities of their athletes.

We had started by testing individuals and teams randomly, but a few days before the showdown with the Hawkeyes, Dr. Murphy came to me saying that we needed to challenge ourselves as to how determined we really were about having a clean program. He suggested that we bring the entire football team in on the Sunday morning after the game (and following a few campus parties, I assumed) and test everyone. No one was to know ahead of time, not even Earle. Our tough logic was that we would be more likely to catch transgressors the morning after a great victory than just about any other time we could think of. And we believed that this action would clearly send the message that we were in earnest about keeping drugs out of Ohio State athletics. I gulped, but I knew Bob was right.

We beat Iowa, 22-13. It was a great victory but I walked out of the stadium worried that half the team might be headed to a Grateful Dead concert. The team always met on Sunday at noon following games to watch film and treat injuries. I called Earle early Sunday morning and told him that we were going to test everyone before they got into their routine. There was a long silence.

"You mean for marijuana?" he asked.

"Yes," I said, "that and a few other illegal substances."

"But last night was Saturday night," he observed, sagely.

"Just my point," I said. "If anyone has a problem, we're more likely to find it now, after a victory worth celebrating. We want the team to know that we want to know."

So we did it and, to our pleasant surprise and great relief, no one tested positive. Of course, we did not test for alcohol and no one was naive enough to think the results would have been the same, had we done so. But the word spread quickly among our athletes that drug testing at Ohio State was a serious matter; you could be tested at any time, including the Sunday after a competition.

Although my drug testing policy became more stringent with each job I had, no one ever challenged it or even criticized it.

By the time I arrived at San Diego State, 20 years later, my policy had evolved to the point that anyone who tested positive a first time was automatically suspended from competition for 20 percent of the season and was required to attend counseling until released by the team physician. Failure to attend counseling or failure to produce a urine specimen at the assigned time and location also counted as a positive test. A second positive at any time over an entire four- to five-year career meant banishment from Aztec athletics.

Ultimately we reduced the penalty for the first positive to 10 percent of the season because we found that 20 percent resulted in some kids giving up instead of working their way back onto the team.

I had two primary goals in implementing drug testing. First, I wanted to protect the image and reputation of the institution. Second, I wanted to provide a deterrent to help keep our student athletes from using drugs. Interestingly, every time I confronted an athlete with a positive test result, he or she ultimately admitted using the drug. In a few instances, the athlete initially swore not to have used marijuana, but claimed to have been around friends using it, thus inadvertently inhaling too much secondhand smoke. However, because we tested at levels so high, the athlete would have had to have been stuck in a phone booth with

15 pot-smoking pals to show up as positive. All eventually came clean.

Starting at Ohio State and ending up at San Diego State, 14 years altogether, I met with about 40 athletes who tested positive. A few who were caught a second time, or who did not complete the rehab process, were eliminated from the program. But most worked their way back onto their teams and successfully withstood further testing over what remained of their careers. At each school, we conducted exit interviews with a sampling of outgoing seniors. When we asked about their opinion of our drug-testing program, all were emphatic that we should continue it. Some urged us to test more often, which we would have done had our budget allowed. Even those kids who felt we might have invaded their privacy were unanimous that the policy had helped them, especially in peer group situations with pot. Because their peers often knew what was at stake for the athletes, they were not as likely to be pressured to smoke the stuff. I was not naïve enough to think we had caught everyone who had ever smoked a joint, but I took satisfaction in knowing that we had provided at least a small deterrent from the use of drugs in our programs.

Having somehow survived both the risk-laden Minnesota trip and the Iowa game drug test, we now had only to whip up on two teams near the bottom of the league, Northwestern and Wisconsin, to get to the annual "championship game" at Michigan. We were tied with Iowa in the conference standings, but our victory over the Hawkeyes gave us the tiebreaker to claim the title if we won out. Northwestern was scrappier than we expected, but we persevered and won, 35-17, in Evanston.

Now, it was back home to dust off Wisconsin in what was considered a "gimmie" by the odds makers before heading to Michigan. I have often wondered how many times in sports a heavily favored team has lost a game to a badly overmatched underdog just prior to a "big game."

Preoccupied with Michigan and all but discounting the Badgers, our boys realized too late in the game that we were in one, and lost, 12-7. As poorly as we played, we were never more than a touchdown behind, and each time we got the ball everyone in the packed stadium was sure that we would find a way to win. But it wasn't to be. Iowa won its game, and was back in the driver's seat. Now we had to beat "that school up north," and Minnesota had to upset Iowa in the final week to give us a chance to go to the Rose Bowl.

It didn't happen. The Wolverines prevailed, 27-17. We got close late in the game when our All-American receiver, Cris Carter, made a circus catch for a touchdown to cut the margin to 20-17. On their ensuing possession, however, Michigan faced a third down and long-yardage situation, which, if unsuccessful, would have forced them to punt, thus changing the momentum of the game in our favor. We blitzed on the play, but its outstanding quarterback, Jim Harbaugh, read it perfectly and threw a long touchdown pass to ice the game for the Maize and Blue. We were 8-3, and our consolation prize was a trip to the Citrus Bowl in Orlando to play Brigham Young University.

Three weeks later the team headed to Florida, the players a lot more resilient than I was. While I was still brooding about the Michigan loss, the team settled into its surroundings nicely. After practice each day there was always a special activity for it, such as a visit to Disney World or Epcot Center. The players had a great time, and still took care of business on the field, beating BYU, 10-7. Old 9-3 Earle finished—what else?—9-3 for the sixth consecutive season.

34

During the three weeks before the bowl game, I was able to turn my attention to Gary Williams' first basketball season as the Buckeyes' coach. The team was off to a rousing 6-0 start, beating three pretty decent Mid-American Conference teams in the process. As I was already aware, Gary was an intense competitor who stalked the sidelines every minute of every game, jabbering at the officials constantly.

As an on-court personality, he was the exact opposite of the stoic Eldon Miller and the fans loved it, especially the students. Having anticipated the reaction to Gary, I had moved the student section from the nosebleed area of the arena to the primo seats, (though they were temporary wooden bleachers) in the lower rung. They were right on top of action, not to mention the officials, the visiting team and the opposing coach, all of whom were now easy targets for the taunts and barbs that students love to lob into enemy territory.

The students wasted no time getting into the spirit of things. The first time Gary came onto the court in his first game, the student section rose to their feet and yelled a drawn out, "Hiiiii, Gary!" Although somewhat surprised, the coach managed a sheepish smile and a brief acknowledgment toward the kids—and a tradition was born. From that point on, a "Hiiiii, Gary," preceded every tipoff. Unfortunately, however, halfway through the season, someone got the bright idea to include me in the fun. Just before one game in January, I happened to walk in front of the student section to attend to something at the scorer's table. Sure enough, the students rose to their feet and gave me a

"Hiiiii, Rick!" A little shocked, I looked over to them, gave a self-conscious salute and went to my seat as fast as I could.

Though faced with a tough rebuilding job, Gary managed to win 20 games in that first season and brought excitement back to Ohio State basketball. Although the Citrus Bowl was on the horizon, and most people in Columbus were still in football mode, the basketball team turned some heads just after Christmas by beating both Kansas and Florida in the Rainbow Classic in Hawaii. Then, after losing its first three Big Ten games on the road against Indiana and both Michigan schools, the team hit its stride winning four straight, including games at Iowa and Minnesota. After that we seemed to alternate winning and losing until the end of the season, when we upset Michigan State for a berth in the NCAA Tournament.

The NCAA selection committee sent Ohio State to Atlanta, where we surprised everyone by beating Kentucky in the first round, 91-77. In the second-round game against Georgetown, we were ahead at halftime and playing well enough to win. But standout scorer Denis Hopson picked up his fourth foul on a questionable call early in the second half, and we were not deep enough in talent to overcome it. With Hopson on the bench most of the final 20 minutes, we lost, 82-79. Still, on a relative basis, we had enjoyed a fine season, finishing 20-13, and 9-9 in the Big Ten. Gary Williams seemed destined to do great things at Ohio State.

It was a marvelous achievement for both Ohio State basketball and Gary Williams. We were back in the NCAA Tournament, and Gary had acquired lots of fans in the process of getting there, not the least of whom was the Buckeye's former great, but bitter head coach, Fred Taylor.

Though his last few teams were his poorest, Fred Taylor had felt unfairly fired, or at least denied his dignity, when athletics director, Ed Weaver, made the necessary change. Taylor left the campus in 1977 to become the manager of The Golf Club, a privately owned men-only course just outside of Columbus, and had never been back. He hated Ed Weaver and Hugh Hindman, and wasn't that excited about meeting me. But I needed all the friends I could get, and I did what I could to let him know that the new regime missed seeing him in St. John Arena. Still, nothing much happened until I introduced him to Gary, who, in turn, invited Fred to attend some of his practices. While I'm not certain what happened, I know that Fred appreciated what we were trying to do, and that he softened toward the athletics department.

Gary wasn't quite so congenial when it came to Buckeye women's basketball. Although well aware of Title IX, he had yet to willingly embrace its principles. He knew how important men's basketball was to the financial health of the athletics program, and he knew that, in that sense, the women's program paled in comparison. When it came to selecting practice times or sharing the court, he clearly felt that the men should have absolute priority.

I had inherited Tara Vanderveer, one of the nation's best, and eventually most celebrated, women's coaches when I arrived in Columbus. But she had always wanted to live in San Francisco and when the Stanford job opened, she jumped at it. By the time Gary Williams came to town, I had hired Nancy Darsch, a Pat Summitt protégé from Tennessee. The two did not get along, mainly, I think, because of Gary's abrasiveness when he was upset. There were constant clashes over who had the gym floor when. The struggle got to a point that Nancy became as stubborn as Gary. Finally, I became tired of the bickering and did what I should have done months before.

"Look," I said, when I had them together, "you both have to begin acting like adults. I'm going to give you one more chance to work out this schedule issue among yourselves. If you can't do it, I will decide the matter for you, with you knowing full well that I will probably make it worse than anything you two could agree on. My decision will be arbitrary and final. So if you want to put your basketball pro-grams' scheduling issues in the hands of an old wrestling coach, be my guests."

They worked it out. I think they had forgotten I was a wrestling coach.

35

The last half of the regular basketball season had included two games in St. John Arena that were marked by bizarre occurrences.

In the final minutes of the Iowa game, the Hawkeyes were running a fast break that seemed certain to result in a key basket that might have won the game for them. But suddenly, in the middle of the action, the game horn sounded, and everyone stopped. The officials went to the scorer's table only to find our man on the time clock somewhat disorientated with no reasonable explanation as why he had sounded the mechanism. The man had been our timer for many years and was embarrassed beyond words.

The Iowa coach, Tom Davis, came over to huddle with Gary and the officials, and I came down from my seat to see what had happened. In as much as even the student section was preoccupied with the conference at the scorer's table, they spared me the "Hi, Rick" greeting.

Iowa's athletics director Bump Elliott happened to be in the stands behind the Hawkeye bench. He had taken the occasion of his team's game against us to visit some relatives in Columbus. Knowing where Bump was sitting, I signaled him to come join the conference, but to my surprise, he waved me off, as if to say, "Hey, buddy, it's *your* game. I'm a guest, and I have my own challenges at Iowa!"

Unfortunately for everyone, especially the Hawks, the only resolution to the matter was to declare the mishap an inadvertent stoppage of play and give Iowa the ball, out of bounds, just beyond mid-court. They did not score on the possession, and we won the game.

At home, later that night, however, I received a call from one of our team physicians telling me that our timer had actually suffered a minor stroke during the game and would not be available the rest of the season.

The other game was even wackier, but did not interfere with the contest itself.

We were about to play Florida International in a rare February non-conference game. Since the game was at mid-week and the opponent relatively unknown, there would have been little interest in the contest except that our star player, Denis Hopson, was primed to break the Buckeyes all-time career scoring record. He needed just 17 points to surpass former Ohio State great Herb Williams, and it seemed certain he would do it against the Golden Panthers from Miami.

Everyone loves a winner, especially Ohio Governor Richard Celeste, who suddenly wanted to jump on our new basketball bandwagon. He was never around when Ohio State athletics could have used him, but he and his staff saw the Hopson milestone as a chance to get some unexpected positive ink. He could have helped us. Our budget would have benefited dramatically from state mandated tuition waivers for scholarship athletes, for example. This had occurred in both Arizona and New Mexico, saving their state university athletic programs hundreds of thousands, if not millions of dollars. But the message from the university administration was that there was no point broaching the issue with the governor's office.

The only time we would see Dick Celeste around athletics was when we were doing well and he needed some publicity. Predictably, then, Celeste became a frequent visitor to St. John Arena in my second year at Ohio State. Gary Williams had stirred up some excitement, and our games were becoming a place to be seen by our heretofore-casual fans.

When it became clear that Hopson was going to break the scoring record, we arranged with Florida International and the referees to stop the game momentarily, so that Williams (who would be seated on the Buckeye bench) could be handed the game ball, walk onto the floor and present it to Hopson. The two would have their picture taken and the game would resume. That would be it. Clean. Simple. Quick.

Also, at halftime we were going to present an award to football player, Eric Kumerow, who had been selected the Big Ten Defensive Player of the Year. His parents would be there; I would present the award following an announcement from the scorer's table. Again, no frills, no speeches. Little pomp and circumstance.

The scant marquee value of our opponent aside, these two brief ceremonies helped generate a good crowd, including Dick Celeste. Fifteen minutes prior to the game, the governor apparently found out about the halftime ceremony, and sent down a messenger who said that Governor Celeste would like to be a part of the football presentation. I sent the messenger back, saying no, that I appreciated the governor's interest, but his involvement would not be appropriate. All was well, for a few minutes, anyway, until Dan Meinert, my assistant athletics director, came to my seat just before tip-off and said the governor had another request. He wanted to be in on the ceremony when Hopson broke the record, to be in the photo with the players. It didn't take a brain surgeon to figure out Celeste's motives. You couldn't buy publicity like this.

I sent another message back—sorry, no way. Again, I said that I felt the governor's involvement would not be appropriate. And secondly, Florida International had agreed to stop the game only momentarily, they had not agreed to a full-blown gubernatorial campaign. Finally, I pointed out that even our coach, Gary Williams, was not going to be in the photo. This was supposed to be a special moment for Hopson and Williams.

We were well into the second half and Hopson was getting close, maybe four points shy. I was standing at the corner of the gym at the end of the Ohio State bench, a usual roosting place, and I looked down the bench. Right behind the team, sitting squashed in the student section, among the kids, was Governor Celeste. He had snuck down from his regular seat, wedged himself between two students and was perched there like a weasel, ready to insert himself into the ceremony.

Sure enough, when Hopson scored the record breaking points, and came over to the bench so that Williams could shake his hand and give him the ball, Celeste jumped through the crowd and nearly over our team bench to congratulate Denis and smile for the camera.

I'll give *The Columbus Dispatch* credit here. They cropped Celeste out of the picture when they ran it in the next day's paper.

One unfortunate incident in the 1986-87 year that carried over from football into basketball involved an African-American female cheerleader, whom I was ordered by the president to add to the squad.

As one might expect, Ohio State cheerleading, or "rally," as it is sometime called, had its own strong traditions. There were cheerleader tryouts in the old field house in late summer. Usually, a large number of young men and women auditioned before a panel of judges who were rally alumni. The tryouts were open to the public, and the fans that attended usually jumped into the spirit of the proceedings and responded enthusiastically to the kids' efforts. The judges, many former cheerleaders, were a diverse group, men and women, black and white and young and old, relatively speaking. I didn't see anyone over 60.

A few months after the composition of the team had been announced, eight men and eight women, I received a call from my faithful secretary, Pat Cropper, who said the president's office was adding another person to the team.

"What?" I exclaimed.

I think Pat was more upset than I was, but she wanted to give me a heads-up before I returned to the office the next morning. She told me that a woman who had tried out but had been left off the squad, had filed an appeal with the school, and when nothing was done for several months, went directly to Jennings on grounds that she had been the victim of racial discrimination. She was African-American. The president, in turn, without any consultation with me, added her to the team. I knew instinctively that he had not carefully considered the matter, especially in terms of the rest of the squad. It appeared that, fearing the situation could become a racial issue, he had elected to preempt any controversy by simply expanding the rally team roster. I believe he thought no one would really care and that we would just slap a uniform on her and let her participate.

As soon as Pat and I had hung up, I called Jennings's office requesting an emergency meeting the next morning, begging him not to announce anything until we had talked. In the meantime, I got ahold of the chairman of the judging committee and was told that the woman not only had failed to make the top eight, but also was barely in the top fifteen. Furthermore, I was told that several other African-American kids had been selected.

When I walked into Ed's office the next morning he was sitting with the university ombudsperson, a white woman, who had heard the woman's appeal and convinced the president to add her to the squad. She said simply that the young cheerleading aspirant had brought this complaint, and that it must be corrected.

I responded heatedly, saying that just because a complaint was brought didn't mean it had merit. I further told them that the judging panel had been diverse, the evaluations fair and documented and that other minorities had been chosen. I also reported that the woman had finished far down the line in the voting and, according to a few judges to whom I spoke, couldn't cheer worth a damn.

All of this fell on deaf ears and I was ordered to put her on the team and to make certain that her teammates treated her with respect. The squad was furious, but, hiding my own anger, I emphasized to the squad the importance of complying with the president's mandate.

Thus, with jaws firmly set, we set about on the first order of business, which was to invite a ninth male to join the squad so that the new member had a partner. With all of the lifting and acrobatics that was involved in rally, the squad needed an equal number of men and women.

But if the students already selected were ready to make the best of it, those who not been selected were not. We started by asking the young man who had finished ninth in the tryouts to join the squad to partner the new woman. He was insulted and refused. We then went to number ten; he had the same reaction. We traveled all the way down the list, perhaps through six to eight names, and it was clear that no one wanted to make the team in this way. And not even the president or the ombudsperson could make them.

So she never did have a partner, and it was a sad sight to see eight couples and then her, standing alone at the end of the row. She quit halfway into the season and I felt sorry for her. She may have instituted the action, but the university should have had more sense than try to appease her in a way that her peers would never accept. She had been embarrassed, but the school made it possible.

36

With both the 1985-86 football and basketball seasons behind me, I turned my full attention to fundraising. The new $10 million athletics center was on the drawing board with its construction pretty much assured. But I had a much larger vision.

We commissioned an architectural firm to draw up a facilities master plan that anticipated renovating virtually all of our facilities, as well as building new ones. The biggest and most expensive projects—an overhaul of ancient Ohio Stadium and a new basketball arena—would require the sale of bonds and would have to wait, for the moment. But in the meantime, I wanted to get people thinking about new baseball and softball stadiums, a medium size arena for the likes of wrestling, gymnastics and volleyball and a new ice hockey building.

We needed to commit to ice hockey or drop the sport. We were spending several hundred thousand dollars a year on the enterprise, but playing in the worst facility outside of Ukraine. For starters, the ice was not officially long enough, but the league, the Central Collegiate Hockey Association (CCHA), let it slide rather than give us one more reason to eliminate the sport. And there was seating on only one side of the playing surface. At most, the place could hold maybe 400 fans, meaning we hardly generated enough revenue to cover the cost of our team's dental bill. As a result, we were not very competitive and getting almost nothing for the investment.

I could see that fundraising was going to be difficult. Except for the donations tied to priority football seating, which were earmarked for scholarships, fundraising had never been attempted within the Buckeye athletics department. Revenue from football and men's basketball paid all the bills, and Ohio State, as Michigan, took great pride in the fact that donations from the masses were not required.

There was another reason. When I was coaching wrestling at Michigan, our athletics director, Fritz Crisler, had eschewed fund raising from alumni, saying that once you took money from a booster, the fan assumed that he (or she) had bought a voice in how the department was run, that he (or she) had a stake in the enterprise. That thinking had changed, as many other major programs across the country were already raising millions, annually, from boosters.

Ohio State and Michigan were among the last schools to solicit their flocks, if for no other reason than they already had huge stadiums, usually filled, which provided the needed revenue. But now, with the proliferation of women's sports, the need for new facilities and increasing inflation, every school needed alternative sources of revenue. Fund-raising was the obvious answer, especially when our programs could entice the most affluent alums with perks, such as preferred seating, sky boxes, free parking, private lunches with the head coach, bench passes and seats on the team plane, to name a few.

But Crisler was right. The more money boosters gave, the more voice they had in the program. My old school, Oregon, was a prime example. Nike founder, Phil Knight, had given tens of millions to Oregon athletics, not to mention the university in general, and he had his own private suite in the stadium with a set of earphones connected to the bench where he could even eavesdrop on the coaches' chatter throughout the game.

Fritz Crisler had to be turning over in his grave.

37

There was one facility at Ohio State that found no trouble generating financial support—the university's golf course, known locally as the Scarlet Course. Located about 15 minutes from the central campus, the university golf complex had two 18-hole tracks and a restaurant.

The Scarlet Course, the longer of the two (the other being the Gray Course), had been the site of many Big Ten and NCAA championship competitions. Jack Nicklaus played his college golf there, as did Tom Weiskopf, Ed Sneed, Joey Sindelar, John Cook, Rosie Jones and Meg Mallon, to name but a few. As with the stadium and the basketball arena, the course needed extensive upgrading.

Under the leadership of long time men's golf coach Jim Brown, we put together a pro-am tournament inviting only those professionals who had golfed at Ohio State. We charged the four-man amateur teams $6,000 each to play with one of these former Buckeyes greats, with the promise that all the money would go exclusively to upgrading the golf courses. Without exception, every one of the pro players, all Buckeyes, played for free and covered their own expenses.

I enjoyed the day immensely. Nicklaus gave a clinic on the first tee. Even Woody came to watch. The first hole on the Scarlet Course is a dogleg left, the corner guarded by a huge oak tree. Without warming up or even taking a practice swing Jack told everyone how, as a college player, he had often tried to take about 70 yards off the hole by hitting his tee shot over the tree, thus cutting the corner. He had never succeeded, he said, but today he was going to show everyone, including himself, that it could be done. With that he teed it up, took his driver and proceeded to hit the ball smack dab into the center of the tree. Everyone had to laugh, including Jack. "I guess it can't be done," he said.

I first met Nicklaus soon after I became athletics director in 1984. One of my associate athletic directors, Al Bohl, who later became the AD at Toledo and Kansas, escorted me down to Jack's corporate offices in West Palm Beach, Florida. We had not spoken very long when, suddenly, Jack said, "Well, when are you going to fire Earle and Eldon?" I was a bit taken aback, and, as the question sank in, more than a little disappointed. I had expected a more convivial conversation. I responded as amiably as possible, saying only that I needed time to personally evaluate both coaches. Jack did not pursue the matter. He didn't have to, as it was easy to guess how he felt. Today there exists on the Ohio State campus a beautiful Jack Nicklaus Golf Museum, but Nicklaus has not always been close to his alma mater. Neither his oldest son, a high school football player, nor his daughter, who played volleyball in high school, were recruited by the Buckeyes, and several people who had known Jack for a long time told me it rankled him. The son, a wide receiver, ended up at Florida State on a football scholarship, and one fall when the Seminoles came to Columbus to play, Nicklaus showed up in the Ohio State press box wearing a Florida State cap. Although, personally, I thought this understandable, the incident did not sit well with the Buckeye brass. Later, however, a younger son, Gary, attended Ohio State on a golf scholarship, and the relationship seemed to thaw a bit.

In my years at Ohio State, I had very little contact with Nicklaus, and I doubt that he would have recognized me on the street. But one day I received a call from the NCAA that would put me in touch with Jack several times over a very short time span. Every year at the NCAA convention the association honored 10 great collegiate athletes, five currently in school, and five whose graduating class was 25 years ago, in other words, a Silver Anniversary class. The

highlight of the luncheon was the introduction of the recipient of the Teddy Award, named for President Theodore
Roosevelt, and awarded to a "great American," who was
also a former collegiate athlete. With more than 1,200 convention delegates present, including every major college
athletics director, and many presidents, it was a big deal.
Vice-President George Bush, a former Yale first baseman,
was to receive the "Teddy," and the master of ceremonies
was none other than perennial *CBS Evening News* anchor-
man Walter Cronkite.

The staff person in charge of the luncheon was public
relations director Dave Caywood. When he phoned that
day to tell me that Nicklaus had been selected as a Silver Anniversary recipient, I was, of course, delighted. But
there was one stipulation. The honorees would not be announced until they had committed to attend the event. "In
other words," Dave said, "Nicklaus is one of the guys unless
he tells us he can't be there, in which case we move on to
the next name on the list. Please contact Nicklaus, and let
us know if he can attend."

When I reached Jack's office in Florida, his assistant
would not put me through, but instead wanted to know the
nature of the call. Patiently, I tried to explain that Jack had
been chosen as a NCAA Silver Anniversary Top Five hon-
oree, but that he must be able to actually attend the ceremony to be announced publicly as a recipient.

"So he's been selected," she said evenly, "but if he
can't be there, he'll be rejected?"

"Not exactly," I said. "It's just that the NCAA wouldn't
have much of a ceremony if none of the honorees could
attend the luncheon." It was the best I could do.

"What's the date," she asked. I told her, and only hoped
that my message to Jack was not lost in translation. The next
day, however, Nicklaus' assistant called to tell me, thanks,
but he can't make it.

"Surely, you understand," she said. "I know this must be special, but his schedule won't allow him to be there."

Finally, I insisted on talking to Jack personally. I told her that, with all due respect, I did not think Jack would be happy if he declined this invitation without fully understanding the significance of the occasion. For both her sake and mine, I said, it would be better if I talked directly to Jack. When Nicklaus came on the line, I explained the concept, the magnitude of the event and that both Bush and Cronkite would be there.

Jack said that he was very busy at the moment and wanted to think it over. He would get back to me. But when he contacted me a couple of days later, he politely declined the invitation. I called David Caywood and expressed my regrets. I was disappointed, but that was life.

A few days later, having all but forgotten the episode, I received another call from Nicklaus' office saying that Jack had reconsidered, and would come to the luncheon. Of course, I immediately called Caywood with the good news.

"Uh, Rick, sorry, but we've already got five," said Dave. "When Nicklaus said no, we moved on and got the backup. We can't go back to him. I don't know what to tell you."

I felt my hands get a little clammy. I told Dave how I dreaded going back to Nicklaus to tell him that he had been de-selected, even though it was his own fault. I was trying to improve Ohio State's relationship with Jack, and this development would not help. Caywood was sympathetic, said there was probably nothing anyone could do, but that he would talk to his boss, NCAA Executive Director Walter Byers.

A couple of days later, Walter called, and said, "Rick, I'm going to save your ass, and improve the Honors Luncheon at the same time. We're getting bigger and need to honor more than five current and former athletes at these affairs. So starting this year, with Mr. Nicklaus joining us, we're making it the 'Top Six.' You owe me one, buddy."

When the luncheon date came, Jack enjoyed himself immensely, even being selected to speak on behalf of his peer group to the audience. This, too, was somewhat of an adventure. I had tactfully warned Jack that he should prepare something, not try it off the cuff. "You'll go second," I told him. "The kid representing the Top Five, (now Top Six), current athletes will respond on behalf of his peers first, and he will be very impressive. They always are." I don't think he paid much attention to me.

There was always a private reception prior to the luncheon where the honorees got to meet one another. The six current athletes were 4.0 students majoring in disciplines such as molecular biology, and were, of course, All-Americans in their respective sports, if not world-record holders and Olympic medalists. The cream of the crop. Once Jack had seen and met these kids, it began to sink in with him that, yes, he had better prepare something. He asked me if I had a pen and spent most of the meal scribbling notes on the back of the program.

Golf was big in Columbus, and in my first summer there I was invited to play in what was billed as a charity event at Muirfield Village Golf Club, located in nearby Dublin, Ohio. The late Dave Thomas, founder of the Wendy's hamburger empire, hosted the event. Unaware of Thomas' penchant for gambling, at least in golf, I eagerly accepted. Later, however, I heard stories that, though not a very good player (to put it mildly), Thomas sometimes played others for as much as $1,000 a hole.

On the day of the event, I was running late and arrived at the course just in time to tee off. The event featured a so-called shotgun start, which meant all the teams started simultaneously, on different holes. One of the bagboys at the club was waiting for me. He threw my clubs into a cart and rushed me out to our starting hole. The other four members of my team (the teams were fivesomes) were just ready to hit when we pulled up.

Immediately one of the guys asked me how many "shares" of our team I wanted to buy. He explained that each share cost $20, and that any prize money we won would be divided among us based upon this buy-in. Having only about $30 on me, I sheepishly said that I had only enough cash for a single share, that I wasn't aware of the format. Someone else offered to stake me, but I politely declined.

As I was the lone newcomer to the group, everyone introduced himself, and we began to play. We appeared to score very well, but I had to leave as soon as our round was completed. I didn't stay for the dinner and never saw the final results. I had completely forgotten about the event, when one day I received in the mail a check for $160, which the enclosed note said was my share of the prize money, based upon my investment. I was shocked, but then someone told me that the Thomas event was notorious for heavy betting. I did the math, and it appeared that our team paid eight to one, when everything was tallied. Later, I heard Muirfield decided to quit hosting the tournament, at least in part, because the stakes were getting out of hand. The club didn't need a gambling investigation, and, as a one-time participant, I didn't either.

38

In the early summer of 1986, I was contacted by the National Association of the Collegiate Directors of Athletics (NACDA) that inquired as to whether Ohio State would be interested in playing in the annual Kickoff Classic game at the Meadowlands in East Rutherford, New Jersey. This was an extra game allowed by the NCAA to raise money for the association, which is the service organization for athletics administrators. The Kickoff Classic, at that time, paid about $750,000 per team and was nationally televised, so I was interested.

Because the game was in late August, however, it meant cutting everyone's summer short and bringing the team back to Columbus for fall practice almost three weeks early. I knew that Earle might not like the idea. Plus, the opponent was Alabama, which meant a 50-50 risk of an early season loss. Knowing that a wise athletics director never schedules a game his coach doesn't want to play, I left the decision to Earle. But I made him seriously consider the possibility by promising that all the money from the game would be dedicated to getting the Woody Hayes Athletics Center off the ground. This new $10 million, state-of-the-art, indoor practice facility was crucial to football, but the central administration was reticent about breaking ground until I had some serious seed money.

Another potential problem that came to light was that we would have almost three weeks *between* the Kickoff Classic and our regular-season opener against Washington, in Seattle. With no classes to attend and summer jobs behind them, the players would be faced with lots of down time. All things considered, while the team was anxious to knock heads with the legendary Alabama Crimson Tide on national TV, Earle and I had reservations about the awkward time span. The summer would be too short, and the time between our first two games too long.

Over the next several days, Earle and I discussed the pros and cons of the issue thoroughly, the coach even consulting with his team captains and several other players. The time sequence was dicey, but it was an unexpected opportunity to break ground early on the new building, a project that would benefit Buckeye football for years to come, and so we accepted NACDA's invitation. That gave us 13 games, assuming another bowl invitation of one kind or another.

I reminded Earle with a wink, "Well, we won't be 9-3 this year."

The few remaining weeks of that summer off-season passed quickly, but no sooner had the team reported for practice than we received the first ominous sign of how the early schedule would go. Earle broke his foot and the injury required him to wear a walking cast that went half way up his calf. During practice, with Earle hobbling around like a penguin, the injury was merely inconvenient, if not a little humorous. But during the game against the Tide on national television, it was a distraction that too often caught the attention of the cameras. This was especially true given the already striking contrasts between the physical statures of the two coaches. Alabama's coach at the time was the dapper Ray Perkins, a Bear Bryant disciple, who was on the sideline in coat and tie and looking very fit. Earle, on the other hand, short and stocky to begin with, was dressed in his gray Buckeye coaching slacks, a nylon golf shirt that barely stretched over his paunch into his ample waistband and his black Woody Hayes baseball cap. In fairness to the coach, he had been a prisoner to his cast for nearly three weeks, and unable to partake even in what little exercise was normal for him.

Perhaps I was oversensitive to the situation, but on the television monitor in the press box it seemed as though there was a split screen of the coaches after every play. One side showed Ray Perkins, upright and purposeful, walking briskly in front of his bench and the other side had Earle, hitching along as best he could, frustrated that he knew how he must look and furious that his injury kept him from feeling more in control of the game than he did.

As expected in a contest matching two pre-season Top 10 teams, the game was evenly played, but Alabama won, 16-10. What was particularly heartbreaking for the Buckeyes, however, was that late in the game we fumbled at the goal line on a play that would have given us the victory.

Before that, I thought it was going to be a perfect week. I had taken the coaches and their wives to a Broadway play, *I'm Not Rappaport*, which had won a Tony for Best Play that year, and starred Cleavon Little and Judd Hirsch, who also won a Tony for his performance. The story involved only these two characters that chance upon one another on a park bench in Central Park, a meeting that leads to several amusing, but provocative conversations. The coaches loved it (a few in spite of themselves), and the wives thanked me for bringing a little culture into their lives— and especially into those of their husbands!

As for the team, New York Yankees owner George Steinbrenner invited us to a ball game at Yankee Stadium. Steinbrenner's in-laws lived in Columbus and were generous contributors to the Buckeye cause, and the Columbus Clippers, the Yankees' Triple A farm team, played its home games not far from the campus. Forever impetuous, the Yankees owner was famous for shuttling slumping players back and forth, from the Big Apple to the Ohio capital, and he, himself, might show up at a Clippers game while visiting. He was interested in Ohio State athletics, and it was this connection that led to my eventual, albeit brief, employment with the Bronx Bombers, two years later.

Steinbrenner sent a car to the hotel to chauffer a few of my associates, including new special assistant Archie Griffin, and me to the stadium. The team went by bus and occupied a block of seats down the left-field line. I took my group to George's private box, which was just outside his office door. We joined a number of well-known personalities.

One was Howard Cosell. As we walked through the door into Steinbrenner's office, Cosell immediately recognized Archie and went into his staccato broadcasting voice, "And here comes the in-compar-able Ar-chie GR-IF-FIN–two-time Heis-man Tro-phy winner, who could not make it in the N-F-L!"

My entire group was embarrassed beyond words, but to Archie's credit, he appeared to take this insensitive jab good naturedly, and walked over to shake hands with Cosell. Whether he had ever met him before, I didn't know and was not about to ask. Of course, I thought this staged comment unnecessary, abrasive and in extremely poor taste, and I felt sorry for Archie. He had been a good pro player for several years, but had had the misfortune of being drafted by the Cincinnati Bengals, a team that lived and died by the forward pass. Perhaps the Bengals felt public pressure to keep Archie in Ohio, but they never utilized his rushing talents in the way that made him one of the greatest running backs in college football history.

39

Within 10 days, the disappointment at the Meadowlands had been absorbed by the all-encompassing anticipation of the trip to Seattle. The Huskies were always tough, but we had a fine team and I felt certain that we would play well in the great Northwest. Our two All-Americas—linebacker Chris Spielman and wide receiver Cris Carter—were the best I had ever seen at their positions. We had one game under our belts and, because of the Kickoff Classic, also had a couple of weeks more practice time than Washington.

I couldn't have been more wrong. The Huskies kicked us, 40-7, in one of the most lop-sided losses in Buckeye history. I don't even remember what went wrong. The plane ride home, long enough under even the most pleasant circumstances, seemed never-ending. It would have been easier to keep going, to Tibet, maybe—anywhere but Columbus. We were now 0-2, the first time that an Ohio State football team had been 0-2 since 1894, when the Bucks lost their first two games to Akron and Wittenberg.

Ironically, however, the trip back reinforced for me what a great football coach I had in Earle Bruce. As miserable as everyone was after the game, I had envisioned a quiet plane trip home, the air putrid with self-pity and sympathy for one another. That was certainly the way I felt, but the coach would have none of that. No sooner did the seatbelt sign go off than Earle summoned all his assistants to the front of the aircraft and, because I was already sitting there, I witnessed a remarkable football staff meeting.

Earle instructed each of his position coaches to begin getting their guys together in small groups around the aircraft, visualizing what had gone wrong (they'd see the film later) and defining what it would take to beat Colorado, the next Saturday. After a short time, Earle made the rounds himself, telling each cluster that, while he appreciated that they had tried hard against Washington, they were much better than they had shown, and that he, Earle, was not going to let them fall short of their potential, by God. They would have to practice hard to get ready for the Buffaloes, and be ready to be pushed, he said, emphatically. The mood was a little too serious for me to remind anyone about Ralphie.

Needless to say, Sunday's *Columbus Dispatch* was brutal. The letters to the sports editor were graphic: Not only did we have a team that was 0-2 for the first time in 101 years, but we had a coach on one leg, who limped up and down the sidelines like a wounded cow. (The Washington game had been on TV, too.) As the week wore on, Earle's physical appearance became even more of an issue, both on the radio talk shows and in the newspaper columns. The cast on his foot, his weight and especially the team's pathetic performance had convinced some observers that he was too old or, at least, lethargic. I had to agree that the team had appeared listless against the Huskies, but it was a big leap to conclude that our coach had grown elderly overnight.

Had we been 2-0, of course, the conversation about Earle's image would have never surfaced. In fact, the campus bookstore would have been restocking its shelves with Earle Bruce caps and coaching shirts. But we were not 2-0. We were 0-2 and there were lots of things to harp on, and one continued to be our coach's sideline appearance.

With this as background, I walked into Earle's office on Tuesday morning with a brainstorm.

"Coach," I said, "I've got an idea for Saturday which I think will blow people away, if you'll do it. You've been getting all this crap about your appearance. What if you led the team out of the tunnel on Saturday in a tuxedo? I'm serious. I think it would show everyone you've got a sense of humor and it would put this sideline appearance controversy to bed once and for all. What do you think?"

Even now I can't believe that I actually suggested a tuxedo. Thank God, he didn't buy it.

"Rick," Earle said, "that's not me."

"That's just the point. It isn't you, and people will see that," I went on.

"No, I couldn't do that," he responded

"Well, what about a coat and tie?" I asked.

He thought for a second, but said, "No, I don't think so."

So that was the end of it. Earle came out in his normal coaching duds on Saturday, and we won our first game of the year, beating Colorado, 13-10. We were lucky though, getting the benefit of a highly questionable pass interference call against the Buffaloes late in the fourth quarter, a play that paved the way for our winning score. The Colorado AD, the aforementioned Bill Marolt, was livid after the game about the call, but calmed down when I agreed with him. I also said that in retrospect I wished I had let them bring Ralphie. With Ralphie on the sideline, I observed, it would have taken some of the attention off Earle's wardrobe.

The Colorado game, close as it was, gave the team a huge lift. We were finally feeling good about ourselves and the next week slaughtered Utah, 64-6. We won again the following Saturday against Illinois (the Big Ten opener that Bo said was so important), and then the season seemed to fly by. We sweated out some close ones, but went on a nine-game winning streak, even beating Wisconsin, which had whipped us four of the last five years. Suddenly, or so it seemed, we were 9-2 and undefeated in the Big Ten with the Michigan game coming up. Some things never change.

In the locker room shortly after we had beaten Wisconsin in Madison, word came that Minnesota had upset Michigan in Ann Arbor. With only our game against the Wolverines remaining, this meant that we could do no worse than tie for the Big Ten championship. But no one was celebrating, because the Rose Bowl was still our goal, and a loss to Michigan the next week would give the Wolverines the tiebreaker and the trip to Pasadena.

The most intriguing question, however, was which bowl would get the Michigan-Ohio State loser. Both the Cotton Bowl and the Orange Bowl wanted whoever it was. After all, they would be getting the Big Ten's co-champion, a team most likely ranked in the Top Ten and a big television draw. The bowls and the television networks liked to have every possible scenario covered before teams played their last game. If the final game was between two national powers, bowl match-ups were usually predetermined.

I couldn't help thinking that if we lost we would be 9-3 again, but not for long. We would have one game left to play and it was my job to get us to a bowl game that gave us the best chance for winning. Ten and three sounded a lot better than 9-4.

Texas A. & M. was already a lock for the Cotton Bowl, as was Oklahoma for the Orange Bowl. Playing the Aggies would be no day at the beach, but the Sooners had one of their best teams ever.

The Cotton Bowl had been following us all season, sending scouts to cultivate personal relationships, even after we opened with two losses. The Cotton Bowl had never hosted a Big Ten team and was extremely eager to do so. The bowl was hoping to strike a deal with both Michigan and us that would guarantee them the loser of our game. The winner, as Big Ten champion, would automatically go the Rose Bowl.

I had already talked with both Earle and President Jennings, and they agreed with my logic that we matched up better against A. & M. The Cotton Bowl was thrilled, but Michigan had yet to agree to the arrangement. A one-way agreement with us really didn't help them, because if we won the game, they had no automatic fallback position with another team unless Michigan consented. Caucusing between conference teams and the bowls took place all the time, so I called Canham.

"Don," I said, "if we lose Saturday we're going to the Cotton Bowl." He asked why. "Because I think we would have a better chance of winning the Cotton Bowl. I don't know about you, but I'm not anxious to play Oklahoma, particularly given our need to finish better than 9-3."

Canham talked with Bo, called me back, and agreed to the Cotton Bowl deal.

In the middle of all this, I got a call from NBC Executive Vice-President Ken Schanzer. His network had the rights to the Orange Bowl, which already had Oklahoma locked up, and they coveted either Michigan or Ohio State as the Sooners' opponent.

"I understand you're about to make a deal with the Cotton Bowl," Schanzer said. (The Cotton Bowl was a CBS property at the time.)

"That's right," I said.

"Rick," he said, "how can you do that?"

"Number one, I think we have a better shot at winning the Cotton Bowl and number two, they have been loyal to us all year," I replied.

"Well, we've been loyal, too," he said.

I was confused. "The Orange Bowl hasn't been around at all," I said.

"No," he said, "I mean NBC. Don't forget our Rose Bowl affiliation." NBC had owned the broadcast rights to the Rose Bowl for many years.

"Well, Ken," I said, "I know all about NBC's connection with the Rose Bowl. But, quite frankly, I don't see what it has to do with anything here. And, again frankly, I'm a little surprised and disappointed that you called. I've never had anyone from a network intervene in our bowl decisions."

"Well," he said, "I'm just telling you…"

And that was it. He didn't try to hammer me. But the pressure was there. Subtle and behind the scenes.

As hip as I thought I was to TV and its interests, I guess my naiveté showed.

A record crowd of 90,674 was on hand for the Michigan game, including representatives from both the Rose and Cotton bowls to make formal invitations, however the game turned out. Also in attendance were Ohio Governor Dick Celeste, and Michigan Governor James Blanchard, who had brought along two high-powered Detroit-area financiers, Al Taubman, a Michigan guy, and Max Fischer, an Ohio State alumnus.

As expected the game was very tight. The Bucks got off to a great start, jumping out to a 14-3 lead, but Michigan closed the gap to 14-6, by halftime. The Wolverines scored a touchdown again early in the third quarter, and minutes later we countered with a field goal.

It was 17-13 Buckeyes, midway through the third period. I was standing with Denice and my invited guests in my suite looking for an opening to bolt to my private box, where I could throw up in peace. Somehow, the door to the suite had been left open and in strolled the Michigan contingent, led by Governor Blanchard. Irritated, but not wanting to be uncouth, I welcomed him to Ohio Stadium and shook hands with the group. But that was about it, because Michigan was driving, and I was totally preoccupied with the action on the field. A minute later the Wolverines scored the go-ahead touchdown, and a big cheer went up from the Blanchard party standing behind me. The veins in my neck were already purple, and I was about to strangle the Governor of Michigan, when I heard Denice say, "Governor, I'm sorry, but if you want to cheer for Michigan, could you please find somewhere else to watch the game." I had never been more proud of her. And with that they were gone and I returned to my vigil.

To make a longer and sad story short, we lost the game, 26-24, missing a game-winning, 45-yard field goal with a minute left. Cris Carter had seven receptions for two touchdowns and Chris Spielman made an amazing 29 tackles, but, in fairness, we had been outplayed. We were 9-3, and going to the Cotton Bowl.

It took a while to get over losing to the *team up north*, but the players were more resilient than anyone else, and a week later everyone was getting excited about going to Dallas.

The trip to Texas was uneventful, and the Cotton Bowl guys entertained us royally. I bumped into many of the athletics directors from Texas A. & M.'s Southwest Conference, and I was surprised, as one after another said to me confidentially that they hoped for a Buckeye victory. It was clear that most of them did not like Jackie Sherrill, the Aggie coach. They thought he cheated and wanted to see him humbled. Our team obliged, winning the game, 28-12, with Spielman making 11 tackles and two interceptions.

I was mostly happy for Earle, who not only was now 10-3, but who shocked Columbus with his attire for the game. In the pre-game warm-up Earle had appeared in his normal coaching gear, except that he looked healthier than he had in the early part of the season. The cast was off, his foot had healed, he had gotten some exercise and his weight was down. Still not svelte by any means, he looked like the Earle of a few years earlier, when his appearance had never been an issue.

The team left the field before the start of the game to allow for all the pre-game, marching band festivities. Traditionally, whenever the Buckeyes came onto the field for the second time, for the kickoff, Coach Bruce led the way, sprinting ahead of the team for as long as he could keep up the pace without being trampled by everyone but the trainers. This time, however, I couldn't locate him from my perch in the press box. But then one of my assistants said, "There he is, the guy in the suit and tie, the guy with the hat!" And so it was! Earle had remembered our September conversation and saved his dapper appearance for this special occasion. The Ohio State media contingent in the press box went nuts, the coach's outfit almost overshadowing the game.

After the game, Chris Spielman was asked what he thought when he saw that Coach Bruce had changed into a suit and fedora just before kickoff. Spielman, who worked himself into a trance before every game, stared blankly at the reporter, and said. "Gosh, I thought that was Mr. Bay." No one could stop laughing. It had been a beautiful day, pure joy.

40

The beginning of the end of my tenure at Ohio State was what some might call "The Earle Bruce Affair," and had its genesis at the NCAA convention in San Diego in January 1987. Maybe if I hadn't intervened there, in a late-night, soul-searching session at the Town and Country Hotel, Earle wouldn't have been fired, because he probably would not have been at Ohio State for the 1987 season.

I received a call from Cedric Dempsey, the athletics director at the University of Arizona, shortly after we beat Texas A. & M. in the Cotton Bowl.

"I'd like permission to talk to Earle," Cedric said, "and I want you to know that I'm coming after him."

I said OK. Dempsey, who later went on to become chief executive officer of the NCAA, had the courtesy to call and I figured it was fair to let him talk to Earle. As I discovered in my basketball coach search, the majority of athletic directors allow their coaches the opportunity to listen to offers, if for no other reason than not wanting someone working for them simply because they felt trapped.

Although I didn't want to lose Earle, I had no qualms about Dempsey talking to him. Earle already had been through a lot in Columbus, especially during the past year. Despite compiling a 10-3 record, including the Cotton Bowl victory, Earle had been beaten up pretty badly. He had taken those shots for the team's performance and his personal appearance at the beginning of the season. I think he was feeling generally underappreciated and that perhaps a change of scenery would do him good.

I don't think Earle wanted to leave Columbus, ever. He was an Ohio State alum. He coached under Woody, went off to do his own thing at University of Tampa and Iowa

State, and now he was back at his alma mater. He was a Buckeye, through and through.

Earle had visited Arizona prior to the NCAA convention. Dempsey had made a very attractive offer—the coach would make more money, and, most importantly, receive a multi-year contract that would probably carry him into retirement. Earle was supposed to give Cedric an answer in San Diego. I earlier told Earle that I didn't want him to leave, but I also told him I wasn't sure I could sweeten his deal at Ohio State.

Privately, I was pretty certain I had no chance of improving his situation with the Buckeyes. Earle wasn't a materialistic guy. He only wanted to be paid commensurate with his peers. His deal at Ohio State was pretty terrific by most standards. His salary was about $95,000, which put him in the top 20 percent of Division I football coaches. He had a radio show that paid him about $45,000 a year, his own TV show and a shoe contract with Nike. All told, he was making about $350,000. It was a Top 20 package, but it should have been better, given he was at Ohio State.

I called Jennings and told him that Arizona was making a big pitch for Earle. I asked if we could do something to encourage Earle to stay and to justify his staying, something, some sort of gesture to show he *was* appreciated at Ohio State, which I think was at the heart of the entire episode. The real appeal in Arizona's offer was that someone else was interested in him. Someone was appreciative of "old 9-3 Earle." Jennings wasn't interested in any of that. He wasn't even interested in doing something symbolic, such as extending Earle's contract. Jennings just wanted Earle to disappear. Watching Earle Bruce walk into a Southwest sunset was an easy way out of a sticky political situation. Naturally, I told Jennings that I thought he was wrong. And, naturally, he remained unmoved.

Meanwhile, a group of Ohio State assistant coaches attending the coaches' convention in San Diego came to me and said that they were afraid that Earle was going to take the Arizona job and that he would then take them all to Arizona, because that was the way the system worked. Most of them would be offered a chance to go with Earle, or take their chances with the new Buckeyes coach, who most likely would be bringing his own guys with him.

They wanted to remain in Columbus—and they wanted Earle there with them. I told them that I had I already told Earle I wanted him to stay. I also told them I had talked to Ed Jennings, and he wasn't making any sort of concession, much less a full-blown counter offer, but they persisted. The nucleus of the Cotton Bowl championship team was returning, linebacker Chris Spielman was coming back, and, at that point, so too was wide receiver Cris Carter. There was enough talent and spirit to overcome adversity, the staff argued. This was the old college try; this was what competition was all about–being courageous in the face of adversity.

I agreed to talk to Earle. Again. Earle, his staff and I gathered in Earle's hotel room. It was late at night.
"Coach," I said, "I don't want you to go to Tucson. We have a great team coming back and you know what I think of the job you've done, and I want to tell you I don't relish the thought of trying to find a new football coach. I think you have a great staff here and I want you to stay," I breathed deeply and reloaded.

"But you also need to know that I talked to Ed Jennings, and we didn't exactly get a vote of confidence. Expectations are incredibly high for next year. People expect us to win the Big Ten and be a contender for the national championship. And that's a helluva way to enter a season, knowing you have to win ten games, minimum, in order to keep the grumbling down. If we lose a couple of games early, it is going to be a bitch."

Despite that dash of cold water, Earle was moved by the support he received that night from me and the staff, even as he felt discouraged and somewhat disillusioned that Jennings would do nothing supportive.

So, there I am saying all this, but I'm also thinking, "Maybe he just should go. It will be better for him and his family in the long run. He is 57 and Arizona would be his last job. He can get a five- or six-year contract going in, and more money. And he'll be better appreciated—at least for a certain period of time."

In the end, Earle just said, "All right, I'm staying. What can I do? You guys are here. You all want me to stay. And I'm a Buckeye. I don't want to go to Arizona; we can have a great year."

There wasn't a lot of flourish to his answer because Earle couldn't out-Gipper Knute Rockne, or even give him a run for his money. But at that time, in that room, you could feel a sense of purpose, a sense of commitment. You could feel the camaraderie of a bunch of football guys rallying to hang on. Sure, it might sound a bit hokey, but it felt good.

Earle gave Dempsey and Arizona his decision as soon as the meeting broke. It must have been around midnight. We had been in the room for several hours. Cedric said later that he thought he had Earle and, in retrospect, given what was coming, I wish he had.

We had a good time in Columbus that winter. Gary Williams and Nancy Darsch were winning basketball games and Earle was the toast of the town. He even had his picture, fedora and all, on the cover of *Columbus Monthly Magazine*. We planned a special ceremony at halftime of a basketball game to present the Cotton Bowl and Big Ten championship trophies to the university. To his credit, Earle, never much of a showman, milked the moment by wearing his suit and fedora. St. John Arena went crazy. A lot of students were wearing look-alike hats. It was nice. It was the warmest reception Earle received from the community. It was a good time. But it wasn't going to last.

41

The 1986-87 basketball season ended successfully with both our teams making it to the NCAA Tournament, and we picked up Big Ten titles in both men's and women's gymnastics that winter.

But on March 12, at about 5:00 a.m., I received a phone call at home from our team physician, Dr. Robert Murphy. Woody Hayes had passed away earlier that morning. Everyone knew that he had not been well and that he probably didn't have long to live. He had not made the trip with us to the Cotton Bowl, which was a sure sign that he was struggling mightily. The announcement was a shock to Columbus, and thousands of messages of condolence began pouring in to Ohio State and his family—wife, Anne, and his son, Steve, a local judge.

Hayes was a great coach and, for most of those who played for him, a great man, as well. Famous for his grind it out, bone-crushing offense, Woody's Ohio State teams were 205-61-10, won five national championships and captured 13 Big Ten titles. He coached 58 All-Americans and four Heisman Trophy winners.

What Vince Lombardi was to professional football, Woody Hayes was to college football. He described his offense as "a crunching frontal assault of muscle against muscle, bone against bone, will against will," and he said it with such affection that you knew that the forward pass was almost non-existent in his thinking. "There are three things that can happen when you throw a pass," he famously said, "and two of them are bad." He was a patriot and a student of military history, and he coached his team like a general leading his troops into battle.

You had only to be around Earle Bruce and Bo Schembechler a day or so and you knew that they must have worked under Woody Hayes. Cut from the same mold, the staff meetings when they coached together were legendary and abound with stories of profane debate and film projectors being hurled across the room, which somehow seemed logical since Woody was one of the first to use film as a teaching and learning tool.

Woody was truly old school, stubbornly set in his ways, tyrannical even; yet he was paradoxical, a man who adapted to the times in which he lived. He was one of the first coaches to recruit and start African-American players in large numbers and to hire African-American assistant coaches. During the campus unrest and racial turmoil that afflicted many schools across the nation in the late '60s and early '70s, he could be seen walking across the university oval and visiting with students. And despite Ohio State's reputation as a football factory, Hayes had a good relationship with the faculty and often ate lunch at the university's Faculty Club, interacting with professors and administrators.

But as the news of Woody's death spread around the country, many of the media could not resist recalling Woody's worst moment on the playing field, his assault of the Clemson player in the 1978 Gator Bowl, the day before he was fired.

Like Bob Knight, Woody Hayes was no stranger to bad behavior and controversy when the Gator Bowl incident occurred. He had been involved in at least two physical altercations with various Rose Bowl media over the years. In the 1971 Ohio State-Michigan game, Hayes ran onto the field to confront an official and finally, in a rage, tore apart the sideline markers in Michigan Stadium. It was pretty spectacular to watch, much less describe as I actually helped broadcast the game. I feel certain that that meltdown would have been his signature piece if it hadn't been for the Clemson game.

Columbus mourned when Woody passed away. I attended two memorial services that, when combined, probably qualified as a state funeral. The first was a private service at the First Community Church in Columbus, attended by 1,400 close friends and admirers from the extended Ohio State family, including President Jennings and me, who officially represented the university.

The most extraordinary aspect of the service was that former United States President Richard Nixon delivered the eulogy. Nixon recalled that he had met Coach Hayes at a reception following a Buckeye victory over Iowa in 1957 and that their friendship had endured. Nixon was in his second term as vice-president at the time, and said that, upon meeting Woody, "I wanted to talk about football and Woody wanted to talk about foreign policy. And you know Woody. We talked about foreign policy." The anecdote lightened the mood of the occasion considerably, and the former president delivered as eloquent a message as I have ever been privileged to hear. He spoke for about twelve minutes without notes and connected with his audience as if he was Billy Graham. People were mesmerized by his presence from the lectern, and the performance belied his presidential reputation as a poor communicator. I remembered well his television debates with John F. Kennedy, during which he appeared nervous and uncomfortable, little beads of sweat forming on his upper lip, just enough for a television camera close-up to capture. But on this day, for his friend Woody Hayes, he was superb.

President Nixon's appearance almost didn't happen. After Nixon accepted the invitation to speak, someone realized that the associate minister at the church was Jeb Magruder, who had been the Nixon's manager for his 1973 inauguration, but later was sent to prison for his role in the failed Watergate burglary and subsequent cover-up.

Magruder was the only direct participant in the scandal to confirm that Nixon had specific foreknowledge of the

Watergate break-in, and that the president actually direct-
ed former Attorney General John Mitchell to proceed with
the break-in, which was organized by G. Gordon Liddy and
E. Howard Hunt. Three months after Nixon's inauguration,
Magruder began cooperating with federal prosecutors,
and was finally allowed to plead guilty in August 1973, to a
one-count indictment of conspiracy to obstruct justice and
eavesdrop on the Democratic Party's national headquarters. For this he was sentenced to four months to 10 years in
prison, but since had graduated from Princeton Seminary
School and been ordained as a Presbyterian minister.

Now, here he was at Woody Hayes' church where his
old boss was to appear. The two men apparently had not
spoken since Watergate and there was great consternation
among those organizing the funeral that the story of their
strange reunion would detract from the tribute to Woody,
and that the situation was simply too awkward.

However the matter was settled, Nixon spoke, and
Magruder, whom I'd met before, did not attend the service.

The next day, more than 15,000 people attended a
public memorial service in Ohio Stadium. The Ohio State
Marching Band ("The Best Damn Band in the Land") played
the alma mater and the Buckeye fight song a few times,
and Bo Schembechler was there to offer the eulogy.

To Woody's delight, I'm sure; Bo's message was hardly
sentimental to begin with. Bo had driven down that morning from "the state up north," and wondered out loud "why
in hell" he was wasting time in the horseshoe when he had
his own spring practice to tend to. Bo finally conceded that
he owed "the old man" (as his assistants called Woody privately) a lot, but said that they had had lots of arguments
and that Woody poured it on the Wolverines whenever he
got the chance. But Woody was a great, great coach, Bo
said, and he and everyone in coaching would miss him a
lot.

Finally, Woody's son, Steve, spoke, praising his father and thanking everyone for coming. He will still be at all the games, Steve said, and from now on, "He will have the best seat in the house."

42

A few weeks later, in early summer, as Denice and I were preparing to travel to New York for a break to see some theater, I received a call from Chris Mortenson, then with the *Atlanta Constitution* and later with ESPN. He hit me with a bombshell.

"Rick," he said, "I am following up a rumor that I believe to be true, that Cris Carter has signed with an agent."

"How do you know that," I asked, terrified to hear the answer.

"I've seen a copy of the contract he signed, and I think he has already taken money," Mortenson said.

We talked for a few minutes, and I think Chris really felt my pain. Unfortunately, I had no comment for him except to say that I would look into it and that, if it was true, I would declare Carter ineligible.

I went immediately to Earle, who was dumbstruck. I said that I wanted to see Carter right away, but Earle asked to talk with him first, which I allowed. A short while later, the coach called me to say that he had just met with Carter, and that the player was on his way over to see me. In the meantime, Carter had sworn to Earle that he had not signed with anyone, and certainly had not accepted cash.

ADs and coaches knew that agents were trying to establish early relationships with players. It was not uncommon for agents to call promising student-athletes, and sometimes to pay them under the table in the hope of obligating them when they turned professional. Some were even so unscrupulous as to entice their victims with small cash gifts which, upon acceptance and if discovered, automatically made the athlete ineligible under NCAA rules. While there were no civil laws at the time that prevented sports agents from signing college or high school athletes with eligibility remaining, the NCAA was a bigger factor.

As he did with Earle, Carter swore up and down to me that he was innocent of any wrongdoing. I told him that there was an appeals procedure with the NCAA, so that if he had signed anything or taken money he should tell me now. He might be penalized a game or two, and would undoubtedly have to make restitution for any cash he had received, but that we could probably salvage his senior season. But I emphasized that if he lied to me, I would do nothing for him. He stuck to his story.

It wasn't long before I not only saw a copy of an agreement Carter had signed with an agent named Norby Walters, but also was subpoenaed to appear before a Federal grand jury in Chicago that was investigating Walters. I had no choice but to declare Cris Carter ineligible for the 1987 season. Carter was a unanimous pre-season All-America, who had caught 69 passes for 1127 yards and 11 touchdowns in 1986. It was a tremendous loss for the team, and Earle was crushed, not only because Cris was disqualified for the year, but also because the player who was almost like a son to the coach had lied to him on several occasions.

It turned out that what had happened at Ohio State had also happened 200 miles east at the University of Pittsburgh, where two Pitt players also had signed with Walters and been declared ineligible. Thus, the Panther AD, Ed Bozik, had also been summoned to appear before the grand jury, as had former University of Iowa running back Ronnie Harmon.

According to news reports, Walters had acknowledged signing representation contracts with many college football and basketball players with eligibility remaining. Also, he had reportedly given some players cash as an inducement to sign post-dated contracts. At the time, neither activity was illegal anywhere, except at the NCAA. The grand jury was interested only in reports that Walters and an associate, Lloyd Bloom, had engaged in threats against the athletes and rival agents to keep the players from deserting them.

It was later documented that Harmon had received $54,000 over two years while still playing for Iowa, before defecting to another agent. Walters finally sued Harmon and several other players for breach of contract. The Harmon case was particularly scary for the NCAA because of the 1986 Rose Bowl, when the running back, who fumbled only once during the regular season, coughed up the ball four times in the *in the first half* in the Hawkeye 45-28 loss to UCLA. Although nothing ever came of it, there were whispered concerns Harmon may have been under outside pressure during the Rose Bowl, a scandal that, if true, would have rivaled Major League Baseball's 1919 Black Sox disgrace.

When indisputable records showed that Cris Carter had received $6,800 from Walters, I dismissed him from the team. It was a sad case, but Buckeye fans had pretty much resigned themselves to a season without the star receiver and had accepted my decision not to appeal Carter's case to the NCAA, because the player had lied to me.

Surprisingly, the only pressure I received from anyone to appeal the matter was from the National Football League, which feared the possibility of being forced to draft Carter *prior* to his graduation. At that time the NFL had an iron-clad policy against drafting underclassmen, and they worried that if Carter could not play in college his senior year, he would sue the professional league on the basis that not drafting him amounted to denying him his right to earn a living in the profession of his choice. This, the NFL feared, would set an unwanted precedent of having to draft *anyone* who applied, thus opening the floodgates to college juniors. (Later, the NFL did begin drafting underclassmen, but not many registered, because those who applied but didn't make a roster were ineligible to return to college football.)

Thus, the NFL people were almost insistent that Ohio State and Pittsburgh appeal their cases, assuming that if we succeeded the athletes would be reinstated and the league would not be faced with the prospect of having to draft any underclass players. Although Pitt AD Bozik seemed amenable to the request, I said that I had no intention of appealing Carter's case, and, besides, professional football in the form of the United States Football League (USFL) had already drafted an underclassman, the great Herschel Walker from Georgia, who had played for the New Jersey Generals and had not sued the NFL. But I was told that the only reason Walker could not successfully sue the NFL then was precisely because the USFL existed and *was* taking underclassmen. Thus, Walker had had an alternative to play professionally without the NFL changing its policy, whereas because the USFL had folded, the Buckeye and Panther players had only one option.

Two months later, in June, there came surprising news from Pittsburgh. One of the Pitt players, Teryl Austin, had won his appeal to the NCAA and his eligibility had been restored. This development set off a firestorm of controversy in Columbus, and immediately it was assumed by some that we would appeal Carter's case. The Pitt player had only to pay back the money he'd received to a charity, and he was to miss a game or two, but that was it.

Based on this precedent, Carter's case seemed a slam-dunk, and it wasn't long before Earle was in my office asking how long the process would take. But to Earle's consternation, I had to remind him that we had decided not to appeal Carter's case, *not because we didn't think we could win*, but rather because the player had lied to us. We believed, or at least I believed, that the infractions were so serious, and so many untruths had been told, that I simply didn't have the stomach to appeal. I didn't feel that

I could have looked anyone in the face if I appealed the case. If we had prevailed, I would have been embarrassed to put a player on the field that everyone knew had been taking money the season before. Earle, of course, who had been furious at Carter for not telling him the truth from the beginning, was now willing to make allowances. It was understandable, because the two had fostered a father-son relationship and Earle was reacting like any forgiving parent.

After announcing my decision not to petition Carter's case, despite the success of the Pitt player, I braced for the backlash in Columbus, but to the credit of the Buckeye faithful, most folks apparently thought I had done the right thing. I think they felt as insulted as I did. Ironically, the only call taking me to task that I remember came from one of the nine university trustees. He was drunk when he called me at home and threatened to have me fired if I didn't get Carter reinstated. He was both profane and belligerent, and I finally told him that if appeasing a guy like him was the only way I could keep my job I didn't want it.

Denice was sitting there listening to my end of the conversation, and asked as soon as I hung up, "Who was that?"

"One of our trustees," I said. "He was drunk."

"Do we still have a job?" she asked, poker faced.

"I think so, but who knows," I replied. Then I called the president and filled him in. He said that he would handle it, and that was all I ever heard.

Finally, Denice and I made it to New York for a weekend. I was beginning to relax when I got a call from Cris Carter's attorney. Would I be willing to meet with him and Cris? I would, I said, but there was no point in it if they expected me to change my mind about the appeal. Still, they wanted to meet right away. When I said that I was in New York and would not be back for a couple of days, they insisted on coming to the Big Apple.

We met in our hotel room where I listened to their pleadings. In truth, I felt very sorry for Cris, whom I liked personally, but I said that there was nothing I could do with respect to restoring his eligibility. However, I said that I would help him in any other way and, ultimately, I did arrange for him to use the Columbus Clippers' stadium to try out for some pro scouts. In the meantime, however, they left New York with nothing altered.

When we returned to Columbus a couple of days later I had one more surprise waiting for me. The president had decided to weigh in on the matter and wanted to meet with Earle and me to review the situation "for the last time." I should have been used to these presidential interjections by then, but somehow I was always surprised. Perhaps the drunken trustee got to Jennings, I just didn't know. But soon word got out to the press that the president was going to meet with Earle and me. As a result, there evolved a perception that he was refereeing a conflict between the AD and the football coach, although I never felt that way. The coach said he still wanted Cris back, that we should appeal, but I never felt that his heart was in it. I think by this time, while he, too, believed that we had done the right thing, Earle may have felt that he owed Cris one last try, despite himself. Later, however, in reflecting upon his days at Ohio State, the coach was asked how he felt when I told him that we were not going to appeal Carter's case. "I wanted to hit him," he said. "But he was right."

In the end, the president supported my decision that Carter be kept off the team and that we would not appeal. Despite everything, I felt badly for the young man. I told him that we would honor his scholarship through graduation, but that football was out of the question. The NFL, deciding to avoid any possible court battle, set up a special supplemental draft, and the Philadelphia Eagles selected Carter. In his third season with the Eagles, he blossomed into one of the premier receivers in the NFL, catching 45 passes, including 11 for touchdowns. But he had a falling out with Eagles coach Buddy Ryan who thought Carter should have been more productive and caught more balls overall. Carter was cut from the squad the following pre-season, with Ryan saying famously, "All he does is catch touchdowns."

Norby Walters, meanwhile, was convicted for fraud and racketeering in April 1988. But before that, while Walters was under investigation, the *Chicago Tribune* ran an article about the federal grand jury's inquiry into the matter, and mistakenly included *my* picture in the story with the caption identifying me as Norby Walters. Living in Columbus, I was unaware of the article until two days later, when I received a copy of the clipping from Notre Dame football coach Lou Holtz. Included in the envelope was a Fighting Irish note card that said: "Rick, did you know that Norby Walters looks a lot like you?" Gallows humor, I guess, but it was hilarious.

43

As the 1987 football season got underway, Earle and I had no idea that it would be our last year with the Buckeyes. We didn't have Cris Carter but we were coming off a Cotton Bowl championship season with a number of great players returning, including All-America linebacker Chris Spielman.

We opened with a 24-3 victory over West Virginia, and a week later beat my old school Oregon, still coached by Rich Brooks, 24-14. Then, on September 26, we headed for Baton Rouge to do battle with the LSU Tigers in the first meeting between the two schools. The Bayou Bengals were the defending Southeastern Conference champions, having finished 9-3 the year before, including a big win over Notre Dame. It was to be a classic match-up between two major conference champions and ABC would be televising the game nationwide.

There is nothing quite like Southeastern Conference football. The pre-game parties begin early in the morning and go well into the evening. About the only break is the four-hour stretch for the game itself, although this is not to say that there is any sort of moratorium on cocktails. It simply means that folks are pretty much confined to the space around their stadium seats, thus temporarily inhibiting the party hopping that goes on in the parking lots. If there was any prohibition against bringing alcohol into the stadium, no one seemed aware of it, or there existed a "don't ask, don't tell" policy that got fans through the turnstiles in a hurry.

I took Denice down onto the field before the game, and we wandered over to the LSU sideline to visit the school's mascot, a huge Bengal tiger in an iron bar cage atop a trailer that could be hauled away at any time. This was a beautiful cat and it pained us to see it so confined, pacing back and forth behind the bars as in a zoo. Having been to Kenya the year before, where we watched the lions roam freely on the Masai Mara, we were more sensitive than ever over what we imagined was the miserable state of this magnificent animal. For a moment I imagined throwing open the cage door and letting the creature loose, which would have been a sobering experience even for this crowd.

But beyond the indignity of incarceration was the fact that the animal's cage contained a microphone, so that its ferocious, or perhaps anguished growl was amplified not only throughout the far reaches of the stadium, but also in cramped quarters of the visitor's locker room. After hearing the Tiger snarl once or twice on the stadium speakers, I wouldn't have been surprised if our team refused to take the field—and that almost happened, although it had nothing to do with the LSU mascot.

After our team's Friday workout in Tiger Stadium (capacity 78,882), Ric LaCivita, the man ABC Sports had sent to Baton Rouge to serve as the network's producer for the game, asked to meet with Earle and me to cover what to expect for the pre-game introductions of the teams. He had already met with the LSU folks, Coach Mike Archer and AD Joe Dean. Ric explained that the Buckeyes would be expected to take the field first and then wait for the LSU squad to come onto the playing area, after which everyone would stand at attention for the playing of the Tiger alma mater. Earle already had his game face on, and this order of events, as outlined by LaCivita, was not what the coach had envisioned, to put it mildly.

"Ric," he said, "you think we're going to come on the field first and then just stand there, while the band plays the fight song and those guys come on, and then we have to listen to the alma mater like it was the National Anthem?

I don't think so. No goddamn way! Those guys go on first, and get all that bullshit out of the way, then we come on, and we kick off!"

Earle said this with such emphasis and enthusiasm that Ric did not even pursue the matter. I didn't have to say anything. Earle was right. It might not fit with ABC's ceremonial plans for a great broadcast opening, but it wasn't fair to our guys to have to stand there with their helmets under their arms while everyone else was intent on firing up the home team. So ABC's plan was quickly altered, and it was agreed that LSU would take the field first and do what it had to do, after which LaCivita would give the signal for the Buckeyes to come out. There would be the coin toss, and the game would begin. That was the new plan, or so we thought.

To this day I am not sure whether LSU was not advised of the revised order of events or whether ABC tried to engage us in a game of "chicken," but the opening of the broadcast the next day had enough dead air to fill the Hindenburg.

Both teams were poised in their respective tunnels as ABC went on the air, and I happened to be standing nearby, ready to head for the press box. We were waiting for LSU to take the field, when suddenly an ABC production assistant who was right next to Earle heard something on his earphones and said to the coach, "Go!" and pointed toward the field. Earle just stared blankly at the guy, not quite comprehending, I thought, when the ABC man again exclaimed, "Go!" this time more urgently. If he hadn't understood the first command, Earle certainly grasped the second. The crowd was becoming both impatient and louder, so the coach had to yell.

"Bullshit," Earl screamed, "They're supposed to go first!" But LSU wasn't moving either.

I don't know what the announcers were saying, but the network was on the air, the precise kickoff time had come and gone and neither team was on the field. It was a first-rate standoff, and though ABC may have been unsure of the outcome, I wasn't. The veins in Earle's neck were popping, and I knew that we would go back to Columbus before taking the field first. Suddenly, I heard a roar and saw the Tigers come charging out of their tunnel. There were fireworks, the band played and the tiger roared. The crowd quieted a little, and then there was a mild chorus of boos as the Buckeyes finally ran onto the stadium turf.

Although I wouldn't call the game anticlimactic, it was a bit pedestrian, ending in a 13-13 tie. In truth, LSU should have won; they had a shot at it. In the closing minute, with the score all even, the Tigers had the ball at midfield and were marching. One more first down would have given them a chance at about a 40-yard field goal for the victory. But, inexplicably, they tried a dangerous pass over the middle that we intercepted, and then ran out the clock. Nobody likes a tie, unless the only alternative is defeat. So we were happy to be 2-0-1 going into the conference schedule.

In the Big Ten opener at Illinois we barely scraped by, winning, 10-6, meaning that in our last three games, although still unbeaten, we had outscored the opposition by a cumulative total of just 14 points. We had been generally unimpressive all season, and the percentages caught up to us the next week in Columbus, as Indiana upset us, 31-10. It was a shocking defeat, our first loss to the Hoosiers in 31 games dating back to 1951, and Coach Bruce called it "the darkest day in Ohio State football" since he had first been associated with the program in 1949. Buckeye "dobbers" were down, as the saying goes, because no one could have imagined a loss to Indiana. Basketball, yes. Football, never.

But Earle never let a team feel sorry for itself and the next week we rallied for a 20-17 victory at Purdue, then came home to trounce Minnesota, 42-9. We were 5-1-1 and appeared to be on a roll with Michigan State next up, at home.

On Friday before we played the Spartans, the crew from CBS, which was televising the game, showed up on campus to prepare for the telecast. Lynn Swann, the former great all-pro of the Pittsburgh Steelers, was the color analyst for the game. I was surprised to see him poke his head in my office late Friday morning. He was agitated, if not angry, that Coach Bruce would not let him attend a Buckeyes' practice to do his homework and get some inside information for the game. Because it was fairly common for coaches to allow announcers to watch practice before games, and, even, to confidentially share some of their game plan with them, Earle's reticence with Swann was unusual. It turned out that the coach was a little paranoid about Swann because the ex-Steeler had played for Michigan State coach George Perles, in Pittsburgh. Although probably ill founded, Earle worried that Swann would see something at his practice that might find its way to Perles before the game. I tried to soothe Swann, telling him not to take it personally, and that Earle was just edgy with a case of pre-game nerves. But Swann said that he was insulted, and left my office in a foul mood. In Swann's defense, I knew that no announcer liked going into a broadcast feeling that he had been denied a chance to become better informed about the game he is covering, but it was Friday and I knew that my coach was getting tight.

The next day, just before the kickoff against the Spartans, I discovered why Earle had been so adamant with Swann. I was down on the field, talking with some of the coaches and meandering among the players who were warming up. This was my way of dealing with pre-game nerves. I finally got over to Earle, who, uncharacteristically in the midst of our small talk, decided to tell me what play the Buckeyes would run the first time we had the ball, the play he hadn't wanted Swann to see.

"We're going to split Everett Ross out to the right and he's going to run a fly pattern straight up the side line. Tupa (our quarterback) is going to throw it as far as he can. I think we can beat their cornerback, and if it works, it's a touchdown," Earle said.

"Sounds good to me," I responded. I shook his hand, wished him luck and headed for the press box to meet my guests for the day.

As it turned out we won the coin toss and elected to receive. As Michigan State was ready to kick off, I told the people standing around me that I wouldn't be surprised if our first play was a long bomb to Ross that would get us on the scoreboard in a hurry. We ran the kickoff back to our own 21-yard line, and, sure enough, on our first play Tupa dropped back and heaved the ball about 50 yards to the spot where Ross had gotten a step on the Spartan cornerback. Ross hauled it in without breaking stride and ran easily into the end zone—a 79-yard touchdown pass to start the game. The boosters I was hosting went nuts and wanted to know how I was able to forecast the play. I modestly mumbled something about having been a quarterback myself, who could recognize a weak defensive cornerback when I saw one.

But my "clairvoyance" had not prepared me for the rest of the game. That one play constituted the Buckeyes' entire highlight reel, as suddenly we went flat and lost the game, 13-7. I guess it was a good thing Swann hadn't seen us practice, or we might have been shut out. We had three games remaining, and needed to win them all just to have, by Ohio State standards, a somewhat acceptable season.

The first of the three was against our nemesis, Wisconsin, in Madison, a team we had beaten only twice in our last six meetings. We made a game of it, but lost another close one, 26-24. Take away our opening win against West Virginia and our blowout victory over Minnesota, and in the other seven games combined we had scored two fewer points than our opponents.

We were struggling big time. At 5-3-1, with only Iowa and Michigan left to play, the best we could hope to be was 7-3-1, or, with a bowl victory, 8-3-1.

44

On the Monday before the Iowa game in Columbus, I was summoned to Ed Jennings office; I knew what was coming. The president told me that he was getting a lot of pressure about Earle and that we might have to consider a coaching change, that I should be prepared. I told him that I really wasn't thinking along those lines, that Earle had done a great job for nearly a decade, and that we shouldn't be thinking about firing him the first time he lost more than three games. I added that if he was saying it was a done deal to fire Earle, than I needed to know. I made the point that a large contingent of bowl reps would be at the Iowa game and that it was very possible that we could receive a bowl invitation as soon as the game was over. I needed to know whether I should simply reject any bowl offer on the basis that Earle and the staff might be fired. And, if we were going to refuse an offer, we had better be prepared to tell the media why. It was clear that the president had not thought of the bowl question, so after pondering the matter for a moment, he said simply that we should talk during the game. I left his office feeling terribly depressed, but determined not to say anything to the coaches until absolutely necessary.

Iowa smelled blood and came in fired up and ready to play. The Hawkeyes had an outstanding team, and the Hawkeye coach, Hayden Fry, who knew lots of college football history, amused the local media by walking them around Ohio Stadium on Friday and showing them "where the bodies were buried." Not meaning any disrespect to Earle, he was referring to all the coaches over time that had lost their jobs by virtue of some game or another in the

'Shoe. Not surprisingly, there were a few Michigan coaches among the corpses, as well.

Surprisingly, we dominated Iowa in the first two quarters, and were leading at halftime. There were a number of bowl scouts at the game and all of them were impressed. Having Ohio State in your bowl game, even a team with three losses, was good business because it meant solid ticket sales and television ratings.

It wasn't long before I ran into the president, who smiled at me and commented on how well we were playing. "If we get an invitation, go ahead and accept."

That was all. But I took it to mean that no one was about to be fired and I felt uplifted, at least for the moment.

We continued to play well in the second half and were leading by five points with less than two minutes to go. Iowa had the ball and was driving, but still had to score a touchdown to win. Finally, with 16 seconds left, and facing a fourth down and 23 yards to go for a first down, and 28 yards to go for a touchdown, the Hawks' quarterback threw an 18-yard pass to his crossing tight end who caught the ball at the 10 and ran into the end zone for the winning score. Never had Ohio Stadium been quieted so quickly. I found it almost impossible to believe, an absolute nightmare.

The Ohio Stadium locker rooms were old, stark and cramped. The team dressed in three different locker rooms and came together in the biggest of the three for pre-and post-game talks from the coaches. The coaches dressed in a fourth room. It was much smaller, more spartan and barren. Wooden benches were bolted into the concrete floor; there are two rows of lockers. The coaches' locker room would have been a perfect setting for one of those Knute Rockne-vintage film clips.

I waited for Earle on a bench in the coaches' quarters. Earle first had to speak to the team and meet with the press. Often, he went upstairs to a room to greet recruits.

I don't recall if he did that day. But, invariably, he was the last person to shower and dress. It probably was about an hour and a half after the game when he arrived to take his shower. The other coaches all had cleared out. Earle and I had to talk. They knew that. It was almost eerily quiet.

"Well, what do you think?" Earle said. He was toweling off in front of this locker.

"I don't know," I said. I told him Jennings said to accept a bowl bid if we won. I interpreted it to mean that unless we were going to send a fired staff to a bowl game, which I thought was unlikely, the staff was secure with a win over Iowa–even if we lost at Ann Arbor the next week and finished 6-4-1. But we didn't defeat Iowa, and I felt less confident about everything right now.

"Earle, I'm not going to ask you to resign," I said. "I never would do that. But I want you to think about a scenario where you resign."

Earle did not interrupt. He allowed me my piece.

"Let's say we survive this and beat Michigan and are invited to a bowl game. We're still 6-4-1 with a team everyone, including you guys, thought should win the national championship. There will be some grumbling. But next year, you will be in the final year of your contract and the first time we lose there won't be any decency about it. It's going to be a bitch the entire year for you and your family. And let's face it; we don't have a lot of horses coming back. We have a tough schedule—LSU is coming in and, well, I just want you to think about it."

Earle still was dressing. He couldn't quite get dried off. It was one of those times where you can't seem to stop perspiring. He put his shirt on and the moisture blotted through.

"I see what you're saying," Earle said, "But I'm not a quitter."

He reacted like a good coach caught in a miserable situation. There was something wonderfully honorable in that. But if someone had taken a photo—a big-time coach sweating profusely as he dressed and his boss sitting on a wooden bench with no answer to offer other than a scenario for resignation—I imagine we would have appeared rather inconceivably pathetic. Especially to fans who saw only the pomp and majesty of intercollegiate athletics, and regaled in the intoxication of Saturday afternoon gridiron fantasies.

But deep in the bowels of a stadium that in its gayest moments fostered sunny possibilities for hundreds of thousands of youngsters and adults alike, a few hours after a discouragingly pivotal loss for one of the most successful coaches in Big Ten history, reality was setting in. And on this bleak, rainy, gray day, the reality was cold, harsh and indisputable; I knew things weren't going to get any easier. And despite Earle's praiseworthy, give-'em-hell attitude, I suspect he knew, too.

Denice and I talked that night. It was a difficult time. I had a pretty good idea that Earle's neck was on the chopping block, but I still felt that firing this coach at this time would disgrace the university. Earle's won-loss record spoke for itself. And aside from the Schlichter/racetrack innuendos, which pretty much had dried up and blown away by now, and Earle's irascibility, which sometimes shone through in press conferences as a lack of tact and was more a public relations concern than anything else, there were no allegations of program scandals or personal problems. None. Terminating Earle Bruce would be interpreted as a firing based solely on the football team's performance, a caving in to outside pressures tied inextricably to success on the field. The image of Ohio State as a football factory, an image we were working hard to eliminate or at least soften, instead would be strongly reinforced. That was of primary concern. But I had another worry, too.

"If Ed is going to come in and fire this guy over my head, I really don't have any credibility left," I said. "I can't get up in the morning and do my job if Ed fires my most important employee over my head. I won't have any meaningful authority."

I'm thinking this and I'm saying this, but I really don't want to believe Earle actually would be fired over my arguments and objections. I hoped that although Jennings might ask me to fire Earle, he would ultimately leave the decision to me. There would be substantial additional pressures from the board of trustees, of course, but I figured that even though people might be upset and angry when I refused to fire Earle, I could ride out their rancor.

I planned to attend the annual Michigan pre-game press conference the next morning. We always held one large media briefing the Sunday prior to the Michigan game in order to keep the contact between the press and the players to a minimum the remainder of the week. I had always made myself scarce on that occasion. The focus was on the coaches and players and the Buckeye-Wolverine rivalry.

"What are you going to say?" Denice asked.

"I'm going to tell everyone that Earle's future does not at all depend on whether the team wins at Ann Arbor," I said, "But Jennings and the trustees are not going to like it."

Denice was with me. I went to the press conference. I told the assembled reporters that, yes, I was disappointed with the Iowa game. I also told them that Earle was my football coach and that Rick Bay, as Ohio State athletics director, intended to honor Earle's contract—that even if we lost 50-0 to the Wolverines and finished the season 5-5-1, Earle was still my coach.

45

My vote of confidence was big news on Monday morning. Denice was at work at the Capitol Club downtown where she ran into Jack Kessler, a well-known Columbus businessman and a member of the Ohio State board of trustees. Jack always liked and supported me, but I don't know if he had the same affinity for Earle.

"It looks as though Rick has really backed himself into a corner."

"No," Denice said, bravely, "Rick has backed the trustees into a corner."

What I certainly had done was lay the groundwork for a discussion with Ed. He phoned my office at about 11 a.m. I had been waiting for his call.

"I read the paper this morning, Rick," Ed said. "You asked me last week whether it was a done deal about Earle being fired. Well, it's a done deal."

Ed's voice was calm, but serious. I took a deep breath, "I'm sorry to hear that, Ed," I said. "I think it's a major mistake on the part of the university. But before you announce anything, I'd at least like the opportunity to talk to you about it." He said fine. We made an appointment to meet after lunch.

I didn't go to lunch. I left my office and took a walk, trying to organize my thoughts. Then I called Denice.

"Ed wants to see me," I said. "It could be all over." She knew how adamant I was. "Are we together on this?" I asked. A real trooper, she said we were. All that was left was meeting with Ed.

Ed was at his desk when I entered his office. He looked concerned, but we shook hands as we always did upon greeting one another. "Helluva way to lose a ballgame," I said. "Really tough."

Ed asked me to sit down, and then said, "I'm getting a lot of pressure about Earle, Rick." He didn't mention the source, but continued, "We just don't have any support for him. We have to make a change."

I said, "Ed, I'm not going to do it. I'll deliver your message, but as I told you last week, this is going to be bad for the university. It is going to be misread. If we think we're seen as a football factory now, think what the perception is going to be if we fire Earle the first time the guy loses four games. He has done all the right things. Nobody is going to understand it. It is going to be a public relations nightmare for the university. I just can't be a part of it, and I'll have to resign."

Ed swallowed and said, "I don't want you to do that. Can't you reconsider?"

The words must have been tough to get out; by this time, I had been a pain in the ass for Ed on numerous issues. I figured this was more or less a courtesy and grist for answers later to questions of whether he tried to change my mind about resigning.

"Thanks for asking," I said, "But, no. The only thing I ask is that I be treated like assistant coaches and be paid through the end of the academic year." Ed said fine.

Then came the kicker. I asked Ed how he wanted to handle the announcement. "I really don't want to announce it until after the Michigan game," he said.

I was incredulous. "Ed, that's just unrealistic," I said. "How are you planning on doing that?"

"We'll just keep it under wraps," he said.

"But Ed," I said, "doesn't the board of trustees know about this?" He said they did, "That's *nine* people just outside this office, at least. You know and I know that there is no way to keep this thing under wraps. Besides, I am being asked all the time by the coaches about their situation, and I can't just lie to them. If this is a done deal, we ought to announce it and provide Earle the courtesy of knowing he is coaching his last game."

"Well," he said, "I really would rather not do that."

"Ed, I have to tell the coaches," I said, "But how do you want to handle it with the media? When are you going to call a press conference?"

"I'm not going to have a press conference," he said. "I'll issue a statement from this office—two lines, something terse—that says the coach has been terminated, and that a search is on for a new coach. Something like that."

"Well, I'm going to call a press conference," I said. "Otherwise we are going to be hounded all week by the media and the distraction won't be fair to the team, to me, to you or the university. We have to get this thing behind us and let these guys concentrate on the Michigan game, instead of letting everyone speculate all week."

"Do what you have to do," he said.

So, I did. I went back to the office and gathered my thoughts. Immediately, then, I drove over to the Woody Hayes complex to meet with Earle. The same $10 million building we had dedicated as one happy family—Earle, the president, me, the board of trustees—just three days earlier. It was about 2:30, and the coach was just about to go into a team meeting before practice.

We went into Earle's office, which he used only in conjunction with practices and other activities inside the building. I had dictated that the cubicles in the Woody Hayes building were for this limited use. The permanent football offices remained in St. John Arena with the rest of us, because I wanted to keep everyone in close proximity to one another. I thought this contributed to better overall staff morale; I didn't like the perception that any one sport, even football, had its own little fiefdom. So Earle's Woody Hayes building office was unadorned, a fitting austere setting for the news I was about to deliver. When I shut the door behind us, Earle, I'm sure, knew what was coming.

"Coach I just met with Ed Jennings," I said, "You've been fired and I resigned."

Earle shook his head, "Aw, Jesus, why?"

"He really didn't say. All he said was that he's been getting a lot of pressure about you, though he never was specific."

"You didn't have to quit," he said.

"Oh, yes, I did," I said, "I didn't do it for you, coach, I did it for me."

He understood.

46

Naturally, I have thought a lot about that decision. If I had just delivered the message that the president had fired Earle, but that I was staying on even though I didn't agree with the decision, I don't think Ed would have fired me. I think even now that I could have gone before the press and said, "I don't agree with this decision, but the president has told me to fire the coach and the president is my boss, so that's what I've done." I think I could have done that and survived. But I couldn't have survived in terms of my own self-respect.

I think Ed had his mind made up a week earlier, after the loss to Wisconsin. But I also felt I had made some impact then, when I argued that Earle's firing would reflect negatively on the university. I also don't think Earle would have been fired if we had beaten Iowa. But once we lost and I went public supporting Earle, Ed was put to the test. Now he had both the trustees and power brokers downtown—and this is all speculation on my part—saying, "Who in hell is the boss over there? You? Or Bay? We've been talking about firing the football coach and, now we're finally down to it, and we're going to let Bay upstage us and decide who is going to be coach?"

So, maybe I forced Ed's hand, though that wasn't my motive. My motive was to support the coaching staff and let people know that if I was going to be overruled in this situation, it was going to be "over my dead body." Besides, I had been promised that any decision relative to firing Earle, or even Eldon for that matter, would be mine. And, finally, if the president could come in and fire my most important employee against my recommendation, what credibility did I have left?

I called a press conference for 4:30 p.m. Before that, I found as many coaches as possible and told them about Earle and about my resignation. One of the coaches I spoke with was Gary Williams, the basketball coach who I had hired away from Boston College just the season before.

"The perspective and everything—it's crazy around here," Gary said.

Then, I went to the press conference. Of course, it was jammed. The Buckeye sports information director introduced me to the throng by saying, "It's a sad day at Ohio State," words that infuriated the university's media relations people who were already reeling in damage control mode. They were trying desperately to spin the story as the president's prerogative, a decision he had been thinking about for awhile in the best interests of the university. Disingenuously, Jennings had said, "We didn't expect this to happen before the Michigan game, but I felt an obligation that if it were to happen, I would give him as much notice as possible."

After I took my last question from the assembled journalists and walked away from the microphone, the reporters broke an unwritten journalistic rule and applauded. The media coverage was sensational and nationwide, and, for me, sometimes embarrassing. Front sports page stories, columns or editorials appeared in major newspapers from New York to Los Angeles and from Knoxville, Tennessee to Bangor, Maine. There was even an op-ed piece in *The Mining Journal* of Marquette, Michigan, and a cutely titled editorial, "Rah, Rick," in my hometown newspaper, the *Waukegan News-Sun*. And the Eugene Register-Guard ran a column describing my departure, entitled "The High Road Led Out of Town."

I received hundreds of letters of support from around the country, and *The Columbus Dispatch* got even more, blaming the Wolfe family, prominent owners of the newspaper who were no fans of Earle, for instigating and forcing the coach's ouster. So intense was the criticism of the publisher that the paper felt compelled to print a rare front-page disclaimer a few days later asserting that the Wolfes had had nothing to do with the firing.

As to the specific reasons Earle was fired, no one ever told me and it might have been because no one really knew. The president said that the coach's dismissal was not because of his win-loss record, but didn't elaborate.

In what one media story called "one-half hooey," a former chair of the athletics council said the university was looking for "dynamic charismatic leadership." He'd also said, "More important than the record on the field is the way the individual represents the university. People are going to have to understand that football is not that important at Ohio State any longer."

But the coach's firing suggested just the opposite, that winning was more crucial than ever (witness Jennings telling me to accept a bowl invitation if we beat Iowa, thus precluding Bruce's demise), and that Earle's alleged failure as a "dynamic charismatic leader" was perfectly acceptable and had been for eight years, unless his team lost four games. One of the trustees, Joel Teaford, a Columbus attorney, admitted that the group often discussed Earle at their board meetings, but denied having taken a straw vote before the Iowa game on whether to retain the coach.

As if he didn't have anything better to do, Governor Richard Celeste weighed in on the matter, telling the Des Moines Register, while on a trip to Iowa, that he knew for some time that Jennings intended to fire Bruce, partly because Jennings had little regard for Bruce's handling of the gambling problems that Ohio State quarterback Art Schlichter displayed while he played for Bruce and the years following. According to a story in the Los Angeles Times, the governor went on to say that Bruce's own fondness for playing the horses, along with Schlichter's gambling, had irritated Jennings for some time. In addition, according to the governor, Bruce no longer had the support of major contributors to the school, and members of the board of trustees didn't believe that his teams could win big games. Celeste said that he had learned that Bruce most likely would be fired a week before the Buckeyes lost to Iowa, 29-27. Finally, Celeste said that he had been asked to intervene with the school's board of trustees on Bruce's behalf because he had appointed six of the nine members, but refused because he didn't want to get involved. He said that Jennings never had much regard for Bruce and intended to fire the coach sometime during the year.

The governor was obviously still miffed at being cropped out of the Denis Hopson-Herb Williams newspaper photo.

Another misconception about Earle was tied to Ohio State's "football factory" image that suggested his players were largely disinterested in school. But while the coach may not have applied the most effective public relations spin to his team's academic success, Buckeye players under Earle's guidance graduated at about 67 percent, which was 14 percent higher than the university average. Finally, he had coached seven first team Academic All-Americas and Ohio State's first Rhodes scholar since 1936.

Whatever the reasons for Earle's firing—the Art Schlichter affair, his public image, his presence at the race track, his sideline appearance, his uncharismatic demeanor or his unpopularity with the Columbus power brokers—one thing is certain. His dismissal sent a message that whatever flaws a college coach may possess are tolerable until he fails to win enough.

Bo Schembechler was incredulous at the mere prospect of Earle being fired. Speaking in Ann Arbor at his own Monday press briefing just two hours before the axe came down in Columbus, Bo said, "It's ridiculous. Earle Bruce is one of the top-notch coaches in the country." Bo said that perhaps Earle had never escaped Woody Hayes' shadow. Asked how Hayes would have weathered such a storm in Columbus, Bo replied, "He was one tough son-of-a-bitch. He would beat 'em down. And Earle will too. He's a Woody Hayes protégé and he's tough. Don't underestimate him."

Bo called Earle a proven winner, recalling that his 56-17 record was the best in the Big Ten over his nine years at Ohio State. "God, I hope he's established himself by now," the Michigan coach said. "I mean what do you have to do? I'm not here to defend Earle Bruce, but all I can say is that it makes Columbus look pretty bad."

To that end, newspaper columnists were pointing out that Earle had one year left on his contract, and that Notre Dame had honored its commitment to the hapless Gerry Faust. *Columbus Dispatch* columnist, Dick Fenlon, wrote, "Notre Dame waited until the end of Gerry Faust's five-year contract before heeding the cries of the subway alumni. It set the school back a year or so on the football field, but you get the idea that the principle of the thing was worth it."

By Monday evening, Earle Bruce was the most empathetic coach in Ohio State athletics history. About 150 of the 220 members of the OSU marching band showed up on his front lawn and serenaded the tearful coach and his wife, Jean, with the school fight song and alma mater, "Fight the Team" and "Carmen Ohio." The news had traveled so fast that several students even made it to my press conference, some wearing "Save Earle" t-shirts. There were spontaneous rallies across the campus in support of the coach and many fans hung their OSU flags at half-mast. As *Columbus Monthly Magazine* later reported, "Ed Jennings had managed to do what Earle Bruce hadn't been able to do—make Bruce a sympathetic figure."

Earle, himself, took it like a pro, but was circumspect in his reaction to what had occurred. Dressed in a suit and tie and speaking before a deluge of reporters after Monday's practice, he asked rhetorically, "What can you say about it? All you can say is that I think they have a right to fire a person, but I think it's very poor timing–right before the Michigan game. I don't think that's quite fair. They can do it any time, but not before the Michigan game ... I'm kind of proud of what I've done here–daggone proud of not only what I've done on the football field, but what I've done in the classroom for our kids getting their education. I'm daggone loyal to Ohio State. I love this football team, and I love Ohio State." Then, he got into his car and drove away.

Meanwhile, the decision to fire the coach was also met with rancor by the Ohio State faithful across the city. A telephone poll by WCMH-TV, in which 12,000 people replied, revealed that over 90 percent opposed Bruce's firing. "Noose Bruce" buttons seen at the Iowa game were now replaced with "Jettison Jennings" bumper stickers. In short, Earle had been screwed, and no one likes to see anyone get a raw deal.

47

What followed leading up to the Michigan game was a week of wackiness. *Columbus Monthly* magazine did a huge cover story about the entire episode, the headline reading, "The Week the Town Went Crazy."

Jennings still hadn't said why Earle was fired, although he once implied that the coach knew why he had been dismissed, leaving the impression that there must be something dark and awful in Earle's past, an implication that without proof was unfair. Ironically, however, this treatment of the coach seemed to trigger questions about the president's own behavior.

According to *Columbus Monthly*, "reporters received anonymous calls filled with innuendo about Jennings and his personal life. The tipsters said that the president—his separation from his wife, Mary Eleanor, had already sparked campus gossip—had been drinking heavily and running around with women, known and not so well known. Start turning over rocks, the reporters were told, and ugly things would crawl out."

Earle's attorney and close personal friend, John Zonak, who was also the Executive Producer of *The Earle Bruce Show* on WSYX-TV, sent a letter to Jennings demanding to know why the coach was fired, but, again, no answer was forthcoming. Because it was a personnel matter, the president said, he was not required to provide any reason for public consumption. But he did acknowledge that Bruce had not broken any OSU rules and was not guilty of any serious misconduct. Still, when asked what qualities he was looking for in a new coach, Jennings said, "An individual who represents the institution well."

And the loquacious trustee, Joel Teaford, said that the Buckeyes' poor season presented "a window of opportunity to get rid of a coach who gave the university a bad image."

By mid-week, Jennings, the OSU Board of Trustees and the publishers of the *Columbus Dispatch* had had enough. After three days of constant thrashing from non-Wolfe-owned Columbus media outlets, *The Cleveland Plain Dealer*, the OSU *Lantern* (the student newspaper) and the court of public opinion, the Dispatch ran an editorial entitled "Jennings Action Proper," which said Bruce "failed to engender good will for the institution" and "failed to subjugate his personal interests to those of the university." The public was reminded that the coach had appeared greedy when he took his television show away from WBNS—a Wolfe station—for more money. The editorial prompted the *Cleveland Plain Dealer* to report that the Wolfes had pressured Jennings to fire Bruce as retribution, precisely *because* the coach moved his television show to a non-Wolfe rival station.

Two trustees, both friends of Denice and me until now, sharply criticized my decision to tell Earle of his firing before the Michigan game, and, of course, the governor had already been widely quoted about Earle's predictable demise.

The president invited the team captains to his office for a sit-down, telling linebacker Chris Spielman during the meeting that, even if the team had finished 10-1, the coach "probably" would have been fired.

This was the most dramatic personnel change in Ohio State University history, and no one–*no one*–could come up with a viable reason for the coach's ouster. And it was evident that even those who tried couldn't get their stories straight, when two trustees told news sources that the board voted informally on November 5, nine days before the Iowa game, that Bruce should be replaced, while others said that no vote was ever conducted.

Clearly, by this time, *The Dispatch* would just as soon have had the story die, but in Cleveland, 120 miles north of Columbus, *The Plain Dealer* continued to pursue unflattering stories about Jennings, saying that community leaders had warned the president that his job was also in jeopardy because of indiscretions in his personal life.

Amidst all this, Earle's football team tried to focus on Michigan, and in the Thursday's final practice before heading to Ann Arbor, in the traditional "senior tackle" ceremony, the coach himself lined up with his senior players and hit the blocking sled for the last time. It was a touching scene, but the way things were going, I could almost envision Earle separating his shoulder and having to roam the Michigan sideline with his arm in a sling. Maybe it would have made people forget his pitiful walking cast in the Alabama game.

Although I was not aware of it, at about the same time Earle was honing in on the blocking sled, his attorney, John Zonak, was entering the clerk's office at Franklin County Common Pleas Court to file a $7.44 million lawsuit against Jennings and "The Ohio State University" for breach of contract, libel and slander. The suit was filed at precisely 4:55 p.m., closing time, so as to miss any press scrutiny until Monday morning and not distract anyone from the game—and so that Zonak, himself, could control the announcement Saturday night. The suit turned the tables on the issue of "character," alleging that Jennings fired Bruce because the coach disapproved of Jennings' personal life. Zonak called the president "weak" and said that Jennings had been under fire from the board of trustees for "his carousing and excessive drinking." And in a final shot, the attorney filed deposition notices for three women: his estranged wife, Mary Eleanor, university fund-raiser, Barbara Real, and trustee, Debbie Casto.

Earle was quoted as saying, "If you are going to attack me and my family, then you'd better be perfect."

One of the most incredible incidents connected with the episode was a rumor that I had resigned as athletic director because I discovered that Denice was having an affair with Jennings. Neither Denice nor I had any idea such a rumor was in the wind until the Saturday of the Ohio State-Michigan game. I was in the visiting director's suite in the Michigan press box and Denice was standing just outside the booth, deep in thought and looking out over the field, when Steve Minick, a Columbus TV reporter, began making small talk with her. The game was about to begin.

Finally, Minick said, "Denice, I have to ask you something or I may lose my job. There is a rumor that Rick resigned because you and Ed Jennings were romantically involved." Minick was a good guy and must have swallowed hard before posing this question, but that didn't make it much easier on Denice. In the first place, Denice didn't like Jennings, or, at least, didn't respect him. In her mind, he was always in my hair.

She was shocked, but had the presence to say, "Good lord, Steve, I have better taste than that!" She had reacted with spunk, but she was mortified and crushed.

I was seriously involved in the game when she came back into the booth, but I could tell she was upset. She told me what had happened. If the rumor weren't so despicable, we could have had a good laugh. But at the moment it was my low point of the entire matter.

The good news is that in the face of so much adversity and heartbreak the team rose to the occasion, showing up on the field wearing "save Earle" headbands. The coach, never one for players wearing "crap" that wasn't part of the official uniform, didn't at first realize what they said and barked at the equipment manager on the field, "Get rid of those goddamn headbands! What the hell's going on," before someone told him they were in his honor.

We beat Michigan, 23-20; the team carried Earle off the field on their shoulders and we finished the season 6-4-1. There would be no bowl game, of course, but the victory meant that Earle had ended his career with a 5-4 record head-to-head against Bo, something even Woody had not achieved.

Bo was classy enough to come into our locker room after the contest to congratulate our team, many of whom had been recruited by him to play for Michigan. Later, that spring, Bo further honored Earle by having him come to Ann Arbor as a guest coach for Michigan's spring football practice, where Earle dutifully wore a Bo Schembechler "M" embroidered coaching cap around the practice field.

After the game, team co-captains, linebacker Chris Spielman and quarterback Tom Tupa, presented me with the game ball. I was in a daze and don't remember exactly what I said to the team, but on the plane ride back to Columbus, I remember sitting with Earle and saying to him, "Amazing isn't it? This is the moment Jennings wanted me to tell you that you are fired."

Aside from this one exchange with Earle, I remember nothing about the ride home, because I was preoccupied with Denice, who was sitting quietly on the other side of me, and trying to figure out how you answer the vicious allegation about her and Jennings without perpetuating it. You simply ignore it, I thought, which obviously is easier said than done.

To the credit of the media, the rumor never even was reported as rumor. In fact, this is the first time it has been discussed in print, though it easily could have been mentioned when the whispers surfaced, or later referred to as an aside when stories in the *Cleveland Plain Dealer* reported Jennings was involved with a woman, a blonde, as was Denice, who was employed in the Ohio State development office.

The local talk shows even protected us. When someone would call in and broach the topic, the host would cut off the caller. One evening we had just gotten in the car, and turned on the Bob Trumpy Show from Cincinnati, when a caller said something about a rumor he had heard about my resignation. The next thing we knew, the caller was off the air. It must have been the station's 10-second delay. Trumpy apologized for cutting off the caller, but said the question was inappropriate.

Still, the rumor hurt terribly. People talked about it. We weren't that naïve to think they didn't. In fact, early the following week, Mary Eleanor Jennings, who was our friend, but whom we hadn't seen since her split with the president, showed up at the Capitol Club to see Denice. She was not hostile, but asked Denice point blank whether she was having an affair with Ed. Denice was taken aback, but said immediately and spontaneously, "Mary Eleanor, you've got to be kidding!" I think that she reacted so sincerely and so quickly that Mary Eleanor never doubted her.

"I didn't think so," she said.

Later, upon reflection, Denice was half embarrassed by her answer, and hoped that she hadn't sounded as insulted as she felt. After all, she had been talking about the man that Mary Eleanor had been married to all these years.

Another reason the rumor was troubling was that it was cold, hard evidence that people needed an explanation other than simple principle for my resignation at Ohio State. Some people, perhaps many, could not believe that I nor anyone else would walk away from a job as manager of one of the foremost intercollegiate programs in the nation just on principle. Some people needed a bigger reason, an ulterior motive, which may say something about the public's perception of the integrity of those running intercollegiate athletics in this day and age. Voila! The president was fooling around with my wife. Or, certainly less viciously, Rick Bay was trying to position himself for the Michigan job, which was coming vacant with Don Canham's announced retirement.

But the truth is that I did just walk away from it. There was nothing else. I didn't have any interest in the Michigan job. I had been happy at Ohio State, and so had Denice. We loved the place, and it remains the best job I have ever had.

Earle's lawsuit against the University and Jennings ended much more quickly than his attorney, Zonak, would have liked. But in his heart the coach did not want to harm the university, and, for them the situation was getting worse. The Monday following the Michigan game the *Plain Dealer* reported that Jennings and one of the women with whom he was rumored to be involved were traveling to London together for a vacation. Although the president's office denied it, the paper had been able to confirm the reservations with the airline. Almost immediately, however, Jennings' reservation was cancelled amidst a report that the woman was making the trip alone.

In the meantime, the university's attorney had moved to settle the case as soon as possible, and Earle really did not have the stomach for what would have been a mucky and scandalous trial. In the end the coach received $471,000, which covered his salary, ancillary income and retirement benefits for the remaining year on his contract, although he told one reporter, "I'd gladly give back the $471,000 plus give them another $100,000 if I could stay and coach the team."

Finally, after learning from the same writer that Jennings said he would be willing to meet with him and divulge the reason he was fired, Earle made an appointment to see the president the Wednesday after the Michigan game. The meeting lasted eight minutes, and, in what has to be the apex of confidentiality, Jennings refused to shed any light on the matter even for his victim, again saying that he didn't have to give a reason.

The assistant coaches and I were to be paid through the end of our appointments in July. In my case, however, the university wasn't quite as forgiving as it first appeared. While the assistant football coaches went largely unmonitored and went about their business finding other jobs, I was re-assigned to another office in a somewhat deserted area of the campus, far from the athletics department. In order to receive my salary, I was expected to report to a cubicle (which had cinderblock walls, a steel desk and covered about 140 square feet), and to be there from 8 a.m. to 5 p.m., every day. I had no specific responsibilities, but the administration was hoping that by making life difficult for me, I would leave the institution before July, or, at least, they would have the satisfaction of exacting some revenge for the trouble they perceived I had inflicted upon them.

After about four days of showing up at 8:00 a.m. and twiddling my thumbs for eight hours, not counting lunch, I started to get inquiries from the press as to what I was doing and what my future held. So, I decided to call Madison Scott, the vice-president for Human Resources.

"Scotty," I said, "the media is looking for me, and when they locate me, it is going to be controversial and the university is going to look foolish. I am over here doing nothing, no one is around, and this office looks like a jail cell." Scott was listening carefully. "I'll make you guys a deal," I continued. "You pay me through March, and I'll disappear right now. Otherwise, without any prompting from me, it won't be long before there will be television pictures from here suggesting that I'm in San Quentin."

"I'll get back to you," he said. And five minutes later he did. "Deal," he said.

Every now and then I am asked, "How many other athletic directors would have done what you did?" I don't know. At the time, resigning didn't seem like a difficult thing to do. I was disappointed that it had come to such a confrontation, but resigning seemed like the only option. I know it is not practical to go to the wall—to demand a showdown—on every issue. At the same time, I felt I needed to make a point. I don't want this to come across as false modesty, but I can't say unequivocally that I would have resigned under different personal circumstances, though I'd like to think I would. At the time, I was convinced I could get another job doing something I enjoyed doing. At 46, I was young for an AD, Denice and I didn't have any children, and she was working. At the very least, we certainly would make do until something else came along. At the time, my action seemed so logical that I didn't think too much about any alternatives.

The Friday night before Earle's last game against Michigan, I attended Don Canham's traditional get-together at his plant in Ann Arbor, which was the headquarters for the mail-order business he had put in a blind trust before becoming the Wolverine athletics director. When I arrived, Canham interrupted the gathering, introduced me and said, "Here's someone you have to hear from. He's just done what all of us like to think we would do given a similar situation, but in reality, I'm not sure anybody would."

It was a nice gesture, and my father would have been proud. He would have been prouder still when, a couple of weeks later, the Columbus City Council honored Earle and me for our "outstanding services to The Ohio State University and the City of Columbus."

Goodbye, Columbus. It was time to move on.

SECTION THREE
100 Days With The Boss

48

It has always seemed funny to me that after a new United States president has been elected, he is subject to a comprehensive performance review by the national media after his "first 100 days" in office. But at the end of his term, when there is far more to evaluate, no one ever analyzes the "last 100 days."

When I unexpectedly and ill advisedly became the chief operating officer of the New York Yankees in 1988, this issue escaped discussion. Because my first 100 days with the Yankees were also my last 100 days—my entire body of work.

That's right. I worked for George Steinbrenner and his Yankees for exactly 100 days. And before anyone laughs, they should keep in mind that my tenure, fleeting though it was, is not a team record for brevity. At least four Yankees managers started a season for the team and were replaced within three months.

Yet I wasn't fired. In fact, George asked me to stay, but the day-to-day frustration of the job and the never-ending state of crisis that menaced the environment in the place was too much to bear.

Almost without exception, when people learn that I worked for the Yankees, their first question is how it was working for Steinbrenner. Even though it was by far the shortest tenure of any job I ever had, and even though I worked with the likes of Woody Hayes and Bo Schembechler, and even though I left Ohio State under the most controversial of circumstances, and even though I was later president of the Cleveland Indians—the first question to me is *always* about the Yankees. And I don't mind.

In retrospect, although professionally disappointing, my time with the team was a fascinating experience, frustrating at the time, but humorous if not downright funny. I am very glad that I did it. And I am glad that I was there when I was—at a time when the club had about as glitzy an all-star cast as one could imagine. Billy Martin was the field manager and Lou Piniella was the general manager. The radio broadcasters for Yankees games were Phil Rizzuto and Bill White; the television announcers were Tony Kubek and Hawk Harrelson; and the venerable Bob Shepherd was the public address announcer. Mel Allen was still around, too, and narrated a video vignette about me when I was hired that played on the Yankee Stadium Jumbotron. Howard Cosell and Donald Trump were regular visitors to the games, and Rickey Henderson, Dave Winfield and Don Mattingly were on the team. It was colorful, if nothing else.

Although I had never met him, Steinbrenner sent me a supportive telegram following my resignation at Ohio State, saying that he thought I had done a great job with the Buckeyes program and that if he could ever help me to let him know.

George followed Ohio State athletics because his wife's family lived in Columbus, and the city was also the home of the Columbus Clippers, the Yankees' Triple A minor-league affiliate. "The Boss," as he was famously known, was notorious for promoting and demoting lots of Clippers players to and from the parent club in New York, sometimes in less than a week or two. A Clippers player might catch George's eye one week, be promoted to the Yankees, make a couple of errors and be sent right back down. People used to joke about the airline "shuttle service" that went back and forth between Columbus and New York.

George became involved more directly in my career when he lent his support in my application for the commissionership of the Southeastern Conference (SEC).

Shortly after I resigned from OSU, SEC commissioner Harvey Schiller informed the conference presidents that he was leaving to become CEO of the United States Olympic Committee. I applied for Harvey's job, just hoping to make the short list of finalists. I had no connections in the South whatsoever, so the best I could hope for would be to get an interview.

The University of Florida was an SEC school and I remembered someone mentioning to me that Steinbrenner had once helped the Gators baseball program and that he was a friend of the university president. While I knew that Steinbrenner's offer of assistance was probably just perfunctory, I decided to call him anyway and ask if he would be comfortable in putting in a good word for me with the president, who was also a member of the search committee for the new commissioner.

When I reached George he came on the phone as though he had known me forever, saying that he would be happy to recommend me. I don't know what he finally said on my behalf, but it was enough to get me in front of the committee for an interview. Predictably, perhaps, I spent most of the session defending my controversial resignation at Ohio State. The debacle in Columbus, I knew, would not be helpful to me with any group of presidents. No president wanted a guy who might make waves by refusing to follow a directive from his CEO.

All of this is speculation on my part because the SEC didn't hire a new commissioner after all. Once Harvey Schiller evaluated what he was really getting into at the USOC, he decided he wanted his old job back. He had performed admirably for the conference and the presidents welcomed his quick return.

The turnabout left me somewhat dejected. I wasn't sure I was that interested in the SEC position, but I had been out of work for about two months and it wasn't any fun sitting around Columbus in the dead of winter. The job offers weren't rolling in. It was a bad time of year for that. Most intercollegiate administrative vacancies occurred in the spring or summer. I probably should have taken some time off, headed somewhere warm and played golf, but I didn't have a financial settlement like Coach Bruce and even though my wife Denice was still working as the sales director for the prestigious Capitol Club in downtown Columbus, we were getting low on cash.

49

I got a phone call from Steinbrenner about a week later. He had heard what had transpired in the commissioner's search and wondered what my plans were now. I confessed that I really didn't have any, but was hoping for something to materialize in the spring. Then he dropped the bombshell.

Rick," he said, "I have this job open. I haven't had a president for the ball club for about three years. I have to get someone with your skills to come and run this thing for me. I've got a couple of sons, but I'm not sure they're interested. And I really have to get away from this damn absentee ownership business, turn the Yankees over to someone and stay in Tampa and run my other businesses. Would you be interested?"

I was speechless and very excited. Despite all the internal turmoil that was constantly reported in the Yankees organization, the thought of working for the club was mesmerizing. I was immediately caught up in the moment and told George that I would love to talk to him about it.

George went on to say that he had a couple of other people in mind and would get back to me. I was pumped up and immediately called Denice, who was thrilled at the thought of moving to the Big Apple. I had taken her to New York for several long theater weekends over the years and she loved the buzz of the city. We not only saw lots of great shows, but almost more enjoyable for us was just walking all over Manhattan, from Greenwich Village to the Upper West Side, and running in Central park on the weekends. Of course, we were getting way ahead of ourselves, but it was fun to visualize the possibilities that arose from that 10-minute phone conversation.

I hunted down Ed Weaver, the former athletics director at Ohio State who had preceded Hugh Hindman, the AD I had replaced. Although Ed was retired, George had made him a Yankees vice-president and set him up in an office at Cooper Stadium, where the Columbus Clippers played. There he hung out with George Sisler, Jr., the Clippers' president and the son of all-time great George Sisler, Sr. who, among other accomplishments, batted over .400 twice in his Major League career. Ed liked me, I think, because I had treated him with great dignity and gratitude, always mentioning his laying the groundwork at Ohio State for any success we might have been enjoying at the moment. It turned out that he had recommended me to Steinbrenner, and promised to keep me posted as to George's thinking on the matter.

Ed Weaver was not the only "vice-president" of the Yankees who lived in Columbus. There was at least one other, a local car dealer. If George liked someone enough, he would arbitrarily make them part of the Yankees family. And the honor went beyond a ceremonial executive title. Weaver and the car dealer proudly wore official Yankees World Series Championship diamond rings, which were nearly the size of a golf ball.

I received another call from George about a week later inviting me to come to Tampa to talk with him about the job. Once the interview was confirmed, I decided to do some homework to learn as much as I could about both the Yankees organization and what it might be like to work for George.

I knew several guys in baseball, including Jim Campbell, president of the Detroit Tigers and an Ohio State alumnus, and Fred Wilpon, the president of the New York Mets and, like me, a Michigan graduate. Sensing my unbridled excitement when I called them, neither wanted to throw a wet blanket on my prospects but both, I could tell, were circumspect in their reactions to the idea. The word that came up most often was "interesting," and generally used in the following context:

"Well, Rick, yes, that would be, well, ah, ur, how would you say *interesting*, your working for George."

Neither man used the words "bizarre" or "challenging" or said what they were really thinking, which I am sure was something like, "DON'T DO IT!" But, even in retrospect, it wouldn't have mattered if they had. Nobody who has lived a life in sports could resist an opportunity to work for the most famous professional franchise in history, notwithstanding the foreknowledge of the many calamities that were certain to befall them in the process. But I blotted all of this from my mind as I boarded the plane and headed for Tampa and my first meeting with The Boss.

We met for breakfast at the Yankee Clipper Hotel, one of George's properties, and he spent two hours telling me about the job. I had been too excited to finish my breakfast and was sipping water to fight off the growing dryness in my mouth. George ate his meal with gusto and, without any small talk, launched into a description of the kind of guy he needed to run the Yankees' front office.

He said that he had just built a new home outside of Tampa, was raising racehorses and, in fact, owned a racetrack in the area. He reiterated what he had said over the phone—that he didn't have time to run the club anymore and wanted someone to take charge as executive vice-president and chief operating officer in charge of administration. He was going to save the title of president for his sons, should one become more interested in baseball later on.

I asked all the right questions and made my position clear. I wanted to be certain I had enough executive authority to run the front office and earn the opportunity to get involved in the baseball end of the operation so that I could someday manage the entire organization.

George was very charming, as he often could be. I believed what he was saying, about relinquishing power and taking a low profile. And I think he believed it, too. But I reminded myself that George probably had made this speech at least once before. I also knew that even if I didn't take the job, and if I was patient, another opportunity in intercollegiate athletics would come along. But I felt a bit tired of college sports, and being in charge of the Yankees would be something different, something beyond my wildest dreams.

Was it ever.

50

George offered me the job four weeks later, but not directly. It was through Ed Weaver. It was a three-year deal at just over $100,000 a year, more than I was making at Ohio State, but surprisingly low by baseball standards. Still, I didn't care. I was on my way to The House That Ruth Built. And like so many Steinbrenner employees before, I figured I had what it took to make the job last without giving much thought to why so many of them had figured wrong.

A few days later, I flew to the Yankees spring training camp in Ft. Lauderdale, Florida. Reality was not far behind.

I can only imagine now what everyone was thinking then. After all, here I was, the guy who was going to reorganize the Yankees, the college-guy hotshot who was going to inherit all the authority George was going to relinquish. I quickly had a publicity photo taken with Yankees manager Billy Martin, who was in his fifth and final stint in the role, having already been fired four other times. Everyone was incredibly polite. Which meant that no one was laughing. But when George introduced me around to some of the team officials, a lot of people had that look on their faces like they knew something I didn't.

I began to understand their reaction the moment I walked into the doublewide trailer the Yankees used for their spring training headquarters. Because the club would be there only about six weeks, there were no permanent offices for the Yankees management at the park. They set up offices in a 40-foot trailer. Even though I knew it was just spring training, this wasn't the environment I envisioned for the perennial world champions. I was already feeling a little disillusioned, and I hadn't even gone inside. When I did, I was dumbfounded.

There, positioned directly in front of me and no more than six feet from the door was George's desk. And right behind George's desk was George. And George wasn't calmly dictating a memo or rifling through a sheaf of papers. No, George was screaming, yelling, bellowing, hollering—goddamn this and goddamn that—at some poor soul on the phone or to just about anyone who crossed his path, which, given the placement of his desk, was everyone.

George's "office" was sandwiched between two others, divided by paper-thin plastic partitions that jutted out only about three-quarters the width of the trailer, leaving a door space—but no actual door—between the adjoining rooms. There was no chance of any privacy, and if George happened to overhear something from one of the other cubicles with which he took issue, he would simply bark a "correction" of sorts in that general direction.

The din was constant and the atmosphere suffocating. I could not imagine working in that kind of atmosphere. But general manager Lou Piniella, who occupied one of the other spaces, was apparently used to it, and would yell right back. These guys could have virtual staff meetings without ever leaving their own offices.

I remember being surprised that George would yell at so many people and on such a regular basis. It wasn't a meanness, exactly, but more a terrific impatience and frustration. Still, I never had been in an environment in which someone conducted regular business that way, with such little regard for civility. I was in shock. If you could walk away from it—and I could at first—you had to laugh. But the incessant haranguing was claustrophobic.

I left the trailer as fast as I could and began to walk around the grounds. I knew that George had a huge philanthropic side to him. It was common knowledge that he took care of some former great athletes, from any sport, who were down on their luck, bringing them to spring training and putting them on the payroll as "special assistants."

Whether it was charity or not, I don't know, but one day I was surprised to see former Heisman Trophy winner Hop Cassady leading the team in jumping jacks. And there were a bunch of old Yankees dressed and on the field as well, instructing here and there, and, I am sure, being paid to do it. This was part of George's soft side, which showed itself more often than people might expect.

One year, he allowed Grambling State, the historic, black college in Louisiana coached by the legendary Eddie Robinson, to play a football game in Yankee Stadium, even though the Yankees were still in the midst of their season, with several home games still to be played. He knew that the football game would tear the field to hell, and it would have to be rebuilt in short order and at great expense to continue the Yankees' season. But Grambling needed the exposure for its program in a major city venue and George was glad to help.

Later, there would be the $1 million check he wrote to Virginia Tech to help the families of those murdered in the 2007 massacre on that campus.

But on this day he wasn't feeling charitable, at least to me. I would like to have circulated among the players for a bit, but fraternizing with the team wasn't my job, as George told me early on.

"Rick," he said, "the players are the enemy. They're labor; we're management. Stay away from the players. They will knife you in the back, if they get the chance."

It was a classic "us versus them" attitude. I was new and idealistic enough to think that I could make us one happy family. But I was also smart enough after two days of spring training to realize that I probably wasn't going to get the chance, and that if George was going to be spending most of his time at spring training, I'd rather be spending mine at Yankee Stadium.

Soon I'd be heading there.

51

Me? Chief operating officer of the New York Yankees? As Casey Stengel might have said, "Whoda thunk it?" But it was true, and, as Casey often *did* say, "You can look it up."

My appointment came as a complete surprise to everyone. Because Steinbrenner's reputation preceded him, many people wondered whether our unlikely alliance could really work. Over the 15 years that he had been principal owner of the Yankees George had played a major role in adding to the nation's unemployment rate, and my actions at Ohio State led some to believe that I was tough to manage, if not downright intractable. But one thing was certain: baseball had always been a part of my life, and I had been captivated by the Yankees since I was nine years old and saw New York first baseman Bill Skowron hit a grand slam home run against the Chicago White Sox. I rushed into the kitchen to tell my dad that Skowron had just walloped a "grand stand" home run.

I had been watching my White Sox suffer yet another defeat on WGN (Channel 9) at the hands of the perennial champions, when the muscular Yankees first baseman sent a moon shot into the upper deck of old Comiskey Park on Chicago's south side. Because I had just started to play age group baseball, my grasp of the game's terminology was just developing. I understood what a "bean ball" was, but I had never encountered a bases loaded, grand slam home run. When Dad finally realized what I was talking about, he tried patiently to explain what announcer Jack Brickhouse had really said, but I was adamant that, no, the ball had wound up in the grandstand. Eventually I understood, of course, but Dad would chuckle about that day the rest of his life.

Skowron's home run is the first memory I have of an exciting moment in sports. I had seen other baseball games on television before that day, but had never experienced such a visceral reaction. I'm not sure what it was, but I think it had to do with the ball flying into the upper deck. I had never imagined anyone hitting a baseball that far, lifting it into outer space like that, though sometime later I saw Mickey Mantle take a Billy Pierce fastball onto the roof of Comiskey, or "OUT OF THE BALLPARK!" as Brickhouse would scream incredulously. But it was Moose's rocket that fired my imagination about sports and sparked in me a lifelong long interest in competitive athletics.

When you grow up next door to the town's fire station and a block from the high school athletic fields, as I did from fifth grade on, and your dad is the school's football and wrestling coach, you've been blessed with a good chance at a wholesome upbringing. I was so favored in the town of Waukegan, Illinois, 40 miles north of Chicago on the shores of Lake Michigan. So perfectly located it was on the lake that Outboard Marine, the world's largest producer of outboard motors, resided there until it went bankrupt and closed in the year 2000.

It was a lakefront that was heavily industrialized, its shores lined for two miles with rusty looking buildings coughing smoke from their chimneys into the already gray skies. The gigantic American Steel and Wire plant (so large that it housed four fire trucks of its own) and Johns-Manville, the largest manufacturer of asbestos in the nation, monopolized the shoreline, along with the Moscow Screw Company and a couple of paint factories. I worked at one of them—Midland Paint—one summer, where my job was to check the viscosity of various lacquers being produced. There was a small sandy beach just beyond the monstrous plants, with a long cement breakwater pier that jutted into Lake

Michigan for at least 100 yards. The pier was used mostly for fishing, and the dunes mostly for parking and necking after dark, the latter activities euphemistically referred to as "watching the submarine races."

With a population of 40,000 and located almost exactly halfway between Chicago and Milwaukee, the city was the Lake County seat and was home to the *Waukegan News-Sun* and radio station WKRS. It was a blue-collar town, with about a 10-percent African-American population, and a high school of 3,000 students, about half of whom went on to college. The town had one of the nation's first McDonald's restaurants (15 cent hamburgers) and claimed both comedian Jack Benny and football great Otto Graham as two of its own.

It was the 1950s. Disneyland had opened and the comic strip "Peanuts" first appeared. Elvis Presley was introduced on the Ed Sullivan Show and the Rose Parade was first televised in color. Oklahoma ruled college football, as did the Yankees in professional baseball. Hugh Hefner shocked the nation with the first issue of "Playboy" and the words "under God" were added to the Pledge of Allegiance. Ted Williams signed a one-year contract with the Boston Red Sox for $125,000, while the average working man's annual salary was $3,000, only a little less than my father made teaching and coaching three sports at Waukegan Township High School (WTHS).

My father, Oscar Arthur "Ott" Bay, was the head varsity football and wrestling coach at Waukegan. He had moved the family to Waukegan from Danville, Illinois, in 1949, specifically to coach football at a big school. And that is where we grew up—me and my younger brothers, Steve and Mike, coach's sons, aspiring athletes with boundless imaginations and enough natural ability to achieve some of our dreams, and Dad's. With Dad coaching us, we all became high school state wrestling champions.

We were immersed in sports. We played them; we watched them; and we talked—no, argued—about almost nothing else. My brothers and I lived vicariously through the ups and downs of the teams and athletes we followed and admired. Our passionate exuberance was such that my father finally banned any discussion of sports at the dinner table, opting to eat in peace rather than mediate an argument as to whether Ernie Banks was a better shortstop than Louie Aparicio. Mike, the youngest by four years, was a hapless Cubs fan, while I, the oldest, followed the White Sox. Our middle brother, Steve, was content to sit placidly and eat his mashed potatoes during these disputes. He was a Yankees fan.

It was easy to be a Yankees fan in the '50s. The Bronx Bombers, managed by Casey Stengel, won six World Series titles during the decade, and their bruising line-up boasted the likes of Mickey Mantle, Yogi Berra, Hank Bauer, Elston Howard, Phil Rizzuto and the aforementioned Skowron. Whitey Ford led the pitching corps, along with Bob Turley and Eddie Lopat, with a fireballer named Ryne Duran in the bullpen. But because they won all the time, it was easy to hate them, too. And I did, something I never told George in our interview.

The Sox always gave the Yankees a run for their money until, it seemed, late August or so, when the Bronx Bombers would come to Chicago for a crucial, four-game series and win them all. The Friday night series-opener often featured a great pitching match-up between Whitey Ford and Billy Pierce, but no matter how well Pierce pitched for the Sox, Ford was better, winning 1-0, 2-1 or 3-2. For six or seven years, the Sox finished second or third in the American League, until they finally broke through to win in 1959.

The Yankees were a great team in the '50s, but blinded as I was by my fierce loyalty to the Sox, I stuck to my nonsensical conviction that they were just lucky. Mantle had been damn lucky to hit 50 home runs, Berra was lucky to win three MVP awards, and Whitey was lucky to lead the league in earned run average. Mickey Mantle was Steve's favorite player, which made him the most contemptible Yankee of all. And because he struck out about three times as often as he homered, I had plenty of opportunities for derisive, if not clever, wisecracks about his failings. But since it was difficult to argue that Jim Busby, the White Sox center fielder, was better than Mantle, I threw my support to Willy Mays and Duke Snider as the game's premier players at Mantle's position. And I even got personal.

"Mantle's a draft dodger!" I exclaimed, having read something about his being rejected as 4F by his draft board because of a chronic knee infection. "He's one of the fastest guys in baseball, and he can't fight in the army? Gimme a break!" I whined.

I never admitted Mantle's undeniable greatness even though I watched him hit a ball completely out of Comiskey Park and saw him hit a line drive home run that cleared the bullpen in center field (415 feet) and crashed into the retaining wall behind it. And infected knees or no, he could run like the wind. The only time I saw him ground into a double play was on a ball he hit so hard it nearly decapitated White Sox second baseman Nellie Fox. The switch-hitting Mick was batting from the left side with a man on first when he ripped a one-hop laser toward second that Fox barely had time to raise his glove to, in what was simply an act of self-defense. Fox actually turned his head completely away from the ball, but it somehow found the webbing of his glove and he was able to flip it to Aparicio who tagged second and threw to first to complete the 4-6-3 double play.

On those weekends, when the Sox would fall from only three games behind New York to seven back because of another Yankees' sweep, I would go into mourning. I would have sold my soul to the devil long before Joe Hardy did in the musical "Damn Yankees" in 1955. And how committed was Hardy anyway–giving in at the last second to save himself, one pitch away from hitting the home run that would have won the pennant for Senators?

Although it was a two-hour train ride to Comiskey Park, I went to as many White Sox games as I could. My older friend Jim "Pinto" Panowski and I would ride from Waukegan to Howard Street and then change to an "el" train that took us very near the ballpark at 35th and Shields. We usually sat in the $2 seats in the lower deck of the left field bleachers, just below the spot where Skowron's "grandstand" home run had landed in the upper tier several years earlier. One season, we won both games of a doubleheader from the Yankees, and Pinto got so excited that he jumped onto the field and slid into second base. I was scared to death because I had never ridden the train by myself, always depending on Jim to lead the way, and I was certain this shenanigan was going to land him in jail. But somehow I got home only to find that Pinto had caught an even earlier train and was already there.

My dad took me to at least one Yankees game in Chicago, and it was one of the most disillusioning moments of my young life. There was a kind of catwalk over the main concourse inside the ballpark that apparently connected the dugout and playing field to the visitor's dressing room. It was about 10 feet above the concourse that served as the main thoroughfare for fans circulating inside the ballpark in a semicircle from first base to third base. The area was always congested, if for no other reason than it housed several restrooms and concessions stands. Many fans hung around there just to see the visiting ballplayers and managers walk by overhead. The catwalk was covered by a kind of cyclone fence, but you could easily converse with a player if he was so inclined.

As I was standing there that day, the aforementioned Casey Stengel, No. 37, shuffled by in his gray, Yankees traveling uniform. I had never seen him in person and I remember him looking so old that he reminded me of a grandfather.

At 10 or 11 years old, I was temporarily mesmerized, until a young boy on the shoulders of another held up a piece of paper and a pencil asking for an autograph—a request that could have easily been filled by passing the paper between the holes in the fence.

"Get lost, kid. I ain't got time for this crap," Casey hissed, and kept on walking.

But there was an even bigger shock in store for me that day. Dad must have known someone in the Sox organization because after the game we were able to go into the team's clubhouse. Many of the players were milling around, some with towels around them as they headed to and from the showers. Without their uniforms, I couldn't really tell who they were, but a couple of them were smoking and as we left I was incredulous to see 10 to 15 cases of beer piled behind the clubhouse door. I was stunned. I knew Dad never allowed his athletes to smoke or drink, and now I saw both things happening in a major league clubhouse. I know I became very quiet, almost breaking into tears, and it wasn't until we were in the car on our way home that I told Dad what was bothering me. He reassured me that smoking, drinking and swearing were still not admirable qualities for an athlete, but that the pros were grown men who made their own decisions. Still, for me, it was a very tough day, one of the first that punctured my innocence and tarnished my idealistic image of professional athletes.

In 1959 when the Go-Go White Sox finally won the American League pennant, I finally quit hating the Yankees. I was fulfilled. Even the World Series against the Dodgers was anti-climactic. As a 17-year-old fan, I had achieved my goal and never felt as passionate again in following any team except those coached by my father. Freed of the blind loyalty that comes with fandom, I began finally to appreciate the Yankees, the greatness of their history and tradition, and the many special players comprising their roster. Even Mickey Mantle.

In 1961, when The Mick and teammate Roger Maris were chasing Babe Ruth's home run record, I was so enthralled that I hitchhiked from Ann Arbor to Cleveland in late August to watch the Yankees play the Indians. I was a freshman on the University of Michigan football team and it was before classes had started. I had to see Mantle and Maris, the so-called M & M boys, challenge history. And they did not disappoint me, both hitting home runs—Maris, his 49th; Mantle, his 46th—in the first game of a doubleheader. The game also featured a tirade by the famously volatile Jimmy Piersall, the Indian's centerfielder and number two hitter in the line-up, who, while waiting in the on-deck circle in the bottom of the first inning, raised hell with the plate umpire over the very first pitch, a called strike, to Ken Aspromonte, Cleveland's leadoff man. The fact that Piersall was not ejected for his histrionics was a testament to the plate umpire's apparent sympathy for the mentally challenged.

Three years later in 1964, Dan Topping and Del Webb, the co-owners of the Yankees (along with Larry McPhail) sold 80 percent of their interest in the club to CBS for a reported $11.2 million. For the next nine seasons the franchise languished, never even advancing to the post-season playoffs. But in 1973, a group led by a 43-year-old entrepreneur named George Steinbrenner bought the club from CBS for $10 million. By 1976 the team was in the World Series and a year later the Yankees were world champions again.

Over the next 12 years, the Yankees signed countless players, employed seven different managers, eight general managers and at least one executive vice-president/chief operating officer—me.

When I told my brother, Steve, that I was the new Yankees chief operating officer, he said, "Bullshit. You can't be. You called Mickey Mantle a draft dodger. I'm going to tell Steinbrenner."

I had to admit that my working with Billy Martin and Lou Piniella at what Yankee pitcher Sparky Lyle called "the

Bronx Zoo" seemed, well, a bit incongruous, but it wasn't as though I was completely out of my element. I had played the game and coached it. One year, I was Waukegan's Little League home run champion, and I stole home with the winning run in the Illinois American Legion state championship game when I was 15. As a high school senior, I was chosen to the Chicago Tribune All-Chicago area all-star team as a catcher/shortstop.

And most relevant? I'd once had a conversation with Casey Stengel.

It happened 50 years earlier when I was a sophomore at the University of Michigan and he was in between jobs—having retired as manager of the greatest franchise in major league history, and steeling himself, I imagined, to manage the worst. From the Yankees to the Mets, from the mountaintop into the abyss. Even Lucifer had not fallen as far. It was 1962 and a friend and I wanted his help on a sports quiz trivia question that could win us some money.

It all began the day Charlie Pascal and I were sitting around in my dorm room in Ann Arbor and decided to enter *Sport Magazine's* annual "Giant Sport Quiz," which had a $5,000 cash prize attached to it. Charlie was from Highland Park, Illinois, just down the road from Waukegan where I'd grown up. We had played high school baseball against one another and loved talking baseball and sports in general. We considered ourselves sports trivia experts; the contest was an exciting challenge and a terrific way to test our knowledge.

The magazine came out monthly and over a three-month period posed 100 challenging questions for, we assumed, thousands of contestants to answer. The contest became our hobby, and by the entry deadline, we knew that we had answered all but one query correctly—actually all but one part of one.

The question in doubt required us to identify three quotes, and the context in which they were made. Two of them were no problem, but the third, "If I can't squeeze when I want to squeeze, where am I?" had us stumped. We couldn't find the answer anywhere in our research, including hours of scanning hundreds of celluloid slides of old newspaper clippings from the University of Michigan undergraduate library. Finally, out of desperation, we decided to try phoning (out of the blue) several famous sports personalities for help; guys we thought might give us at least a clue, if not the answer itself. We were actually able to talk with Howard Cosell, who, amused by our cheek, tried to help us, but couldn't.

"Squeeze" was a baseball term primarily, but maybe that was too obvious, we thought, and tried to think of other sports to which it might apply. Around that time, golfer Ken Venturi had been going through some problems with his hands, so we said, why not, and called Venturi, who didn't know what the hell we were talking about.

"No, fellas," he said politely, "I don't think I ever said that."

Finally, we thought of Casey Stengel, who was famous for talking in circles–"Stengelese," the media called it. Somehow, I knew that Stengel made his home in Glendale, California, so, on a hunch, we called directory information, but the operator had no one listed under "Casey Stengel." But then a light bulb went on, and I said to the operator, "What about a Charles Dillon Stengel?" Bingo! We got the number and called. An elderly woman's voice answered, which we assumed belonged to Mrs. Stengel. Our hearts stopped when she asked us to wait a moment, and then we heard, "Casey, it's for you." We nearly collapsed. Mr. Stengel, as we addressed him, listened patiently to our ridiculous story, but in what seemed like Stengelese, said, "I don't think I said it, unless somebody said I did."

We were finished. I don't recall what we submitted as the answer, but it was just a guess. We never discovered the source of that quote then, but later found out that it was the old Brooklyn Dodger manager, Charlie Dressen, but in what context Dressen had said it we never knew. When the answers were printed it was the only question, or one third of a question, we had missed.

Silly as it may seem, these were the moments that came flashing back to me when George Steinbrenner offered me the job—Bill Skowron's "grandstand" home run, Mickey Mantle's double play ball, the trip to Cleveland to watch the M & M boys, the beer in the White Sox clubhouse, Casey Stengel's blowing off a kid wanting his autograph and, finally, my brief phone conversation with Casey about the sports quiz. As for my many years as a Yankees hater, they were immediately forgotten in the euphoria of the moment and would further disappear as I prepared to head to Yankee Stadium.

52

I knew that there was nothing simple about George Stein-brenner. He could be a sympathetic, concerned patriarch one moment and a browbeating bully the next. The problem most people had in dealing with George was his total unpredictability. When baseball announcers describe a schizophrenic team, they often use the cliché, "You just never know which team is going to show up, the team that hit five home runs two nights ago, or the club that couldn't get a ball out of the infield last night." Well, it was the same with George. You just never knew which Steinbrenner was going to phone or come through your office door. Perhaps that was his edge, his way of keeping people off balance. My problem was I signed on to run the Yankees, not walk a tightrope.

As it turned out, George flew to New York with me. Surprisingly, we sat together in coach at the back of the plane. George wanted to personally introduce me to everyone at the Yankees' offices, which were set back from the mezzanine seats in the second deck at Yankee Stadium, overlooking the field. On the flight I asked him to sketch the club's current organizational chart. The truth was he didn't have an organizational chart, but he devised one off the top of his head. However, he did have an "enemies list" of the New York media—who I could trust and whom I couldn't—and the bad outnumbered the good by about three to one.

The surprises didn't stop once we reached the stadium. For starters, no one had mentioned my hiring to Bill Dowling, the team's chief legal counsel, who had acted as George's COO for about two years, and whom I'd never met. Unfortunately, Dowling had read about my hiring in the newspapers. I was extremely embarrassed that this had happened, but Bill, when we shook hands that day, just shrugged it off, and welcomed me to the team. It was another bad sign of what constituted business as usual.

George escorted me into his office, the floor covered by a huge dark blue wall-to-wall carpet with a giant white baseball, the Yankees' logo in the center. At the far end of the room, which overlooked the third base side of the field, was a glass door that led outside to about 20 seats, spread among four rows. This was the viewing area for George's personal guests. At the other end, nearest the entrance to the office was George's desk, a gigantic, circular, richly finished wooden table, perhaps five feet in diameter. Behind the table sat a large, beautiful, tan, genuine leather chair for George, and on the table rested only a platform-type telephone with six lines. The leather furniture in the room's sitting area matched the desk chair, but the easy chairs were designed to look like baseball gloves, like an Oldenburg sculpture. There was a television, of course, but the room was surprisingly free of baseball memorabilia. It was a magnificent space. The stylishness of the office wasn't the surprise. No, the surprise came when George said, "Well, Rick, here we are. Here is your office."

I was more than a little taken aback, "But George," I said, haltingly, "this is *your* office."

"No," he said, "you'll work from here."

"But what about when you come to town? Why don't I just find something down the hall," I responded, almost plaintively.

But George insisted, saying that, first, he wasn't going to be in town very often. He had a lot going on in Tampa, and, when he did come, he said that he would work from his suite at the Regency Hotel, in mid-town Manhattan.

That settled, he led me on a tour of the other cubicles and offices comprising the club's modestly laid out executive floor. I met some of the other staff, including Bob Quinn, the vice-president for baseball operations. Bob was a veteran baseball administrator, whose son went to Ohio State. He knew of me, but when we met, he gave me the same look I had experienced at spring training, almost as if to say, "What the hell are you doing? You just left a firestorm at Ohio State, and now you're jumping into this crazy job?"

George's first day in New York didn't last very long. Right after our tour of the office, George called an ad hoc staff meeting and went around the table introducing me to those I hadn't already met, including long-time ticket director Frank Swain.

Frank was a wonderful man, very soft-spoken and polite. He'd been in this thankless job for many years and I sensed immediately that he had been through this hellish drill before. With stress oozing from every pore in his face, he looked to be 80 years old, when he may have been 60. The public relations director, John Fugazy, was there, too, along with the media director, Harvey Greene, who also looked gaunt and nervous. Everyone around the table looked on edge, like those awaiting a countdown for the launching of a rocket into space, or the detonation of a condemned building. George started going through some business, wanting to know what promotional days were on tap for the season—bat day, bobblehead day, etc.–and grilling Harvey about the "goddam media," and why he wasn't getting better press.

Then he turned his attention to the ticket operation. Because the season hadn't started, tickets had not yet been mailed, and George wanted to know where the VIPs would be sitting. Swain had brought a huge tray of tickets–I'd say at least 500–all precisely organized by row and seat number, so that if George didn't like the seating arrangement Frank could change it on the spot. Frank started to answer when, for no apparent reason, George grew terribly agitated. There was some sort of problem with the tickets, and where certain people had been assigned their seats.

"You can't put those people together, Frank. Jesus Christ, use your head."

I had never heard anyone berated like this in a staff meeting. I was stunned. Then George, his patience exhausted after only 10 minutes, grabbed a handful of tickets out of the tray and threw them in the air.

Meeting over. George was leaving. His final words to me were something along the lines of, "I don't want to fuck around with this stuff anymore. I'm going back to Tampa. It's your mess now."

But it never really was my mess. I would have enjoyed the challenge. Instead, I ended up constantly *being challenged*. On just about everything. George called one day when Judy, his (and my) secretary was absent. She had gone to the dentist with an abscess. I answered on his private line, which I could tell surprised him.

"Rick," he said, rather puzzled, "where's Judy?"

I told him about her tooth. The line went silent. Then George spoke again. His voice dripped with disappointment.

"Awwwww, Rick," he said. "Rick, Rick, Rick. Why did you let her do that? That's not the kind of toughness I'm looking for." And before I could respond, he hung up.

By this time, I had discovered that George did a good bit of yelling over the phone and that he had a rather impolite propensity for hanging up without saying goodbye, sometimes in the middle of conversations. He didn't necessarily do this angrily, but almost absentmindedly, as though he was through with the person on the other end and a "goodbye" was simply superfluous.

It always threw me for a loop when I was on the receiving end of this insult, especially when other people were in the room with me.

On at least two occasions, I was in the middle of a small staff meeting in my office (George's office) when Judy buzzed me that "Mr. Steinbrenner" was on the line.

There was no saying, "Ask him if I could call him back," because the answer would have been too violent to endure. So I would have to ask everyone sitting around my desk to wait a moment while I took the call, which I didn't dare take on the speakerphone, and then George would be talking in my ear. As I would start to respond, there would be a click and I would realize that he had hung up while I was in mid-sentence. To avoid the embarrassment of letting everyone else in the room become aware of this humiliation, I would keep chattering into the dead line for a minute or so. "Right, George," I'd say to the dial tone, "I'll take care of it. By the way, how is Joan (his wife) doing? (pause) Good. Well, tell her I said hello." What else could I do?

Staying on the line for at least a few seconds in these situations was also a matter of self defense, because if you weren't sure about the click, and he *did* happen to still be on the line, you could be accused of hanging up on him. Phone calls from George were stressful, but really, it was comical when you thought about yourself sitting there, listening intently, hoping to hear either a click or George breathing, some signal for what to do or say next.

53

A few weeks later–but still before the season opener–
George came to New York, pretty much unannounced.
His driver, Mike, called me on his way to Teeterboro Airport
to pick him up. He had flown into town on his private jet.

"I'm bringing him to the stadium," Mike warned. "I
didn't know if you knew."

There was nothing going on in the ballpark and I was
puzzled, because George had told me that he was going
to work out of his suite at the Regency unless there was a
game.

But he didn't work at his suite. He came to the stadium
and plopped himself right down at *his* desk. Or, rather, *our*
desk. He didn't kick me out of the office. He wanted me to
work right there, right next to him, almost elbow to elbow.

He said, "No, Rick, stay here. It's all right," as I was scram-
bling to get my things together and move down the hall.

So there he was, the owner of the Yankees, with the
executive vice-president and COO of the team right beside
him, almost sitting in his lap. Two grown men, executives,
the top guys at the New York Yankees, sitting and working
at the same desk, with one telephone between them. I just
hoped that Denice wouldn't call. "Rick, it's for you," I could
almost hear George say.

When it came to being out of the office, the secretary
snafu was not my only naïve indiscretion; I also unwittingly
violated the eat-lunch-at-your-desk edict, even though I did
not often eat lunch. If I had time at noon, I would go to the
umpires' dressing room, change into jogging clothes and
run laps at a public park beyond left-center field, outside
the stadium. George called once when I was out. Naturally,
I returned the call. George was not a happy Yankee.

"Rick," he said with some urgency, "where were you?"

"I was out running," I said, "getting some exercise."

"Awwww, Rick," he said, his voice again heavy with dismay. "We can't have that."

"George," I said. "This is my lunch hour. I do this instead of eating."

"Awwww, Rick," he said, "You don't have time to exercise."

He had called one other time, when I was actually out for lunch. But when I told him so, he sighed.

"Rick, around here we eat lunch at our desks. You need to be available."

And so it became evident rather early that morale might be a bit of a problem, both for me and everyone else in the administrative offices. I was trying, though, attempting to do things as simple as putting together an organizational chart. But the minute I'd get something in place and try to build some staff confidence in it, George would come in and blow it to smithereens, with some executive order from the top that compromised the entire management hierarchy. He had no use for any chain of command. If he wanted to talk with the assistant to the assistant of media relations, he would just call him directly. What was worse was that this assistant to the assistant was expected to call George directly, too, if it was something "The Boss" had inquired about.

George was inexplicably and indiscriminately dictatorial, which, incidentally, complemented nicely his tendency to bully people who wouldn't stand up to him. And not many people did. His rage sometimes was so abusive that I expected people to say, "This just isn't worth it," rather than have George come in every other day and disparage them. To the contrary, it was as though most Yankee employees seemed able just to go along with the program, attempting to stay in hiding when George was on the prowl, trying their damndest not even to pass him in the hallway.

And there was some wonderful camaraderie in the attempt.

Bill Squires, director of stadium operations, was one of the good soldiers in the front office. Squires, a Navy veteran, was in charge of security. Bill could stand at attention and take whatever George dished out. Maybe it had something to do with his military experience. Anyway, whenever George was en route to the stadium, his limousine driver, Mike, would phone ahead to Bill.

The call usually came when the car was about 10 minutes out. When Squires received the initial call, he would go to the side entrance and wait for the limo. The driver would pull up to the door so George could enter the stadium unobserved. As soon as George passed Squires on his way into the stadium, Squires would key his walkie-talkie, which transmitted over the office phone-intercom system, and a droll voice would come on and say, "The ... package ... has ... arrived!" And everyone would duck for cover.

For a while, every day held some sort of surprise. Generally, it involved George, who sometimes would come in loaded for bear and other times be in and out of the stadium in a flash. His schedule often was as unpredictable as his behavior.

But George, himself, wasn't always the cause of astonishment, For instance, there was the "protection money" the Yankees paid to keep the outside walls of Yankee Stadium free from graffiti. This deal didn't seem to be much different from the extortion that occurs outside an arena when a neighborhood tough says, "Watch your car for $5, mister?" Except this payoff was about real money, Tony Soprano stuff—pay up or your stadium walls will look like a Jackson Pollock canvas in the morning.

As COO, I had to approve all payments, and co-sign all checks. One day, I came across a request for a payment of $17,500 for services from someone named Muhammad, a person I'd never heard of. I asked our controller Bob Stoffel about the invoice. Bob, a little embarrassed at his mission, just wanted me to sign it, hoping, I think, that I wouldn't ask any questions. When I pressed him, Stoffel reluctantly told me, "It keeps the outside walls clean, you know, no graffiti."

My eyes must have widened, "You mean protection money! Does George know about this?" Of course, Bob said, continuing, that the practice had been going on for years.

The next morning, as I was walking to the stadium from the nearby subway station, I realized for the first time that while all the buildings around the ballpark were thickly covered with graffiti, the white walls on the outside of Yankee Stadium were pristine. The space was as inviting a canvas as any spray paint artist could dream of, but there was not a speck of color anywhere. Apparently, no one messed with Muhammad, and, clearly, the 17 grand was money well spent.

Speaking of money, I was also responsible for signing the ballplayers' paychecks, and, initially, the numbers shocked me. Major league players were paid once every two weeks, but only over the seven months of the season. Don Mattingly was then the Yankees' highest paid player, making $2 million annually, chump change by today's standards when you consider Alex Rodriguez's current $25 million annual salary. But I will never forget signing those checks for Mattingly: *he took home around $115,000 every two weeks.*

54

With Opening Day fast approaching and Denice still living in Columbus, I was trying to find a place for us to live. My first four weeks in the city had been both lonely and discouraging. Denice was still working at the Capitol Club in Columbus and I missed her terribly. We had quickly sold our home there, but still had not closed. Soon, however, we would have to move our furniture either into storage or a place in New York.

In the meantime, Steinbrenner was putting me up in a small suite at the posh Regency Hotel, where he lived while in the city. I also had the use of George's car and his driver, Mike, to get me around to see some places. Mike had gotten into trouble the last time George had come to town by getting into the owner's Tic-Tacs, a supply of which he kept in the limo's glove compartment. The driver had opened a new box and helped himself to two or three of the tiny mints, and foolishly left the evidence in the car. George was nothing if not fastidious, and when he saw the broken seal, he chewed out Mike, and told me to keep an eye on him.

Denice loved her job and probably sensed that I was unhappy from our many phone conversations. She would visit me every other weekend, but we spent most of the time looking for a place to live. It was nothing reminiscent of the wonderful long weekends we had spent visiting the city in the past, when we had seen four or five plays, run in Central Park and toured the galleries.

Mike, George's driver, had survived "Tic-Tac Gate" and patiently drove us all over Manhattan, until we finally found a ground floor co-op in the East Village, near New York University, at the corner of Fourth Avenue and Ninth Street.

The apartment was a bi-level, with the main floor featuring 12-foot ceilings, a single sprawling great room, brick walls, wood floors, and a small nook up a fireman's ladder that could serve as an extra sleeping space.

It stretched us financially, but it was some consolation when my friend from CBS Sports, Ric LaCivita, a New York veteran, said, "Now this is truly a Manhattan loft!"

The only problems were that it had no air-conditioning and that it was on the ground floor, and, though it had big windows, they faced an outdoor space guarded by three, tall, adjacent buildings that blocked out most of the sunlight. If things weren't going well in the outside world, the place could feel dark and depressing. A few weeks before we were due to close on the place I actually inquired about backing out, but the seller wouldn't budge.

Denice had promised her Columbus club to stay on a few weeks after we had to be out of our home there, moving into a local hotel in the interim. Meanwhile, all our furniture had been shipped to New York and dumped in a heap into the middle of our new apartment.

The seller had agreed to paint the unit, so I couldn't arrange any of the furniture until that was completed. I felt completely at loose ends. Nothing was in its proper place. I was in an expensive loft that I shouldn't have bought, the job wasn't working out, the apartment was in shambles, Denice was leaving a job she loved, and the weather was turning warm, making the apartment feel a lot stickier than the seller had promised. I had moved too quickly, something even George had warned me against, although I don't think he had any premonition that our partnership wouldn't work.

I felt as though I was working at cross-purposes and it made no sense. Deep down I knew the Yankees job was not going to work, but I refused to admit it even to myself. I thought that if I had slowed down on finding a permanent residence that it was tantamount to acknowledging that I had made a huge mistake in coming to work for George.

On the positive side, Denice's company immediately placed her in a new sales position in New York as the membership director of a private health club at the beautiful Equitable Center Building, near the theater district. The building featured a huge Lichtenstein painting on one of the exterior walls in the foyer.

The subway stations Denice and I used were very close and we soon became experienced commuters. Denice took a local train to Midtown, and I took the Number 4 express train from 14th Street to 159th to the stadium in just four stops and 35 minutes. Then I walked from the station about two blocks along Muhammad's beautiful unscarred stadium walls to the entrance to the ballpark. I took the same line home, unless the club played a night game, in which case I took a private car.

On the weekends, Denice and I loved to take the subway to 59th Street and 5th Avenue, to run our old route along the perimeter of Central Park, which went as far north as 109th before turning back toward Midtown. Every three weeks or so we might rent a car and drive out to Long Island to get away from the concrete jungle that surrounded us daily, and, despite the ongoing misgivings about my job, we renewed our love affair with the city. We walked everywhere, although Denice's natural inclination to be street friendly got her some curious glances in the Village and her charitable nature made her an easy target for the beggars in the subway stations.

Oddly, though we were only minutes from Broadway, we didn't go to much theater. We saw a few productions here and there, but nothing like our previous play-packed extravaganzas. Maybe it was just that I had all the drama I could handle each day at Yankee Stadium.

55

Finally, Opening Day at Yankee Stadium arrived. The ballpark looked pristine. Every wall and corridor had been scrubbed and freshly painted; on the field not a blade of grass was out of place. And, presumably, thanks to Muhammad, the outside of the stadium was fresh-looking and spotless. The team's 22 world championship pennants rippled softly in the breeze above the rooftop, and Monument Park in left-center field was ready for the thousands of fans who would wander among the twelve plaques, commemorating the greatest Yankees players of all-time. The setting was electric.

But, as often happened with the Yankees, the great occasion was clouded by an off-the-field controversy.

There was tension in the Yankees camp as the season approached, mainly due to deteriorating relations between George and star outfielder Dave Winfield. Steinbrenner and Winfield never really got along, but when it leaked out that Winfield was writing a book, George became paranoid and wanted to put a stop to it. He was certain that the book, entitled *Winfield*, would be disparaging to him and the Yankees and demanded to see the galley proof of the book in advance, even hiring an attorney to work on it. But the book was published just as the season got underway, and George's suspicions about the content were confirmed. For starters, there were statements in the book attributed to the club's African-American second baseman, Willie Randolph, suggesting that the Yankees were a racist organization. Randolph later denied making the comments.

There were other things, too. Winfield made the accusation that the Yankees lost the 1985 American League pennant because Steinbrenner's interference with his players had lowered their morale. To make matters worse, George made it quite clear publicly that he disapproved of the book, and that he was trying to trade Winfield. It was open warfare.

Steinbrenner had made headlines in 1980 by signing Winfield to a 10-year, $23 million contract. In 1985, with Winfield struggling at the plate during the critical stretch run, the Yankees lost the American League East to Toronto on the second- to-last day in the season. George later derisively referred to Winfield—a great early season hitter—as "Mr. May" to the local media, an obvious negative comparison to Reggie Jackson, who was nicknamed "Mr. October" for his post-season heroics.

The Steinbrenner-Winfield feud was in full swing when Opening Day arrived on April 5, and the local media were poised for the apocalypse. Still, it was a glorious occasion. The defending World Champion Minnesota Twins and pitcher Frank Viola were the opponents. A regular-season record crowd of 55,303 showed up. As always on this day, *promise* was in the air—the promise of a summer of excitement and the promise that baseball would push the George vs. Winfield battle into the shadows.

Eventually, anyway.

But there was a problem brewing for the occasion that no one had anticipated. Call it the Great Opening Day Gaffe, for which I was partly responsible.

Opening Day was a VIP special occasion in the stands. People were dressed up, and in George's private box, located just outside his office on the third base side, the stars were out *en masse*. Actually, on a slightly lesser scale, this wasn't unusual at any time during the season. George did not attend many games, maybe one weekend series a month, so in his absence I hosted the suite, and met some very famous and interesting people in the process. Because these folks often came alone, I had a chance to sit and visit with the likes of Donald Trump, Mike Wallace, Lee Iacocca,

Howard Cosell, opera star Robert Merrill and New York mayor, Ed Koch.

Mayor Koch's grand entry into Yankee Stadium on this Opening Day was a thing of beauty. I noticed that he wasn't in George's box as the game began, but then during the first inning there was a commotion near the left-field foul pole. People began standing and pointing, and finally I saw His Honor and his large entourage on the cement walkway between the last row of the box seats, and the first row of the loge seats, about ten rows up from the field and in full view of most of the stadium. The walkway encircled the stadium, and the mayor, who could be a divisive and controversial figure, strolled all the way around the park from the left-field foul pole to the right-field foul pole, smiling and waving as he went, throwing kisses, soaking up the cheers of his adoring supporters, while apparently oblivious to the boos and cat calls that were at least equal in number and volume.

Like my boss, "The Boss," Mayor Koch was flamboyant if nothing else. I once sat in a meeting between the two in the mayor's office in Manhattan. Steinbrenner was there with Bill Dowling and me to impress upon the city that he had no intention of extending his stadium lease with New York, which expired in 2002, unless he received more favorable consideration for such revenue streams as skyboxes and parking. George constantly talked publicly about the possibility of moving the Yankees across the Hudson River to New Jersey when the lease ended. There was nothing subtle about this. This was not an implied threat, because there was nothing "implied" about it.

Mayor Koch, who knew nothing about baseball and resented the leverage the club had, had two of his staff in the room with us. Once the Mayor and George started talking, they acted as if their staff people weren't even there. We were referred to in the third person. At one point, George pointed to one of Koch's staff and said, "This asshole keeps saying that this is your best offer," and the conversation went downhill from there.

On this Opening Day, however, the mayor was grateful to have Major League Baseball in his city and was taking full advantage of the public stage it provided him.

56

If there was one problem with Opening Day, it was that the event was such a happening that almost all the tickets were bought up early at premium prices by VIPs and corporations, leaving a lot of kids shut out. Often school was in session and it didn't matter. But in 1988, school happened to be in recess during the first week of the baseball season and vice-president for public relations John Fugazy came to me and suggested that we have a second opening day, make it something like Kids' Opening Day, and go through the same pomp and circumstance as the day before. It meant we would introduce the players again, one by one, before the game, and have them line up on the foul lines. I thought it was a terrific idea and mentioned it to George. He OK'd it, and we were on.

But on that first day, the official Opening Day, the game took a back seat to the Steinbrenner-Winfield matter, at least in the beginning. The crowd was into it, and it soon became obvious with whom they were siding. Winfield was the Yankee cleanup hitter, and as soon as Don Mattingly, the third place hitter in the line-up was announced and began trotting from the dugout to the foul line, the roar began. It was for Winfield, and it easily was the largest ovation of the afternoon.

Then things became a little ugly. Suddenly, people in the stands turned toward George's box and started chanting, "Trade the owner, trade the owner," which, though embarrassing to George, still seemed rather tame to me by New York standards. George handled it well, however. He sort of smirked and walked away.

He didn't do as well on Opening Day II. We all were in the box again–me, John Fugazy, George, and some guests—and were enjoying the festivities until the Twins were introduced, and were standing on the third base foul line, waiting for the introduction of the Yankees.

Then it hit John and me at the same time—it was going to happen again! Winfield was going to be cheered, and "The Boss" was going to be jeered.

George, not thinking clearly, said something like, "What the hell is going on? We've got to put a stop to this!"

Of course, it was impossible. The Twins were already lined up; a local band was poised in center field to play the national anthem; Rickey Henderson and Willie Randolph—the first two batters in the Yankee line-up—had already been introduced; Don Mattingly, again the batter before Winfield, was jogging forward as his name was being called—and George wanted to call the whole thing off. Now! But there was no time to do anything, and the crowd embraced Winfield as his name was called.

George went a little nuts. Forgetting that he, himself, had approved the idea of a second "opening day," George said to Fugazy, "What asshole thought of this brilliant idea?"

Wanting to protect John, I said quickly, "George, it was my idea. It wasn't John's fault." Then, trying to defuse the moment, I said, "Come on, George, it's no big deal."

George just looked at me. "Well, of course, it's no big deal to you. It's not your ass that's getting booed!"

Well, he had a point there.

At least the season was underway, which I figured would bring some normalcy. I was correct except that my concept of normalcy and the Yankees notion weren't quite the same.

57

We won our first five games, taking two from the Twins and three from the Brewers. It was the best Yankee start in 55 years. The streak ended there.

George didn't take 5-1 lightly. Game six was an afternoon affair in Toronto, on April 11. I didn't make the trip, nor did Piniella or Bob Quinn. We were watching the game on television in my office. Our guys jumped off to a big lead in the first inning, but in the bottom of the inning, shortstop Rafael Santana committed an error at second base on a double-play ball. The miscue led to six runs, four unearned, and was the catalyst for a Blue Jays 17-9 win.

Santana had been acquired from the Mets over the winter in the first ever trade between the two New York teams. Raffy, as he was known, was a career .245 hitter, but was solid defensively. The Yankees had been playing musical chairs at the shortstop position for years, and the feeling was that Santana, at age 30, would anchor the infield.

But no sooner was the inning over, than George was on the phone from Tampa to the Yankees clubhouse in Toronto chewing out manager Billy Martin's ass about Santana.

"That was a Little League play," he said. "Why did we ever trade for this guy in the first place?" And so on.

Piniella, Quinn and I were still blithely watching the TV, having no idea the phone lines from Florida to Ontario were afire—until about halfway through the second inning, when Piniella's phone rang. It was Martin calling from the clubhouse in Toronto. After parroting the ranting he'd just endured from George, he told Lou, "We've gotta trade this sonuvabitch!"

It was only moments later when George called the stadium. Lou quickly reminded him that it was only our seventh

game, that we had 155 to go and that the team was playing in such cold weather in Toronto that was amazing anyone could hold onto the ball. I was almost sure that I heard
a click from Lou's phone in the midst of this reasonable explanation. Lou rolled his eyes and put down the phone, only
to have it ring again. It was George, amending his trade-
the-SOB order with: "And start working on it, NOW!"

Crisis management was again in high gear in the Bronx.
Piniella started working the phones, and finally, toward the
end of the game, he had something tentative worked out
with Philadelphia Phillies general manager, Woody Woodward, who had recently left the Yankees, and who was, fortunately, not watching our game on TV. Lou told Woodward
that that we had a young shortstop in the system we wanted to bring up (on the Columbus shuttle, no doubt), which
had made Santana, who was 30 (and had aged considerably in one afternoon) expendable. A lot of bullshit, of
course, and Woodward knew it. Still, he needed a shortstop
and was interested. Woody told Piniella that he would call
him the next day to see if they could consummate the deal.

But nothing was quite that simple with the Yankees. After the game, Martin met with the press and proceeded to
rip Santana big time. Martin said that Raffy couldn't play,
that he'd lost his touch. The brutal, seat-of-the pants assess-
ment made for colorful copy in the morning papers. And
though Woodward, who knew Billy, took all of this with a
grain of salt, he was now faced with trading for a shortstop
that the Yankees had said publicly wasn't worth a damn–
and, not surprisingly, the deal fell through.

The irony of the mess was that Santana was voted the
"Good Guy Award" by the New York baseball writers at the
end of the season, and he wound up playing in 148 games,
the fourth highest total by a Yankee shortstop since 1952. He
batted .240, which was about what was expected, led the
Yankees in assists and had a 32-game errorless streak late
in the season. In all, nothing spectacular, but solid, and not

bad for a guy whom everyone wanted to trade when he muffed a double-play ball on a cold day in Toronto, on the sixth day of the season.

Although things eventually cooled off for Santana, the dugout or clubhouse phone calls between George and Billy didn't. While I was surprised by the Santana discussions—I didn't think things like that took place *during* a game—I was astounded when on another occasion the in-game discussion centered on the team's alcohol policy.

A few weeks later, the team was finishing up a road trip in Texas. It was a Sunday morning, and Denice and I left our apartment to get some breakfast. We sat down. Then I opened the paper and nearly gagged on my orange juice. There was a big story from Texas and it wasn't about the game. Martin had been in a fight in the restroom of a topless bar near Dallas. I began to hyperventilate thinking about damage control, when I realized that no one had even called me about it. I assumed Steinbrenner knew, and Piniella, but it was another strong indication of how unimportant my role with the club really was. No one contacted me the rest of the weekend and so I took the subway to Yankee Stadium on Monday, as though it were just another day, even though the papers were having a field day about Martin's fight.

The club had returned from Texas Sunday night for a two-week home stand, after which they would be heading to California on a charter flight for a West Coast swing, starting in Anaheim. Just before the final game of the home stand on Sunday against Oakland, George called me, concerned about Martin's drinking. Apparently the Texas episode had finally brought management to the realization that Billy had a problem, although it had been common knowledge long before. George wanted to know what I thought about eliminating booze from the team charter to California. Being a college guy, I never felt that it was good policy to serve alcohol on a team plane or in the clubhouse. It encouraged drinking and could only lead to trouble. I gave George my opinion and he agreed.

The game had started by the time I called our traveling secretary and told him not to stock the charter with any alcoholic beverages. It wasn't long, however, before word reached the dugout about the decision. When Billy got the news, he immediately got on the clubhouse phone and began to raise hell with the traveling secretary. Again, this while the game was in progress. The next thing I knew George was in on the discussion, and for several innings the game became secondary. Having been bypassed again, I don't know exactly how many phone calls were made, or what exactly was said, but the parties reached a compromise—beer and wine only. What a zoo!

All of this was vintage Martin. Because I wasn't really involved in the baseball side of the organization, I had very little contact with the Yankees manager. He was a bit of a recluse, comfortable only in the clubhouse or on the field. The fans loved him because of his feistiness and his reputation as a fighter, and not just on the diamond. Early on in his playing career, Martin and several Yankee teammates, including Mickey Mantle and Yogi Berra, were involved in a celebrated brawl at the famous Copacabana nightclub in Miami, Florida. In 1960, he broke the jaw of Chicago pitcher Jim Brewer and ended up in a lawsuit that cost him $10,000. In 1979, Martin infamously fought a guy in a bar who turned out to be a marshmallow salesman. And in 1985 he had another highly publicized row with one of his own players, pitcher Ed Whitson, in a Baltimore hotel, in which the manager suffered a broken arm.

Aside from the publicity picture of us together taken at spring training, I never really saw Martin again until early in the season, when I had to go to the clubhouse to read Major League Baseball's gambling policy to the team. Bobby Brown, the American League president, had declared that the policy must be read aloud, that it wasn't enough just to post the rules on the bulletin board. The players were milling around when I walked into the clubhouse. I spotted Martin, and asked him if would get everyone's attention so that I could begin. Because I had spent such little time at spring training, almost none of the players knew who I was, and I thought Billy might at least give me a short introduction. But, instead, he simply whistled to get the players' attention, and said, brusquely, "This guy has something to read to you." Then he walked into the manager's office, and closed the door. It was, how shall I say, rather awkward.

A couple of days later, however, George called me. "Rick, I heard you were in the clubhouse."

"That's right," I said. "The commissioner's office instructed me to read the gambling rules to the team."

There was a brief silence. Then, "Rick, I told you before. Stay away from the players."

58

About two months into the season, I knew that the job was not going to work out. It wasn't that George was such an ogre, but it was that everything was always in crisis mode and the day-to-day environment was so stressful. I made up my mind to quit.

But as I was strategizing how to break the news to George, Lou Piniella, our general manager, beat me to it. Lou had had enough, as well, called George and resigned. He had threatened this action many times before, but when he finally did it, George swore us all to secrecy. Piniella was very popular with Yankee fans and George wanted to put the best possible spin on the announcement, in such a way that it didn't look like Lou was being forced out or that the club was coming apart at the seams so early in the season. I gulped when I heard this because I was about to drop my own bombshell. Now it seemed better to wait.

The news, of course, leaked out. This was, after all, New York. And, given George's track record, the press attacked the story like a pack of wolves after a carcass. George was furious and called in Bill Dowling, who was now solely the club's general counsel, and asked how in hell the news of Piniella's resignation got out, and who leaked it? Dowling didn't know and had no answer. So, George told Bill that he was calling in a private investigator that was going to administer lie detector tests for everyone, including me.

"Bill," I said, when he told me, "I didn't leak anything, but I'm not taking a lie detector test, simply on principle."

"Rick," Dowling said, pleadingly, "George says everyone has to take one."

Finally standing up for myself in this mad house, I said, "Well, just tell George to shove it up his whatever, because I'm not going to do it."

Bill sort of nodded. Then I said, "Come on, Bill, are *you* going to take one?"

He looked at me. "Well, not this time."

I was incredulous, "THIS TIME? You mean you've taken one before?"

Bill said yes, that there was a problem in the business area a few years back. George had been suspicious of some employees and had someone administer tests and eventually flushed out a few people involved in some financial shenanigans.

Thankfully, the tests never occurred. George cooled down, and told everyone that Lou would become a "special assistant," freeing him up from the daily grind of the front office, and allowing him to take a broader look at the organization. George considered this spin control, as if there had never been any kind of blow-up or disagreement with Piniella.

Lou's decision was no surprise to me. He had the office two doors down from mine, with Bill Dowling's office in between us. There were adjoining doors in all three spaces, so that Piniella could easily walk through Dowling's office to get to mine, which he did, often. Lou was a great guy, with a well-known fiery disposition. Every baseball fan has seen Lou Piniella highlights of his many blow-ups with umpires as a field manager. No one has ever kicked more dirt on home plate; flung his hat to the ground any harder or so brutally ripped second base from its fittings in a rage as Lou. So, it was never surprising to hear his raised voice bellowing through the office during one of his four or five daily phone conversations–or arguments–with George.

By the end of the day, this dapper Italian was wearing his designer shirttail out, had his necktie askew, and his hair disheveled. He would walk into my office and collapse onto the beautiful leather sofa, just inside the adjoining door.

"I'm telling you, Rick, this fucking guy is nuts! Jesus Christ!" And then he would take a short nap while I continued to work at my desk. Usually this happened after the office had closed at 5 p.m., but before the game began a couple of hours later.

When the team was in town for a home stand, our days were long, all of us arriving by nine, and not leaving until the game ended. Or, I should say, until 25 minutes *after* the game ended.

George had a rule that all the executives had to attend every home game and not leave the ballpark until 25 minutes after the final out. It was crazy. There was no need for everyone to be at every game, or to hang around that long afterward, but I guess George wanted to make sure he was getting his money's worth. It would have made a lot more sense for the executives to alternate the duty so that people could be a little more rested, especially if there were three or four night games in a row.

Some of us had to be there all the time, including the baseball guys and me. It was the 25-minute rule that killed everyone; often it wasn't observed and I had to cover for someone. Bob Quinn, our vice-president for baseball operations, lived in a suburb about an hour from the stadium, so he often left the game early, winking at me as he went out, as if to say, "I know you'll cover for me." Piniella had to see every game to do his job because he was constantly evaluating the team. Lou never left the game early, but he wasn't exactly compliant with the 25-minute rule, either. Often, during the game, he had to take several more calls from George, who was watching on closed circuit television in Tampa. He was frazzled by the time the last out was made and was out the door almost before the teams had left the field, saying to me as he flew by, "I'm telling you, Rick, I've got to get the fuck out of here!"

Then, I would sit there by myself waiting for the phone to ring, which it did, exactly 25 minutes later.

"Rick, let me talk to Piniella," George would say, by way of a greeting.

"Uh, he's not in his office right now, George," I would respond.

"I know he's not in his goddamn office. I just tried him there!"

"Uh, he must be headed down to the clubhouse to see Billy," I would offer, hopefully. Lou had a cell phone but the technology wasn't good enough then to pick up a signal in the bowels of a dungeon like Yankee Stadium. So, just because George couldn't reach Lou on his cell didn't necessarily mean he wasn't there.

George knew this, but it didn't stop him from screaming, "Goddamit, he left, didn't he?"

"No, George, I ..." (CLICK). Then I went home.

In fact, my cover for Lou wasn't really that believable, because he and Billy rarely spoke. Lou was ok with the manager, but Billy was suspicious of Lou, imagining that he was the guy waiting to take over when he was fired–again.

It had already happened once before at the end of the '85 season when Billy was axed and replaced by Piniella. Piniella guided the club on the field for the next two seasons, while Billy cooled his heels as a "special advisor" to Steinbrenner. Now, in 1988, the roles were reversed, with Piniella kicked upstairs as vice-president and general manager and Martin taking over in the dugout. But who was to say that the switch couldn't happen again. After all, this was the fifth time that Martin had managed the Yankees, an all-time major league record for the most times as manager of one club.

So one can imagine how Billy saw it when, one day, Lou was on the field in the batting cage working with Yankees' star Don Mattingly, who had asked Piniella to look at his hitting stroke. Martin felt threatened and his already cool relationship with Lou turned icy.

59

Once Piniella announced that he was quitting as general manager, I began looking for the right time to tell George that *I* was leaving. Actually, I felt a little guilty. George had given me this opportunity when I was down and out and I thought maybe I should just gut it out for a year, if only for the sake of appearances and spare both of us the public embarrassment of ending our partnership so prematurely. And I might have done it had it not been for the switchboard episode.

Perhaps it was fitting that the final straw of my brief tenure had to do with telephones, which had always played such a key role in George's iron-fisted control of everything within the organization. This situation, however, had nothing to do with trading players between innings or discussing evening libations between balls and strikes. It involved the stadium switchboard operators.

In retrospect, it was a crisis waiting to happen. We had a relatively new phone system in the administrative offices, some young and inexperienced operators, and an owner who called frequently and was easily agitated if he was cut off or if his call was misrouted. These switchboard jobs didn't pay enough to warrant taking very much abuse and turnover was a constant problem.

Finally, we hired three young individuals, two of whom were African-American. They were being trained and were learning to cope with the pressure of trying to route George's phone calls all over the administrative offices without error. But George was demanding and they made mistakes. I would have to admit that if I were George, I might have gotten a bit frustrated every now and then, too. These guys weren't perfect, but they were improving. Still, every now and then George would get cut off, and he would call me and say, "Rick, we have to do something about the switchboard. Go out and get the best people you can find. Find out who the *experts* are. Do your homework. Get the best!"

I was living in the real world, however, and I realized that the jobs didn't exactly attract people with doctorates in communications or master's degrees in electrical engineering. So, I would say, "George, just let me work with them. They are getting better."

And George would say, "Well, I'm just telling you to get it straightened out."

Every time George kicked into his switchboard tirade, I'd listen, and then call in the operators and say, "Now, you know Mr. Steinbrenner can be excitable. But when he calls, don't let him intimidate you to the point you can't operate the board effectively. Take your time. Do your best."

But none of that—neither the operators' improvement nor my attention to the problem—mollified George. Finally, he said, "Look, Rick, I'm just telling you and I don't want to tell you again—GET SOME BETTER SWITCHBOARD OPERATORS!"

Naturally, I didn't. The group was improving, and starting from scratch would have just made the problem worse.

One day I was so sick that I just couldn't make it to the stadium. I had to stay home. I was resting on the couch when George called. He was upset.

"Rick, where are you?" he said, even though he had just dialed my home number. I told him I was home with the flu, but that I felt reasonably sure I would be back at work tomorrow.

"Rick," he said, "I've told you about the switchboard operators." I asked what had happened.

"Rick, I called today and, goddamn it, I got cut off again! How many times do I have to tell you to get rid of the fucking switchboard operators? I want you to get in there tomorrow and fire them all. All of them. Get some new people!"

I could tell this wasn't going to be an enjoyable conversation. I was feeling just sick enough not to give a damn, so I said, "George, look, we have been working with the operators and they are getting better. We have a new phone system and we are almost a third of the way through the season. By the time we fire these operators and hire new people and train them, it will be more trouble than it is worth. And things will get worse before they get better."

I'm not sure George was listening but, flu and all, I felt as though I was on a roll. "And besides, George, you know that the organization has just been accused in Winfield's book, a nationally distributed book, of being racist. Two of the new people are African-American."

George was not deterred. "I don't care about that," he said.

I didn't let him finish and I didn't want him to hang up on me. "George, I'm not saying it should be your primary concern, but it is a part of the situation. I'm just trying to protect you from yourself. We don't need that sort of thing. It will be misread."

There was a long silence. This was one of the few times I had ever had his attention on the phone. Finally, he said, "One thing you better learn is that I don't care about any of that. Now, just get rid of them."

What came next was less influenced by George's attitude than the fact I finally was convinced George never was going to allow me to be what he hired me to be. I said, "George, I'm never going to be able to please you. My style of management isn't compatible with the way you want your club operated. I think I ought to start looking around."

George was silent for a moment, and then said, "OK, you take it easy. I'll see you."

I never did fire the switchboard operators and George never brought up the subject again. I don't know if the operators survived or not. And they weren't the first people I didn't fire after being ordered to do so.

The editor of *Yankees Magazine,* an in-house publication that went to our season ticket holders periodically, was castigated early in the season for a cover story he had done on slugger Jack Clark. The club had acquired Clark in the off-season from the St. Louis Cardinals. Clark was extremely strong and had a bull-like body that had "power" written all over it. The editor put the words "The Animal" with his picture, and George went ballistic. The guy tried to explain that Jack had been referred to in that way in St. Louis, once he started hitting prodigious home runs.

But George didn't want to hear any of that. He felt that we had insulted our newest player and told the editor he was finished, to "get out." The editor's wife also worked for the club and had just taken maternity leave. If he lost his job, the couple would have been in trouble. Later, I told him not to worry, but just to lie low and keep doing his job. His office was in the bowels of the stadium anyway, and he just skulked around down there like the Phantom of the Opera for a couple of months. I don't think George ever saw him again or, if he did, he had forgotten about the incident, which happened often after such blow-ups.

A few days after our final phone conversation about the switchboard, George surprised me by asking why I was leaving. I told him it was because he didn't need a chief operating officer, that he was that guy. Finally, I said, "George, I don't really do anything."

He looked at me, and said, "Rick, you don't have to do anything. Just don't rush into anything." In its own way it was a magnanimous gesture, but I told him that I needed a challenge, and would start looking.

Five years later, in 1994, when *Seinfeld's* George Costanza began working for the Yankees, I was nearly convinced his role was based on me. In retrospect the experience was that comical.

I resigned from the Yankees on June 1, 1988, to join my friend Ric LaCivita, the former television director from CBS Sports, who was starting up his own television production company. So calloused were the New York sportswriters to the endless turnover in the club's front office that my leaving didn't even cause a murmur in the media.

I had been a Yankee for a brief, but hectic, 100 days.

60

When people ask me what I learned during my experiences in professional baseball and how it compares to intercollegiate athletics, I can only generalize.

I did get the impression that many owners are eccentric. George was one of a kind, but I attended enough owners meetings to know that there were others like him. I also sensed a rather cavalier approach to off-the-field matters. The Yankees, for instance, seemed relatively unconcerned with their public image, aside from winning, and at times, even apathetic about operating within the rules governing Major League Baseball.

While I was COO, the Yankees were the only team in the major leagues without a specific—and required–substance abuse rehabilitation program for its employees, and the league office would remind us of this distinction fairly regularly. But George always found an excuse not to have one. I think it just was his way of saying, *"I'm in charge of the Yankees!"* I talked to him about it being a problem both politically and from an image standpoint, especially given Billy Martin's well-publicized escapades in and out of bars. And considering the disturbing substance abuse problem in the country, not to mention New York City, the Yankees could have set an example, been out front. But there was no sensitivity to that sort of issue. George would say, "We don't have a problem on this team, and if we do have one, we can take care of it then." The league office never gave us an ultimatum. But it was just that kind of thinking that made it tough for me to feel good about the club.

Neither was there any attempt by the ownership to generate a family feeling in the organization. The team was run via a deluge of phone calls out of Tampa. There was no structure, no *esprit de corps*. "Yankee pride" was limited to the field, while off it, it was every person for himself in a cut-throat environment, if only to survive.

I wrote a memo to George early on, suggesting that we meet privately a couple of times a month to review how things were going, and discuss what we could do to improve office morale. A few days later, George called me, saying that he had received my memo about "morale."

"Rick," he said, "Fuck morale. Morale will take care of itself."

Several years later, while I was the athletics director at San Diego State, I attended a San Diego Padres game and ran into former Pittsburgh Pirates general manager Sid Thrift. Thrift was doing some consulting work for the Padres and had worked briefly for the Yankees after I left. I introduced myself; we shook hands and I could tell that Thrift was trying to place me. Finally, he said, "You're that Rick Bay who worked for the Yankees."

"That's me," I said.

He chuckled, "I've got to tell you something. One day I was going through some old files at Yankee Stadium, and I came across a memo you wrote to George about front office morale. I never laughed so hard in my life. George never gave a damn about morale. I can just see him reading that. That was hilarious!"

As for George, well, I liked George, simply because George was truly likeable. Plus he gave me a job when I didn't have one and he sang my praises to the media three years later when I became president of the Cleveland Indians. In between, he always treated me with respect, relatively speaking, of course. With a guy as enigmatic as George, everything was relative, especially his personal relationships.

Two years after leaving the Yankees, while I was the athletics director at Minnesota, our men's basketball team made the NCAA Tournament and was sent to the Meadowlands in New Jersey for the first- and second-round games. I called George and asked him to be my guest at the first game against Duke. He declined, but offered me the use of his car and driver while I was in town. In 1998, when I was AD at San Diego State, he did the unimaginable and brought the Yankees to play an exhibition game against our Aztecs team in *our* tiny 3,000-seat stadium.

And no one can discount his business acumen. The Yankees are the most famous professional sports franchise in history. With the opening of its new stadium in 2009, the franchise is estimated to be worth well more than $3 billion. George Steinbrenner bought the team from CBS in 1973 for $10 million. And during his 37 years of ownership, the Yankees won seven world championships, the most of any major league club, while creating their own cable television network. Despite the dysfunctional nature of the organization on a day-to-day basis, George clearly made enough brilliant decisions along the way to become an incredible success.

George was an interesting guy in his own right. He graduated from Williams College, where he majored in English literature, was an outstanding hurdler on the track team, played halfback on the football team his senior year and played piano in the symphony band. He earned a Master's Degree in physical education from Ohio State, where he was also a graduate assistant football coach for Woody Hayes. And he later was an assistant football coach at both Northwestern and Purdue. In fact, his football mentality was one of his problems with the baseball club. It was not unusual for him to march into the clubhouse, and try to fire up the players with a Knute Rockne-type halftime speech. One of the players told me that he once did this after the club had lost two games in a row early in the season. Once he had cooled down, one of the executives told him, "George, take it easy. There are 150 games left."

Finally, a new high school in Tampa, Florida, opened in 2009, is named George Steinbrenner High School in honor of his community service in the area.

In a strange way, George and I were very much alike. We both always loved sports and the cultural arts, and neither of us was ever good at compromising our beliefs. This was the second job I had left because my bosses refused to let me manage what they had expressly hired me to do. And George was not about to loosen his hold overseeing his ball club, no matter what he might have promised in good faith at the time.

Toward the end, George and his wife, Joan, celebrated their 32nd wedding anniversary at Yankee Stadium before a game. All their family was there, including the grandchildren. Denice took the train to the stadium, as well, to take part in the celebration. During the party, Denice and I approached Joan, and Denice said to her, "Congratulations! That's wonderful!"

"Wonderful?" Joan said, without missing a beat. "It's a GODDAMN MIRACLE!"

Considering my 100 days, I couldn't argue with her.

EPILOGUE

My job with Ric LaCivita's fledgling new television production company Starbright lasted only five months. Ric was a creative innovator and his ideas for the future of television were cutting edge. We made a presentation to the NCAA, encouraging the organization to establish its own television cable channel, perhaps partnering with Major League Baseball to guarantee year-round programming, using the NCAA basketball tournament and the World Series as anchor events to attract subscribers. We got nowhere then, but today MLB, the NFL, and the Big Ten Conference, to name a few, have their own cable channels. But Starbright was under-capitalized from the beginning, and though Ric was ahead of his time in his thinking, the company didn't have the staying power to remain viable long enough for him to find an underwriter.

The Yankees' season continued its turbulent pattern. Billy Martin's paranoia over Lou Piniella's batting cage session with Don Mattingly turned out to be justified. On June 23, Martin was fired as the club's manager for the fifth time; Piniella took over—and almost predictably—Lou himself was replaced at the end of the season. The club finished fifth in the tough American League East, but only three and a half games behind first-place Boston. The Yankees had been 40-28 under Martin and 45-48 under Piniella.

Dave Winfield, despite his feud with The Boss, led the team with a .322 batting average, and "The Animal," Jack Clark, led the club in home runs with 27, though he struck out 141 times in 150 games. Mattingly hit .311, and both he and Ricky Henderson made the American League All-Star team.

In the fall, when it began to appear that Starbright was not going to make it, I applied for the commissionership of the Big Ten Conference. Given my long history at Michigan and my tenure at Ohio State, I had the right pedigree. But the nature of my exit at Ohio State killed my chances. Although OSU President Ed Jennings had assured me that he would not object to my candidacy, the chairman of the search committee intimated otherwise, saying, "Rick, we have to have someone everybody can agree upon."

In November, the University of Minnesota recruited me for their newly vacated athletics directorship and Denice and I moved to the Twin Cities in December to start the job. We rented out our New York co-op and took up residence in the Radisson Hotel on the campus, where we lived for the next six months. The hardest part was that we had to park our car in an open parking structure all winter, which meant plugging in our battery overnight so that we had a 50-50 chance of being able to start the vehicle in the morning. Denice found a job at the Minneapolis Athletic Club working in her specialty, membership sales.

The first year of my job was dominated by two NCAA investigations that I'd inherited, one involving a university administrator who had embezzled $200,000, some of which he claimed to have given Gophers athletes, and another to do with recruiting violations in football. Suddenly the Yankees' problems didn't seem so awful.

After three years at Minnesota and a successful, but truncated stay with the Cleveland Indians, and a much longer but turbulent tenure as the athletics director at San Diego State, Denice and I retired to Palm Desert, California in 2003.

But in August of 2007, in the most tragic event of my life, Denice was killed in a single car accident in Morro Bay, California, at the age of 54. Two weeks later, crushed and despondent, I was climbing Mount Kilimanjaro in Tanzania, Africa, with her ashes. There, on the continent Denice had visited and loved, at the highest point in Africa, on the summit of the tallest free standing mountain in the world, at an elevation of nearly 20,000 feet, I spread her remains as close to God as I could carry them.

ABOUT THE AUTHOR

Rick Bay was a sports executive for 25 years, in both collegiate and professional sports. He was the athletics director at the University of Oregon, the University of Minnesota, San Diego State University and The Ohio State University.

He also worked for George Steinbrenner as the Chief Operating Officer for the New York Yankees, and was the President of the Cleveland Indians.

Rick graduated from the University of Michigan, where he played football and was an All-American wrestler. He later coached wrestling at his *alma mater*. His last two Wolverine teams were undefeated, won a Big 10 championship and finished third and second in the NCAA Tournament—and Rick was voted the National Wrestling Coach of the Year.

Rick has been inducted into both the University of Michigan Hall of Honor and the National Association of College Athletic Directors Hall of Fame (NACDA) Hall of Fame.

He is married to Dr. Julie Kerry of Ann Arbor, Michigan.

Rick's website can be found at www.thebaywatch.com.

CPSIA information can be obtained at www.ICGtesting.com
Printed in the USA
LVOW07s2232151015

458511LV00014B/135/P

9 781477 464199